**WITHDRAWN
UTSA LIBRARIES**

RENEWALS 691-4574
DATE DUE

Microcomputers in Urban Planning and Management

Microcomputers in Urban Planning and Management

Richard K. Brail

Copyright © 1987 by Rutgers, The State University of New Jersey

Published by the Center for Urban Policy Research
Building 4051 - Kilmer Campus
New Brunswick, New Jersey 08903

All rights reserved
Printed in the United States of America

Library of Congress Cataloging-in-Publication Data

Brail, Richard K.
    Microcomputers in urban planning and management

    Bibliography: p. 309
    Includes index.
       1. City planning—Data processing. 2. Municipal
government—Data processing. 3. Microcomputers.
I. Title.
HT166.B715   1987   307.1'2'0285416   86-31767
ISBN 0-88285-121-7

For Nancy, Gregory and Samantha

Thanks for the good times

Contents

EXHIBITS xiii

PREFACE xvii

ACKNOWLEDGMENTS xviii

1 THE MICROCOMPUTER AS A PLANNING AND MANAGEMENT TOOL 1

    Introduction 1
    Evolving Technology 2
    The Era of Microtechnology 4
    The Hacker Ethic 5
    A Historical Perspective on Utilization 6
    Conclusion 10

2 HARDWARE 11

    Introduction 11
    A Brief History of Computers 11
    Counting Systems 13
    Bits and Bytes 15
    The Internal Structure of a Microprocessor 16
    The Pieces of a Microcomputer System 19
        The Main Unit 19
        The Video Display 20
        Storage Devices 22
        Printers 23
        Other Peripherals 23

Conclusion 24

3 SOFTWARE FOR PLANNING AND MANAGEMENT 25

Introduction 25

Operating Systems 26
An Overview 26
The MS-DOS Operating System 28

Applications Software 30
1. The Electronic Spreadsheet 31
2. The Database Management System 31
3. The Project Scheduler 31
4. The Graphics Generator 32
5. The Telecommunications Package 33
6. The Statistical Package 34
7. The Wordprocessor 34
8. Integrated Packages 34

Current Utilization of Microcomputers in Planning 35

Two Examples of Micorcomputer Applications 38

Issues in Hardware and Software Selection 40
The Rapid Evolution of Technology 41
Availability of Software 41
The Viability and Costs of Custom Software 42
Selecting a Particular Package 42

Future Directions in Software Development 45

Conclusion 46

4 INTRODUCTION TO ELECTRONIC SPREADSHEETS 49

Introduction 49

The Concept 50

A Simple Population Projection Example 51

Introduction to the Population Projection Spreadsheet 54

The Linear Model 56

The Command Structure of an Electronic Spreadsheet 58

A Second Example 59
The Exponential Model 63
The Modified Exponential Model 66
A Simple Multiplier Model 67

A Constrained Regional Model 70
A Perspective on the Population Problem 71
Conclusion 71

5 MODELING WITH ELECTRONIC SPREADSHEETS 73

Introduction 73
Modeling Urban and Regional Development 73
A Population Allocation Model 75
  The Concept 75
  The Spreadsheet 76
  Alternatives Analysis 80
The Lowry Model of a Metropolis 80
  The Concept 80
  The Spreadsheet 86
An Employment Projection Model 94
  The Concept 94
  The Spreadsheet 95
The Urban Transportation Planning Model 108
  The Concept 108
  The Spreadsheet 112
A Comparative Cost Model 125
Developing Better Spreadsheets 136
Conclusion 137

6 PROGRAMMING: MINIMAL BASIC 139

Introduction 139
Why Programming? 140
The Five Pieces of the Puzzle 141
Variable and Constant Specification 142
Input and Output 144
  The Output Unit 145
  Location 145
  Numeric Formats 147
  File Characteristics and Manipulation 148
Mathematical and Logical Operations 151
Branching 152

Loops   153
Writing a Program   154
A Set of BASIC Commands   157
A Program to Compute an Average   158
Conclusion   161

7 STRUCTURED PROGRAMMING   163

Introduction   163
The Development of Structured BASIC   163
The Characteristics of Structured BASIC   166
  Introduction   166
  Top-Down Programming with Modules   166
  Pre-Declaration of Variables   168
  Program Legibility   168
The Linear Model Revisited   169
A Three Model Projection Program   171
Programming the Population Allocation Model   179
The Fiscal Impact Model   184
  The Concept   184
  The Computer Program   189
The Interface between BASIC and Electronic Spreadsheets   205
Pascal: A Programming Alternative   208
Conclusion   211

8 FILE AND DATABASE MANAGEMENT   213

Introduction   213
The Functions of a File or Database Manager   215
A Simple File Manager   217
  The General Concept   217
  The State Park Example   218
  The Role of a File Management Program   221
Using Spreadsheets as File Managers   222
Database Management Systems   226
The Relational Model   226
  Introduction   226

The Transportation Improvement Program Example 227
Using dBASE III PLUS 231
   Introduction 231
   Creating a File 232
   Entering the Data 234
   Querying the File 236
   Generating Reports 237
Linking Files in a Relational Model 238
   The Conceptual Basis 238
   The Relational Model in the Marketplace 243
Accessing Multiple Files in dBASE III PLUS 244
Other Database Systems 246
Conclusion 248

9 FUTURE DIRECTIONS 249

Introduction 249

Developing and Using Expert Systems 250
   Introduction 250
   Using a Programming Language 252
   Prolog as an Expert System Tool 253
   Commercial Expert System Packages 260
   Conclusion 260

Mapping the Urban Environment 261
Managing the Electronic Office 263
Conclusion 265

APPENDIX 269

REFERENCES 309

GLOSSARY 317

TRADEMARKS 321

INDEX 323

Exhibits

2-1 A Conceptual View of a Microcomputer   16
2-2 Random Access Memory in a Microcomputer   19
4-1 A Blank Lotus 1-2-3 Worksheet   52
4-2 Regional Population Projection Model, Version 1   54
4-3 Cell Listing, Regional Population Projection Model, Version 1   55
4-4 The Linear Model   57
4-5 Lotus 1-2-3 Worksheet Commands   60
4-6 Regional Population Projection Model, Version 2   64
4-7 The Exponential Model   65
4-8 Cell Listing, Regional Population Projection Model, Version 2   68
4-9 The Modified Exponential Model   69
5-1 An Urban Modeling Framework   74
5-2 Population Allocation Model   77
5-3 Cell Listing, Population Allocation Model   79
5-4 The Lowry Model of Urban Development   82
5-5 Cell Listing, The Lowry Model   88
5-6 Regional Employment Model   96
5-7 Cell Listing, Regional Employment Model   102
5-8 Typical Coding of a Highway Network   111
5-9 The Branchbrook Transportation System   111
5-10 The Branchbrook Transportation Planning Study   114
5-11 Travel Times in the Branchbrook System   124

5-12	Traffic Assignment in the Branchbrook System 126	
5-13	A Comparative Cost Model Spreadsheet 130	
5-14	Spreadsheet Map, Comparative Cost Model 132	
5-15	Menu and Parameter Sections, Comparative Cost Model 133	
5-16	Macro Listing, Comparative Cost Model 134	
5-17	Description and Range Names, Comparative Cost Model 135	
5-18	Graph of Discounted Values, Comparative Cost Model 136	
6-1	Components of a Flowchart 156	
6-2	A Program to Compute an Average 159	
6-3	Flowchart of the Average Program 159	
6-4	An Example of Output from the Average Program 161	
7-1	Largest Number Program, Unstructured 164	
7-2	Largest Number Program, Structured 165	
7-3	Structure Chart, Largest Number Program 167	
7-4	Structure Chart, Linear Model 169	
7-5	Listing, Linear Model Program 172	
7-6	Listing, Three Model Program 175	
7-7	Structure Chart, Population Allocation Model 179	
7-8	Listing, Population Allocation Model 182	
7-9	Structure Chart, Fiscal Impact Model 190	
7-10	Listing, Fiscal Impact Model 194	
7-11	Listing, a DIF File Read Program in BASIC 206	
7-12	Spreadsheet Data for DIF Transfer 207	
7-13	The DIF File Listing 207	
7-14	Listing, Linear Model in Pascal 210	
8-1	A General Representation of a Database 215	
8-2	The Opening Menu of PC-FILE III 218	
8-3	The State Park File Database 219	

Exhibits xv

8-4	The Field Definitions in the State Park File	220
8-5	Adding a Record in PC-FILE III	220
8-6	A List in PC-FILE III	221
8-7	The Screen Display of the Smiley County File	223
8-8	The Opening Menu of the Smiley County Spreadsheet	224
8-9	The Smiley County Spreadsheet Map	224
8-10	Data Input Form, Smiley County Spreadsheet	225
8-11	The Structure of the TIP Database	227
8-12	The TIP File Data	228
8-13	The NETWORK File Data	229
8-14	The MUNI File Data	230
8-15	The LINKSET File Data	230
8-16	A Screen in dBASE III PLUS Assistant	233
8-17	The Creation of the NETWORK File	233
8-18	Adding a Record to the NETWORK File	235
8-19	A Customized NETWORK Data Entry Screen	235
8-20	Displaying Records in the NETWORK File	236
8-21	Displaying Records in NETWORK Surveyed after June, 1986	237
8-22	Report on the NETWORK File	238
8-23	Non-Normalized and Normalized LINKSET Files	240
8-24	Third Normal Form File Structures	241
8-25	Relating the TIP and MUNI Files	246
8-26	The State Park File as a Hierarchical Structure	247
9-1	The Structure of an Expert System	251
9-2	A Traffic Impact Expert System in Prolog	256
A-1	Cell Listing, Urban Transportation Planning Model	270

A-2	Cell Listing, Comparative Cost Model	296
A-3	Cell Listing, Smiley County Information System	301

Preface

The purpose of this book is to introduce microcomputer applications to the urban planner, the public sector manager, and the student. There is no doubt that we are seeing an increase in computing power in this decade which will profoundly affect all of us. Microprocessors are found in automobiles, household appliances, and audio equipment. For the urban planner or manager, the development of very powerful and inexpensive microcomputers is perhaps more important than for many other professionals. The corporate manager or university researcher has had access to large central computers for three decades. Large organizations could afford expensive computers; the small urban planning office or city administration could not.

I recall teaching computer applications courses to graduate planning students in the early 1970's. The course used a large central computer to run FORTRAN programs and statistical packages. The students would write a program on coding sheets, type the program lines on punch cards, and submit the "job." If lucky, the output would come back from the computer the same day. Often, it would be the next day or later when the output would appear in the student's mailbox. Typically, the programs would not run the first few times submitted. The whole process was cumbersome and often frustrating. Moreover, when the students later took jobs, there was little opportunity to use a computer. I stopped teaching the course.

I am again teaching computer applications courses in the mid-1980's. The changes in the decade between the old courses and the new courses are remarkable. The new computer courses use microcomputers, and teach much of what is in this book. The students learn a great deal, and more importantly, use the skills developed in the jobs they take. Local planning offices have microcomputers, and these machines are being used for increasingly more complex tasks.

This book is one effort to bring some of the current materials before the professional and the student. The publication of the book itself is an experiment in using microtechnology. The book was produced with a text-formatting software package, scLASERplus, from Software Channels, Inc. The final camera-ready copy was produced on a Hewlett-Packard LaserJet Plus printer. This package is not a true "what you see is what you get" (WYSIWYG) desktop publishing package. The actual layout of the graphics on the page and the page breaks could not be seen on the computer screen. The pages of the book had to be printed on the LaserJet in order to see what they would look like. This disadvantage was offset by the ability to use this system on a standard IBM personal computer, and by the quality of the output. Traditional typesetting was unnecessary. The errors which sometimes occur in the translation of typed copy into a finished book were avoided because the final product is an edited version of the original manuscript, created using a wordprocessing program.

The emerging desktop publishing industry is one example of the power of the microcomputer. This book will introduce others using examples from the urban planning and management fields.

Acknowledgments

The production of this book owes a great deal to many individuals. My students in the graduate planning program at Rutgers have contributed insights and have pointed out errors. In particular, Samy Amer and Tim Fluck have provided important and willing assistance. I am grateful to my colleagues, in particular to James Hughes and Donald Krueckeberg, for suggestions and guidance.

The Center for Urban Policy Research has given its usual capable support. George Sternlieb, Director, provided insightful comments and supported the concept and implementation of a microcomputer-focused book. Carole Baker was especially important to the book production process — reading, commenting, and making excellent suggestions. Mary Picarella capably supervised the book production process, and provided excellent insights into the nature of book design. Arlene Pashman did a fine job of final proofreading.

Others were very instrumental as well. Tanner Gay did an excellent job of editing the book, while Valerie LaPorte did the indexing. Leslie Mullen did the cover design based on a microcomputer graphic developed by Samy Amer.

I am profoundly grateful to all mentioned above, as well as to those unmentioned who have contributed. Any errors or omissions are mine alone.

1

The Microcomputer as a Planning and Management Tool

Introduction

This book will focus on the potential use of the microcomputer in urban planning and management. There are many applications of the microcomputer which are directly connected to planning and policy analytic situations. These applications span the wide range of activities which planners, policy analysts and managers perform. The power of the microcomputer centers on its accessibility to a wide number of individuals at reasonable cost and its capacity to do relatively large and complicated tasks which were formerly either done with large "main frame" computers on one side, or with paper, pencil, typewriter and hand calculator at the other.

The development of the microcomputer represents the democratization of computing power in society. Not only is the microcomputer hardware becoming increasingly inexpensive, making microcomputers accessible to more and more individuals and groups, but also the software is becoming increasingly powerful and user-friendly. The technology is making such rapid advances in increased memory availability and processor speed that it is entirely possible that the mainframe computer, which five years ago would have taken up a good-sized chunk of a room, is now sitting on the desktop. This means that the software can take advantage of this increased memory and speed to provide the user with both more capacity and greater ease of use. Also, the increased capacity of microcomputers means that it is now possible to put databases of some size on them.

This book will introduce the reader to the use of microcomputers in planning, policy analysis and management. The examples will be drawn from planning and public sector management areas. This book will not attempt to replicate the multitude of microcomputer books already available which encompass a wide range of materials from introductory to advanced techniques in programming. Rather, this work will attempt to answer the question: **If I am a planner, policy analyst or public sector manager, what do I need to know to effectively use the microcomputer in my activities?** Of necessity the topics covered will be similar to other books in the area. Thus we will discuss spreadsheet programs, programming and database management. However, the orientation will be toward potential situations which the planner or manager can understand. Unfortunately, many of the available books use what are often irrelevant or silly examples. One current book on database management uses a liquor store example, classifying the merchandise by brand and size. Unless you either are a heavy drinker or have an extensive wine cellar, the liquor store example, while competently presented, does little to help you relate that example to work activities.

It is also common for professors who write books on programming to make the calculation of student grades into a series of problems. As a professor writing this book, I totally disavow such programs here. Of course, if you are moonlighting at a local school to earn a little extra holiday money, you may be saddened by my decision; to you I apologize. There is yet one more item on my "little list," to draw on Gilbert and Sullivan's *Mikado*. To illustrate character-manipulation techniques, books on programming will often ask the student to print out someone's name backwards. Unless you plan on joining Alice in Computerwonderland, I do not see the point. Surely there must be a more creative way to illustrate the programming concept involved. Unfortunately, the writers of computer books do not often have the necessary backgrounds in substantive areas to connect their knowledge of computers with the professions. My teaching and research activities in quantitative techniques and computer techniques have convinced me of the essential need to relate the analytic tools to the substantive field. While I will have to simplify for instructional purposes, I will attempt to relate the materials to concept and application in urban planning and management.

Evolving Technology

A number of popular authors have commented on evolving technology and its impact on society (Toffler, 1980; Deken, 1981). These authors have discussed the "electronic cottage" — the decentralization of various work, maintenance and recreational activities to the home — and the widespread impacts of technological change on public and private organizations. The public to which planners respond will be increasingly surrounded by everyday uses of microtechnology, whether it be electronic banking, touch screens in shopping centers, or computers in the home or on the desk at work. The larger society will expect technological competence in all phases of government and business activities.

It has also become clear that, in fact, societal observers may have understated the rate of technological change. Few would have predicted two years ago that today one can get a home computer for less than $100. Advertisements have appeared offering home computers as a bonus for opening a bank account or for purchasing some amount of carpeting.

At the root of this phenomenon is the tremendous development of more powerful microprocessors and random access memory along with a rapid decline in prices. The microprocessor is the "engine" which drives the microcomputer. We have rapidly moved from the 8-bit engines with 16-bit address registers which directly access about 64,000 bytes (or characters), through 16-bit engines with 20-bit address registers which can address over a million bytes, to 32-bit microprocessors which can access over a billion bytes. These newer engines will also work faster. This means that more complex tasks can be done on a microcomputer parallelling the power of the large central computers or "mainframes."

The microcomputer internally stores programs and data in random access memory (RAM) chips. These chips contain thousands of individual bits which can possess one of two states — on or off — permitting binary arithmetic. The rapid technological developments of the past decade have meant the movement from the 4K (1 K equals 1,024 bits) memory chips developed in the early 1970's to the 256K RAM chips of 1984 — an increase in memory power over a decade of 64 times, or 6,400 percent. The 1,024K chip, with a million bits, is next on the scene.

While microtechnology is increasing at a powerful rate, so is telecommunication. It is common now for computers in business and government to communicate by telephone and satellite. Often these organizations use "terminals," which unlike a microcomputer have no independent computing power. Either terminal or micro can be used for telecommunications linkages, although the microcomputer is more flexible because it can process programs and information on its own.

The Era of Microtechnology

Central to understanding the relationship between planning and management and microtechnology is the rapidity of change. The capacity of the microcomputer which will be discussed in this book will be only a pale shadow of the emerging machines of next decade. The initial development of the microcomputer in the early 1970's started with machines which had only a few thousand bytes, or characters, of memory. In January, 1975, a New Mexico company called MITS introduced the Altair computer in *Popular Electronics*.

At that time there were a number of computer clubs whose members shared information, exchanged equipment, and discussed the dream of having a computer in one's own home. Two of these organizations based on the West Coast had the populist philosophy, believing that computers should be widely available to the public. One group, called Community Memory, was established in Berkeley in the early 1970's. Community Memory connected a set of terminals to a central computer containing a community database. The database could be queried through the terminals to ask, for example, for all health clinics in the area and receive a list, or to enter comments on a local restaurant. Such a database was intended to act as a continually evolving collective of community information. The project lasted only a year and a half, in part because the equipment was not reliable enough at the time (Levy 1984). One of the founders of this group, Lee Felsenstein, later went on to design the Osborne 1 portable microcomputer and in the 1980's once again started Community Memory. A second group, called the People's Computer Company (PCC), published a newspaper, one of the first special-interest publications in the field.

The Homebrew Computer Club was founded to respond to the need of computer enthusiasts, or "hackers," for an organization in which they could discuss hardware developments and machine construction. At its first meeting in March, 1975, 32 people showed up. Among them was Steve Wozniak, one of the founders of the Apple Computer company. Soon over a hundred hackers were coming to meetings, including many who would eventually be leaders in this emerging microtechnology.

The Hacker Ethic

In these early explorations of microcomputer development and applications, hackers were sailing in uncharted waters. They lived by what was called "the Hacker Ethic" by Levy (1984). This ethic was defined by a willingness to share information and to explore uncharted electronic regions. This meant that there were no secrets: all information about hardware developments or new software programs was to be shared. The software developed for larger machines had to be rewritten for the smaller and slower micros essentially from scratch. Hackers would write this software and exchange it, building the base for the development of the current software for micros. Along the way hackers discovered, as did others, that one can profit financially from microcomputers.

The Apple II microcomputer, designed by Steve Wozniak, made its debut in 1977 with a memory of 16K (thousand) bytes expandable to 48K. By 1983, the standard IBM PC (Personal Computer) was being sold with 128K of memory. In 1984 typical systems in use would contain 256K or more of memory. In 1986 the typical IBM PC system contained 640K bytes of memory, while the IBM PC AT (Advanced Technology) microcomputer could contain over one million bytes. The Apple Macintosh Plus microcomputer came standard with 1 million bytes and more could be added. These machines offer extremely powerful and friendly programs for a wide variety of tasks.

There is a lesson for urban planning and management both from the hacker ethic and from the rapid shifts in technology which will be occurring over the next decade. Planners, consultants, and urban analysts and managers will need to be extremely flexible in hardware and software choices, comfortable with the dynamics of sometimes very rapid change, and, most importantly, knowledgeable about computers. The exploratory work done by hackers at the initial stages of the microtechnological evolution was essential to the development of the field. Correspondingly, the current state of planning is such that we are also at an exploratory stage in terms of the potential uses of microtechnology in practice and research. The field needs to create an environment where hacking — the exploratory use of hardware and the development of new software — can occur. In a small field such as urban planning and management, there is a distinct need to continually develop new responses to both changing hardware and changing societal issues.

It is clear that the rapid hardware developments will make any effort to stabilize on one machine very difficult. Also, planning-focused software is often expensive since the market is small and the needs are very specialized. For example, the price of MINUTP, a transportation planning package designed by COMSIS Corporation to run in an IBM PC environment, was $5,000 in 1985. However, prices are coming down to the point where specialty software in planning is becoming affordable to a wider range of users. Some of the currently emerging land-based graphics mapping systems, such as ATLAS AMP, which can digitize and display maps coded with various demographic information, are available for under $1,000 for a single-machine license.

However, many planning agencies, private consultants, and public sector organizations will face difficult budgetary squeezes in their efforts to integrate the microcomputer into the workplace. One or more machines can be purchased after budgetary approval, but necessary and ongoing software needs may subsequently be overlooked by the budget-makers. What is needed is a return to the Hacker Ethic by planners and managers — the sharing of software developments and programs either freely or at modest costs. The hacker would often have to develop his or her own software exactly because it was not available. In a field like urban planning or public management where policy mandates can shift radically, there are always new topics which require analysis and decisions.

For example, the environmental movement of the past decades in the United States has introduced a whole set of air, water and solid waste issues to local communities. Each set of new problems has brought the need for a different kind of analysis. More recently, toxic wastes has emerged as an important topic. Insofar as computer-based analysis is important to planning and the issues in planning keep changing, then flexibility in software and hardware utilization become important. Planners, consultants and public managers need to maintain the "hacker" spirit, and attempt to share where possible.

A Historical Perspective on Utilization

Planners and managers have used computers to assist decision-making and do repetitive tasks for the past three decades. A number of studies have been done to examine the impacts of computers in local government. Kindleberger (1982) queried 26 large American cities about current computer applications and prospects for computer future utilization.

The study shows that the pace of computer developments in local government during the 1960's and 1970's was slower than anticipated by the respondents. The excitement exhibited during the 1960's for large-scale simulation efforts, integrated information systems, and computer mapping systems was not matched by accomplishments in many situations. A number of exciting projects were instituted, but the impacts were widely spread and not a part of an overall computer applications environment. The innovations were "lumpy" in terms of their effect on the planning and public management landscape.

The survey also points out that the development of the microcomputer has been viewed as an important step in broadening computer literacy and in expanding the role of computers in local government. The increased knowledge of professional staffs about the potential of the computer in planning and management activities will improve the environment for better computer utilization in future years. One anonymous response to the Kindleberger survey sets out the change which has occurred with the advent of the microcomputer:

> In the past, the degree of use of computers in local government planning seems to have been more dependent upon congruence of acceptance among planners, computer specialists, budget staffs, and policy makers, than upon any natural affinity between planning and computer technology.
>
> The introduction of microcomputers (which can operate independently or as remote terminals providing access to centralized mainframe computers), and the availability of hundreds of 'user-friendly' software packages, will undoubtedly change the balance of understanding between planners and other city departments. (Kindleberger, 1982)

Other observers have confirmed Kindleberger's comments about the disappointments of the 1960's with regard to the potential for computers in local government. Kraemer, Dutton and Northrup (1981) examined 42 cities on their experiences with computing in six "information-processing tasks" (IPT). These tasks were selected to represent different types of information-processing activities. The authors have identified six different IPT's in local government:

1. Record-keeping — The entry, updating, and storage of information. Example: traffic-ticket processing

2. Calculating and printing — The sorting, calculating and printing of data. Example: budget control and reporting
3. Record searching — The primary activity is querying data files. Example: detective investigative support
4. Record restructuring — The reorganization of diverse datasets to develop new summaries. Example: urban information systems for policy analysis
5. Sophisticated analysis — Mathematical model-building and complex analytical techniques. Example: police patrol manpower allocation
6. Process control — The cybernetic use of data through continual monitoring and adjustment (feedback) to achieve established performance standards. Example: local government budget monitoring and control

The examples listed above for each of the six categories of processing are the IPT's which Kraemer, Dutton and Northrup (1981) used in their study. The authors found that the development of computer technology in these six categories had mixed results in their effects on local government. Two of the areas — detective investigative support (a record searching activity) and police manpower allocation (complex analytic techniques) — did not generally show improvements in operational performance through use of computer technology. The other four IPT's studied did show some improvements in performance when computers were used. All six areas studied, however, showed one unintended outcome: the creation of a positive work environment. Workers in general liked to use computers in their work; it made their jobs easier.

Laudon (1974) carried out an earlier study which tended to confirm the limited impacts of mainframe computers on public organizations. He studied the relationship between computer information systems and bureaucratic change. He started his study seeking to determine the effects of technology on organizations, and quickly reformulated his question to ask how organizations shape the use of this new technology. In general, Laudon found in four case studies that computer systems increased the efficiency of line operations but did not impact the broader elements of social policy. He says:

> At best, however, the impact of computers has been to increase the efficiency of line personnel acting within the context of traditional public policies. Policemen can now make more efficient

and thorough arrests based on better information; more stolen automobiles are recovered; welfare and medical assistance programs have less fraud; budgets are more current and more thorough. (Laudon, 1974:302)

These studies point to the fact that in the 1960's and 1970's the computer did not radically affect the structure of decision-making, public organizations or society. There are situations in which the computer played a particularly important role in planning — the development of large-scale transportation and land use models, for example. It is hard to visualize how transportation planning as it is practiced today would be possible without computers. However, computers in the late 1960's and the early 1970's were not generally instruments of social change, but rather devices for improving the efficiency of already-established systems.

Kraemer, Dutton and Northrop offer some guidelines for the introduction of computer technology into local government which have direct bearing on the use of microtechnology in planning and management. For routine tasks such as traffic ticket administration, which are characterized by large processing volumes and a high degree of repetitiveness, computer systems should be centralized. However, for non-routine tasks, characterized by flexibility of response, changing environments, and experimental activities, the authors suggest that computing should be decentralized. They suggest that "The more direct and personal the involvement of users with the technology, the greater their ability to mold it to their specific and changing needs." (Kraemer, Dutton and Northrup, 1981: 340)

Even more, the users should be directly involved with the computer applications, and should have access to equipment without inhibiting resource constraints, such as charges for computer time. Kraemer and colleagues were studying large computer systems, not the micro-environment, so computer charges were an issue.

The lessons for urban planning and management in an emerging era of powerful and ubiquitous microtechnology are clear. While some activities are clearly routine — building permits, zoning applications — many are non-routine, requiring solutions which change in response to dynamic socio-political and physical environments. For planning and management of routine activities in an urban and regional context, a centralized computer system may be extremely useful. Microcomputers, however, allow a degree of flexibility, power and access that was not mentioned in the report of Kraemer and colleagues. As important elements in the evolution of technology, microcomputers appear to be useful in these dynamic situations where flexibility and quick response are necessary.

Conclusion

The sobering comments in this chapter on what computers did not do in the 1960's and 1970's for society are important to understanding the role of microtechnology in the 1980's and 1990's. Two key words have defined the distinction between the past and the future — **power** and **ubiquity**. Hardware and software are much more powerful today and microcomputers are everywhere. This does not mean that society will necessarily be affected in a significant way, that cities will be more beautiful, or that poverty will diminish. However, to compete in this increasingly technological world, the planner or public manager will need to know what a microcomputer is and how to use it. To this end the following chapters are directed.

2

Hardware

Introduction

The driving force behind the rapid evolution of computer utilization in planning and management is hardware technology. It would have been impossible a decade ago to foresee the wide-scale availability of microcomputers which has occurred in the 1980's. This dissemination of computing capacity will continue into the next decade. There are three areas of concern in understanding the technology of microcomputing in the next decade. First, there is the need to understand some of the history of computing as a background to current developments. Second, it is important to know how the microprocessor works in general terms. Third, it is important to examine the components of a microcomputer system as a base to knowing how it can be used.

A Brief History of Computers

The invention of the modern computer has both a distant and a recent history. Stonehenge, the circular arrangement of large stones in southern England, has been called the "stone age computer" (Holoien, 1977). It has been theorized that the construction of large stones as arches and pillars, and the 56 holes dug in a circle around the construction, operated as a large astronomical forecasting device which predicted solar and lunar phenomena such as eclipses. Stonehenge operated as a special-purpose computer. Ironically, a modern computer was used to figure out the purpose of Stonehenge (Holoien, 1977).

In the 17th century Blaise Pascal developed a calculating machine which used interconnected wheels to do arithmetic operations. Pascal, of course, was also a brilliant philosopher and mathematician whose name has been given to one of our popular higher-level computer languages. In the beginning of the 19th century, Joseph Marie Jacquard improved on existing looms used to weave cloth by developing a way to code a cloth design. Appropriately placed holes were punched in a card mounted to the loom. By using sets of different cards, a weaver could control cloth design. Information coded into cards was used in a production setting: this concept was used for decades in the form of punch card data entry to computer systems.

Charles Babbage is important because of his design and development of the Difference Engine and the conceptualization of the Analytical Engine. The Difference Engine could calculate mathematical differences required for the accurate design of navigational tables. Its construction took many years, in part because Babbage was continually improving the design. The primary improvement, never actually constructed in his time, was the idea of the Analytical Engine. Babbage conceived of a machine which could be programmed to do any mathematical task through a set of cards. These sets of cards could be developed for different formulas and stored until used. Babbage thought up the concept of programs (or sets of instructions) which could be stored in the first software library (Holoien, 1977). Ada Augusta Lovelace, for whom the recently developed computer language Ada is named, extended the Analytical Engine concept to areas beyond mathematical formula solution. The engine could be used, she argued, in any area which had a coherent logical foundation, such as the creation of musical pieces.

The next development of note was the introduction of punch card processing. Herman Hollerith developed the system consisting of cards containing punches and machines to read the punches for the 1890 U.S. Census. His system was estimated to have saved the Census Bureau $650,000 in costs for the analysis of the 1890 census data as well as producing the results in record time (Holoien, 1977). Interestingly, the punch card system developed by Hollerith was first used in a public sector project, although Hollerith quickly formed a company to produce the tabulating equipment. This company, the Tabulating Machine Company, eventually merged with other companies and became the International Business Machine Corporation (IBM).

A succession of individuals over the period of the 1930's and 1940's developed the conceptual basis and actual operation of the electronic computer. Howard Aiken developed the Mark I computer at Harvard University during the early 1940's. It was electromechanical: electricity drove a series of mechanical relay switches. The first vacuum tube computer built by John Atanasoff and Clifford Berry was completed at Iowa State University in 1942. The most famous of the pioneer totally electronic computers was ENIAC (Electronic Numerical Integrator and Calculator), developed at the University of Pennsylvania and completed in 1946. This machine weighed 30 tons, contained 19,000 vacuum tubes, and used 150,000 watts of power, dimming the lights of northern Philadelphia when turned on. The smallest microcomputer today has more capacity than ENIAC.

To this point the computers which had been developed were fed instructions by punched paper tape or wired circuit boards. John von Neumann developed the concept of storing the computer program in the memory of the machine along with the data. The EDSAC (Electronic Delay Storage Automatic Calculator), developed at Cambridge University in England and completed in 1949, was the first stored program computer.

The first commercially available computer, the Univac I, was delivered to the Census Bureau in 1951 by Remington-Rand. Once again, as with the Hollerith machines, a public sector organization was the first to use the innovation. The vacuum tube technology in these early computers was soon replaced by transistor-based machines in the late 1950's and early 1960's. Finally, the integrated circuit, which made possible the microcomputer, was introduced.

Counting Systems

There are a number of basic elements of microtechnology which should be understood. There is the distinction between decimal, binary and hexadecimal counting systems. We are used to counting by 10's, using the decimal system. Computers, on the other hand, use both binary and hexadecimal counting systems. The binary system counts by two's. By convention, the two states in a binary system are called "0" and "1," or "off" and "on." It was simpler to design computers with vacuum tubes to represent on and off than it was to represent the 10 different states needed for a decimal representation. In the decimal system the number 138 can be represented by:

$$(1 \times 10^2) + (3 \times 10^1) + (8 \times 10^0)$$

where: $10^2 = 100$ and $10^1 = 10$ and $10^0 = 1$

In other words:

$$(1 \times 100) + (3 \times 10) + (8 \times 1) = 138$$

Note that each position in the number corresponds to some power of 10. One simply starts at the rightmost position from the decimal (the units position) and adds one to the exponent of base 10. Hence, the number 1,479 could be represented:

$1 \times 10^3 =$	1,000	The thousands digit
$4 \times 10^2 =$	400	The hundreds digit
$7 \times 10^1 =$	70	The tens digit
$9 \times 10^0 =$	9	The units digit
Total	1,479	

In the decimal system the base is 10: in the binary system the base is 2. A binary number contains only 0's and 1's, so the number 9 in binary would look like this:

$$1001 \text{ (binary)} = 9 \text{ (decimal)}$$

Using the base 2 and writing the number in extended notation:

$$1 \times 2^3 = 8$$
$$0 \times 2^2 = 0$$
$$0 \times 2^1 = 0$$
$$1 \times 2^0 = 1$$
$$\text{Total} \quad 9$$

Note that the system for calculating a binary equivalent to a decimal number is comparable to the system discussed above for decimal numbers, except that the base is changed. The largest four-digit binary number is "1111," which translates into 15 in decimal, as follows:

$$1 \times 2^3 = 8$$
$$1 \times 2^2 = 4$$
$$1 \times 2^1 = 2$$
$$1 \times 2^0 = 1$$
$$\text{Total} \quad 15$$

The smallest four-digit binary number which is not negative is "0000", or "0" in decimal. This means that a four-digit number can take on 16 different values (0 through 15), which, in fact, is mathematically correct. Since a binary number can take on one of two values (0 or 1), there are 2 to the n power different ways in which n binary values can be uniquely represented. In other words there are 16 different ways in which a four-digit binary number can uniquely occur:

$$2^4 = 16$$

These start with "0000," end with "1111," taking on all other combinations, such as "0001," "0100," and so on.

This discussion about binary numbers is limited to presenting the general concept. A much more detailed discussion can be found in Osborne and Bunnell (1982). The binary number concept is important to the understanding of how the computer works with bits, bytes and words.

Hexadecimal notation is also important to the understanding of how a computer works. In hexadecimal, one counts by 16's, with the curious fact that letters represent the decimal equivalents of 10 through 15. Hence, a decimal "10" is equivalent to a hexadecimal "A," "11" equivalent to "B," up to decimal "15" or "F". In a computer using a binary system, four bits can represent one hexadecimal character using the sixteen different bit structures "0000" to "1111" to represent the hexadecimal characters. Any four-bit chunk of memory can be represented by a hexadecimal character.

Bits and Bytes

The basic unit which the computer contains is a "bit," which is an electronic single binary digit with states 0 or 1. Bytes are groupings of bits, usually eight bits to a byte. Since there are eight binary bits to a byte, then there are 256 different alternative configurations in an 8-bit byte:

$$2^8 = 256$$

In fact, the number 256 will show up in a wide variety of places in microcomputer technology. For example, the Apple II microcomputer stores data on floppy disks in 256 byte chunks. More directly, since it is conventional to store a single character in a single byte in many applications, this 256 number means that there are 256 different characters which can be uniquely represented in a single byte.

The relationship between these 256 different representations of 8 binary bits or byte has been partially codified into the standard classification scheme. The first 128 characters have been organized into the American Standard Code for Information Interchange (ASCII), while the next 128 are left to the devices of the various computer manufacturers and vary among the different machines. This classification scheme is the most popular one at this time for microcomputers.

The Internal Structure of a Microprocessor

The microprocessor chip is the "engine" of the microcomputer. This chip is a powerful collection of computer functions which will be briefly discussed. Essentially, the engine of a microcomputer can be generally represented by the diagram in Exhibit 2-1.

Exhibit 2-1

A Conceptual View of a Microcomputer

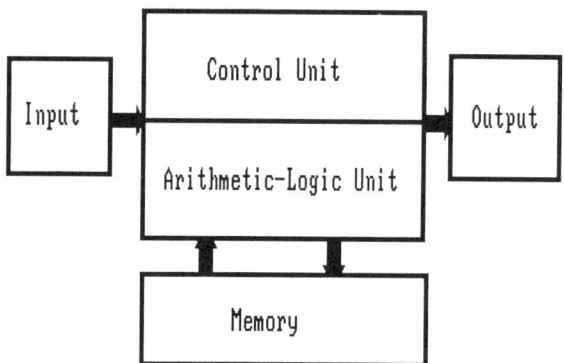

The microprocessor has a central processing unit (CPU) which is made up of two elements — the control unit and the ALU (arithmetic-logic unit). While the ALU does the arithmetical and logical operations necessary for the the computer program to run, the control unit operates as a manager of the flow of data (Zaks, 1980; Osborne and Bunnell, 1982). While it is not important here to understand how the CPU operates in detail, it is important to understand the relationships between buses, registers and the CPU.

Buses are the pathways or communication lines along which data is transferred between elements in the system. It is easiest to think of buses as multiple-lane highways. Travelling on each lane is a stream of bits which carry the electronic equivalents of either 0's or 1's. The number of lanes in the bus is a function of the particular microprocessor. Many of the microprocessors developed in the 1970's contained 8 lanes of parallel data transfer, and were called 8-bit microprocessors. The Apple II computer series contained the 6502, an 8-bit microprocessor.

Registers are banks of binary switches which hold some number useful to the microprocessor. For example, the ALU needs registers to hold the inputs and outputs of an arithmetic operation. Also, address registers are needed to hold the address in memory of the next instruction of the program. Typically, in an 8-bit microprocessor the data registers are 8 bits wide, but the address registers are 16 bits long. This is an important point. Recalling binary notation, a 16-bit address register can hold the number 65,536, or 2 to the 16th power. This means that a microprocessor with a 16-bit address register can directly address in memory the information stored in the byte associated with highest storage location 65,536. Since by convention 1 K (K for 1,000) of memory is really 1,024 bytes, then a microprocessor with a 16-bit address register is called a 64K machine.

The early popular microprocessors of the 1970's contained 8-bit data buses and data registers while using 16-bit address registers and buses. These included the already mentioned 6502 used in Apple II microcomputers and the Z80 chip used in a wide variety of micros, such as Kaypro, Radio Shack, and Osborne. These systems were called "8-bit" microprocessors with internal and external data buses 8 bits wide. These 8-bit machines usually had 64K of random access memory exactly because that was the largest amount which could be directly addressed with 16-bit registers. In the early 1980's many of these 8-bit microcomputers were advertised with 128K of memory. In fact, the microprocessor remained the same, but the circuitry was designed to address this 128K in 64K banks: this "trick" is called bank-switching.

The introduction of the IBM Personal Computer(PC) in late 1981 legitimized the "16-bit" microprocessor with a much greater memory addressing capacity. The 8088 microprocessor in the IBM PC does its internal manipulations in 16-bit data buses but communicates externally outside the processor to the rest of the computer in 8-bit buses. Technically the 8088 microprocessor is an "8/16" because of the different sizes of the buses internally and externally.

The power of the 8088 microprocessor in the IBM PC or similar machines is in its addressing capacity. The address space is 20 bits long, meaning that the computer can directly address 1,048,576 different bytes in memory, or 1,024K. A million bytes of addressable storage in a microcomputer in the early 1980's was a seemingly large amount of memory, although the more powerful programs which subsequently emerged easily used this amount. It should be noted that the 8088 does use 16-bit registers in combination to yield a 20-bit address.

As shown in Exhibit 2-1, the CPU (made up of the control unit and the ALU) is fed by input devices such as a keyboard and puts out results to the screen or to disk. There are two kinds of memory which interact with the CPU — random access memory (RAM) and read only memory (ROM). The contents in RAM can be both read by the CPU and changed by the CPU. There is two-way interaction between the microprocessor and the memory. ROM, on the other hand, can only be read by the CPU. It cannot be altered by the microprocessor (Zaks, 1980:107-120). While RAM is used for general storage of programs and data which change continually, ROM generally holds programs which are essential to the operation of the machine. In the IBM PC, for example, a minimal BASIC language has been put onto a ROM chip because it is assumed to be widely needed.

There is an increasing trend to place a wide variety of programs on ROM chips. For example, Hewlett-Packard has announced a portable microcomputer with Lotus 1-2-3 located on a ROM chip. Whether emerging software is on floppy disk, is located in ROM, or placed on cartridges, such as are found with inexpensive home computers, the fact is that it will become increasingly complex and require both more memory and better performance from the hardware with which it will be used.

The random access memory of a microcomputer is used for a variety of purposes. Different areas are assigned different functions. In Exhibit 2-2, RAM is divided into a section containing (1) the operating system, doing system management; (2) an application program, Lotus 1-2-3; and (3) an area for storage of data, or in the case of Lotus 1-2-3, an actual worksheet containing data and formulas. Information is brought into the central processor, altered if necessary, and sent back out.

Hardware 19

Exhibit 2-2

Random Access Memory in a Microcomputer

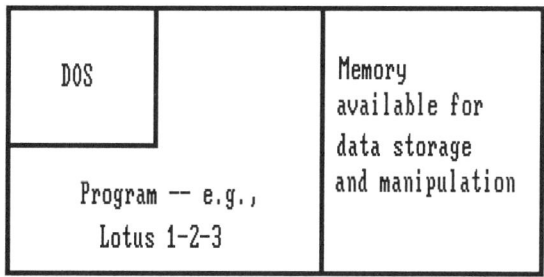

The microcomputer has developed beyond the 8088 chip designed by the Intel Corporation. In 1984 the IBM AT (Advanced Technology) computer came into prominence powered by the Intel 80286 chip. This chip had a 16-bit wide data path and a 24-bit wide address register. It was considerably faster than the 8088 and will be widely used in the late 1980's. In 1986, machines using the Intel 80386 chip made their appearance. This chip approaches the power of mini-computers, containing a 32-bit data path and address registers, and permitting powerful applications to be carried out on the micro. Also, the 68000 chip made by Motorola and found in the Apple Macintosh, Atari ST series machines, and the Commodore Amiga, has evolved also with the announcement of the more powerful 68020 chip. The current and emerging developments in microcomputer technology will assure that most serious applications in a public sector or private consulting office can be done on a modestly priced machine.

The Pieces of a Microcomputer System

The microcomputer system contains two kinds of components — required and optional. The required elements of the system make up the basic system. At many stages of developing a microcomputer system the builder will be confronted with a variety of choices.

The Main Unit

All microcomputers have a central unit which will house electronic components located on one or more circuit boards. These circuit boards contain the main microprocessor chip, such as the Intel 8088 or Motorola 68000. The boards will also contain computer memory — random access memory (RAM) and read only memory (ROM). Typically, a main unit can hold from 256K to two million bytes on the main circuit board, called a "mother board." The mother board will also usually contain slots into which additional boards, or cards, can be plugged. The main unit is driven by a power supply which supplies low-voltage current to the electronic components.

Either attached or built into the main unit is a keyboard. The keyboard will vary among different micros in terms of the placement of the keys and the number of specialized keys contained. As one might expect, there are IBM-type keyboards which have become standard containing either 10 or 12 function keys which can be programmed to generate any selected commands. The electronic circuitry inside the main unit will also include video display components.

The Video Display

Microcomputer designers have disagreed as to whether the video display circuits should be on plug-in modules or not. While IBM has opted in its personal computer series to put the video circuitry on a plug-in card, the original Apple Macintosh built the video circuitry into the main electronic board. The advantage of the plug-in strategy is obvious — as video displays improve, the IBM can be upgraded much more easily than the Macintosh. The disadvantage of the plug-in strategy is that the sometimes confused user will not know what card to install.

The primary display device for microcomputers is the **raster scan** cathode ray tube (CRT). The television screen is a raster scan type, made up of rows of horizontally scanned dots, or pixels, and the microcomputer displays use this television technology. Earlier graphics workstations used vector graphics displays, in which the pictures were made up of a series of straight lines (Carter, 1984). At this time the raster scan tube has become dominant because of cost, ability to use color, and intuitive attractiveness. Essentially, the question of video resolution centers on the number of pixels (dots) which can be displayed horizontally and vertically on a raster type screen, and the number of colors which can be displayed simultaneously. A two-color display is the monochrome version — white, green or amber on black are typical.

The term "video display" as used here refers to both the video circuit card to be installed in the microcomputer, and the appropriate display monitor which works with the particular card selected. Not all cards work with all monitor types. Some current options for the IBM-type computers include:

1. The standard color/graphics video display — 320 by 200 pixels in 4 colors, and 640 by 200 in 2 colors with on-screen display of graphics.
2. The monochrome display with no on-screen graphics — 720 by 348 pixels in two colors.
3. The "Hercules" version of the monochrome display — 720 by 348 pixels with graphics on-screen.
4. The enhanced graphics video display — 640 by 350 pixels in 16 colors with graphics on-screen.
5. Other higher resolution systems up to 1,024 by 1,024 pixels in many colors — 256 colors, for example, simultaneously out of a color palette of thousands.

By comparison, the original Apple Macintosh, a well-known graphics-based system, has a standard display of 512 by 350 pixels in two colors. As one might expect, the movement is toward higher resolution video displays. One limiting factor on the development of these higher resolution displays is the amount of memory contained on the video cards dedicated to the screen display.

In simplest terms, visualize the computer screen as a picture of memory. Recall that a single bit of memory can have two states — "on" and "off." If "off" is associated with a color, say black, and "on" with the color white, then in the screen display with 640 horizontal pixels and 200 vertical pixels, there are 128,000 different screen pixels and a corresponding 128,000 bits turned either on or off. These 128,000 pixels correspond to 16K of bytes, at 8 bits per byte. And in fact, the standard color/graphics video card by IBM with a 640 by 200 pixel resolution has 16K of memory on it. This direct pixel-to-bit correspondence is what is known as a "bit-mapped" video display, and is essential to the on-screen presentation of graphics.

When one moves to higher resolution the memory needs for video become more extensive. For example, a 640 by 350 pixel screen in two colors would require 224,000 pixels or bits, while 1,024 by 1,024 pixel resolution would require over a million bits of memory. The issue is further compounded when color is introduced. Recalling our binary arithmetic, it would take 4 binary bits to represent 16 different colors since $2^4 = 16$. This means that a 16-color 640 by 350 pixel resolution video display would require 896,000 bits (640 pixels X 350 pixels X 4 bits) in memory dedicated to screen display, or 112,000 bytes. A bit-mapped video display at higher resolutions and in color is memory-intensive. Also, because there are more bits to manipulate in the display, the higher resolution screens require a higher microprocessor speed to have the display generated quickly.

Storage Devices

The third component of a microcomputer system is the availability of storage devices to hold programs and data. The typical microcomputer comes with one or two floppy disk units and possibly a hard disk system as well. The current generation of floppy disk units utilizes removable disks which are either approximately 5 inches or 3 inches in diameter. The 5 inch system actually uses a semi-rigid disk rotating in a flexible sleeve. The 3 inch "shirtpocket" floppy is encased in rigid plastic and is the emerging format in many applications. These floppies typically hold between 300,000 to 1.2 million bytes of data. Each byte consisting of 8 bits can hold a single alphabetic character in a standard format. In some applications the bytes may be grouped in special configurations to represent programming commands or compacted numeric data.

Hard disks are non-removable rigid sets of high-speed rotating platters which are accessed by multiple heads which read from and write to the moving surface of the disks. The early versions for microcomputers could hold about 10 million bytes, while current ones typically hold 30 million or more. A hard disk unit has become essential for many applications because programs have become so big, typically taking up a number of floppy disks. For example, WordPerfect 4.1, a word processing package, is contained on 5 disks.

Optical storage devices, employing laser technology, are emerging as a potentially powerful storage media holding hundreds of millions of bytes on a single, virtually indestructible disk. While not a widespread storage choice in the mid-1980's, there is every indication that the media will be of major importance within the next decade. The particularly data-intensive field of urban planning and management will gain from these technological developments. There are plans to produce the 1990 U. S. census data on optical disks, making a large and valuable dataset available to a wide audience. An optical disk player, similar to a floppy disk drive, can be attached to a microcomputer and can access these datasets given appropriate software.

Printers

The printer is the primary output device in a microcomputer system. Three kinds of technology are the most popular — impact dot-matrix printers, fully formed character ("daisy wheel") printers, and laser printers. The cheapest early solution was the dot-matrix variety in which a print head made of 9 pins moved across the page. In a 9-pin head dot-matrix printer, the vertically located pins could be impacted on the page through a ribbon. The quality of the dot-matrix printer has improved considerably with the introduction of the 24-pin head variety. The print quality is better and approaches that of an electric typewriter.

The daisy wheel printer is also an impact device. The printer uses a round wheel with petals containing fully formed characters. The print quality is high but the machines are generally slow. Laser printers, such as the Apple LaserWriter or Hewlett-Packard LaserJet, are the emerging technology. Silent, fast, and durable, they permit the integration of text and graphics at a high resolution. The field of desktop publishing is emerging as a consequence of the laser printers. It is entirely possible to produce newsletters, reports, and books with current desktop publishing software and a laser printer.

Other Peripherals

Beyond the basics of a microcomputer and a printer there are many other peripherals which are useful. Modems can be connected to a micro to make it into a smart terminal which can communicate with large mainframe computers or other micros over telephone lines. This permits the "telecommuting" — working at home while communicating with the office through a modem. The development of electronic mail services, from such companies as MCI and AT&T, make it possible to communicate instantly around the country and the world. Also, a number of service companies now provide data useful to planners and public managers.

The mouse, a small movable desktop pointing device, has come into vogue recently on such machines as the Apple Macintosh. Particularly useful in a graphics-based system of computer interaction, the mouse will become increasingly prevalent on emerging microcomputer systems which use a graphics interface. Finally, there is the plotter which uses a set of pens to draw intricate maps and designs. The current generation of mapping packages for the microcomputer assumes that the plotter is the primary output device.

Conclusion

Much more could be said about the components of a microcomputer system. The potential purchaser will be blessed with a wide range of choices when he or she decides to act. Only the very basics have been outlined here, precisely because the field is so dynamic. New advances are coming out all the time.

One general guideline emerges from the analysis presented here — buy equipment that is **more powerful** than you need and equipment that is **upgradable**. This means that if you can afford the machine with more memory or more processor speed, get it now. Then you will be ready for the next generation of available software which will utilize the faster speed and greater capacity.

The first IBM personal computer, using the 8088 chip, is simply not fast enough for the graphics interface software of the late 1980's. It is at this point that the upgradability issue enters. Hardware fixes are available for this slow IBM PC to make it faster. Machines with "open architecture" — slots or connectors into which new electronic components can be plugged — are inherently more flexible than machines which do not have such slots or connectors.

Beyond this general recommendation to buy power and flexibility, it is difficult to separate the purchase of hardware from the software which will be used on the machine. There is a balance between buying too much machine and bringing home a system that is already obsolete. Any detailed discussion of a strategy for hardware choices in a dynamic environment requires a concurrent discussion of the current and emerging state of software development.

3

Software for Planning and Management

Introduction

Software is a general term which refers to the programs that generate the instructions which operate the hardware. Hardware has had impressive development in the past decade, and will continue to improve steadily in the next decade. Software's development pattern has followed a slower path. The amount of time required to improve software is virtually proportional to the time spent on the tasks at hand. Complex programs require extensive efforts at error checking and logical construction. This logic is human logic, subject to all the potential flaws of incorrect or sloppy reasoning. Computer hardware will do what it is told, and incorrect or inappropriate programming logic will be carried out by the machine regardless of the consequences.

The public or private sector planner or manager will most likely spend much more time on software selection and learning than on hardware purchases or maintenance. There are continuing efforts at developing more powerful programs. Unfortunately, these increasingly complex programs will require increasingly powerful sets of commands to operate the programs to their capacity. The user cannot assume that a program is easily mastered just because it claims to be "user-friendly" while harnessing the power of the sun! In a subsequent section on electronic spreadsheets, we will discuss the evolution of one spreadsheet program, VisiCalc, into a much more powerful offspring, Lotus 1-2-3. VisiCalc is a much simpler program to use; correspondingly, it is much less powerful.

There are a number of software categorizations which computer systems use. A general distinction can be made between operating systems software and applications software. Operating systems software is the "manager" which controls work flow, the peripheral equipment, and the linkages between applications programs. Often, an operating system will contain a number of utility programs which allow the user to perform various functions on disk files. For example, the command "DIR" (directory) in PC-DOS, the most widely used operating system for the IBM PC, will call up a program to list disk files on the screen. On the other side, applications software is the stuff of the real world. Applications software does the work of calculating, word processing, modeling, etc. for which the microcomputer was intended.

Operating Systems

An Overview

The operating system, or more often the disk operating system (DOS), can be thought of as an "envelope" within which applications can be carried out. Often, the DOS will be loaded into computer memory from a disk when the machine is turned on. In some situations the DOS is in non-volatile memory in the machine, always resident and ready for use. The operating system has one fundamental characteristic which makes for confusion and difficulty. It is wedded to the particular microprocessor in the machine. Each DOS is written to optimize the particular instruction set of the microprocessor chip.

For example, the first widely used "traditional" operating system was CP/M (Control Program/Monitor) designed for the 8080 and Z80 microprocessors. Introduced in 1973 by Gary Kindall, now head of Digital Research, Inc., a major software firm, CP/M permitted computer systems using different disk drive configurations to all have a common operating system as long as the "engine" of the machine was an 8080 or Z80. The success of the Apple II computer in the late 1970's meant that another microprocessor, the 6502, came forward. It had its own operating system, Apple DOS, which looked different from CP/M and, in fact, was completely incompatible. Disks and programs designed for a CP/M machine could not be used in an Apple II.

Both the Z80/8080 and 6502 were 8-bit processors capable of directly addressing 64K of memory (65,536 bytes). The movement to the so-called 16-bit processors represented by the 8088 and 8086, as found in the IBM PC and comparable machines, created the need for a new operating system. IBM commissioned Microsoft, a large software firm, to develop a new operating system and called it PC-DOS. The operating system was originally designed for the 8088/8086 family of microprocessors designed by Intel.

There are two important points about the introduction of PC-DOS. First, the operating system is being constantly updated and becoming increasingly like Unix. Developed by Bell Laboratories, the Unix operating system is a highly flexible package that uses a wide variety of important concepts which ease use, such as hierarchical file structure, multitasking (allowing multiple programs to run at the same time), and easy changing of input and output sources. Moreover, unlike the microprocessor specific operating systems like MS-DOS, Unix is portable. It can be used by a wide variety of microprocessors including the Intel 8088, 80286 and 80386, and the Motorola 68000 family. Unfortunately, the Unix operating system is large in size and does not fit easily on a typical microcomputer installation without a hard disk for program storage. Unix does exist on micros, including a derivative called Xenix, and there are those who argue that it will be an increasingly popular choice in future years. PC-DOS itself may eventually be very similar to Unix in terms of language and operation.

There is a second important point about PC-DOS. Its development has concretized the current operating system environment. The IBM family of personal computers has become an industry standard in terms of microprocessor selection, disk configuration, and operating system choice. Microsoft produces versions of PC-DOS, called MS-DOS, for a wide variety of machines which use the Intel family of microprocessors. The PC-DOS, or structurally similar MS-DOS operating system, can be used on machines with the 8088 chip, machines like the IBM AT (Advanced Technology) micro with the 80286 chip, and the emerging 80386 based machines. Since the instruction sets of these Intel processors are similar, a common operating system can be used. In this sense, MS-DOS is upwardly migrant to the newer, more powerful machines.

There are many manufacturers which produce machines similar to the IBM family. These machines are referred to as the "clones," and use MS-DOS as an operating system. Since these clones cut into the sales of IBM machines, a new proprietary operating system controlled by IBM may emerge at any time. The advantage for IBM is obvious: more expected sales since other manufacturers will be closed out of the market. The disadvantage for the consumer is also obvious: a commonly shared operating system, MS-DOS, replaced with a privately controlled alternative. The very ubiquity of MS-DOS may doom such a proprietary move by IBM. At best, MS-DOS may evolve into a more powerful form which will support the needs of the more powerful processors emerging.

Along with MS-DOS and Unix there is another operating system for microcomputers which has received wide attention — the UCSD p-System developed at the University of California, San Diego (hence UCSD). Currently offered by Softech Microsystems, the operating system is available for a wide range of microcomputers and allows for programs written for one machine to be moved to another machine without undue effort. The concept of the p-System is interesting. Most operating systems have compiler programs which convert source code (a language such as BASIC) directly into machine language (understandable by the computer). This means that any time one would want to move a program developed for the Apple to an IBM PC, it would have to be transferred over, possibly even by retyping the entire program, and recompiled after changing the program to reflect the peculiarities of the new machine. The p-System instead offers a common programming structure in which a program is compiled in "pseudo-code" (hence p-code) which is like a universal machine language. When the program is actually run, an interpreter converts the p-code into the specific machine language of the machine being used. The advantage is program convertibility among machines. The disadvantage is that the p-System is slow in processing because of the necessary conversion of p-code to machine-specific language at runtime. While Unix is emerging as an operating systems on micros, the p-System is already here and has been used successfully by major software developers.

The MS-DOS Operating System

While Unix and the UCSD p-System have received a good deal of attention, the MS-DOS environment is the predominant one at this time. Below is a set of basic commands in the MS-DOS operating system. These commands represent basic operations needed on a microcomputer to manage the work flow. Similar commands are found in other operating systems.

Program and data files stored on disk have names which follow a particular convention. By using these names, one can create and retrieve files. In MS-DOS, a filename can be 1 to 8 characters, either letters or numbers, which may be followed by a 3-character extension.

For example, the word processing file of a report on population change in the community to the year 2000 might be labeled POP2000.CHG In this case, the user has supplied the full name including the extension, "CHG". In many situations, the program itself will supply the extension. For example, in the BASIC programming language any program saved to disk automatically has "BAS" put after the name as the extension. A BASIC program written to compute an average, named "AVERAGE" by the programmer, would be stored on disk as AVERAGE.BAS.

Following is a basic set of MS-DOS commands explaining how to list a directory of disk files, copy from one disk to another, and set up, or format, a disk for use by MS-DOS. There are different versions of MS-DOS such as 2.1, 3.1, and 3.2. The higher the version number, the more recently it was introduced. Each successive version is increasingly more complex and powerful. By convention each floppy or hard disk in a system is labeled. In MS-DOS, the first floppy is labeled "A:," the second "B:," and the first hard disk "C:". At any one time, one of the disk drives is "logged in," meaning that the user can assume that any disk command not specifying a drive will refer to the logged drive. The following commands are typed in response to a computer-generated prompt — "A>," meaning the disk drive labeled A is logged in.

DIR	Lists the directory of the A: disk drive.
DIR B:	Lists the directory of the B: disk drive.
COPY AVERAGE.BAS B:	Copies the file in drive A: named AVERAGE.BAS to the disk in B: using the same name.
COPY *.* B:	Copies all files (global command) to B:.
FORMAT B:/S	Formats a new blank disk located in drive B: so it can be used by the computer. /S puts the operating system files on the disk. This means that the disk can be used to initialize the computer when first turned on. Formatting a disk will destroy whatever was stored before.

FORMAT   Formats without the operating system being placed on the disk.

DATE   Permits the user to enter the current date into a computer which does not have an internal clock. This date is stamped on a file whenever it is saved to disk, and can be read along with the file name whenever a directory is read using the DIR command.

TIME   Same explanation as the DATE command.

There are many other commands which make up the MS-DOS operating system. Following the lead of Unix, one of the major elements of the MS-DOS operating system is the use of hierarchical file structures. Essentially, this "tree-structured" approach means that a directory can contain sub-directories of files. These sub-directories in turn can be split into further sub-directories. Using backslashes, "\," to split directory, sub-directory, and file names, then the program POP2000.CHG stored in the COUNTY directory and the POPULATN sub-directory would have the full designation:

\COUNTY\POPULATN\POP2000.CHG

Since the creation of many-layered sub-directories is possible, a full file name can be quite long. The tree-structured approach refers to the fact that a tree has roots with smaller roots branching off. This hierarchical file approach makes it easier to find a particular file because it has been classified in a category. Each directory and sub-directory can be individually listed so a file buried away can be found. A hard disk can hold hundreds of files and a hierarchical structure is virtually essential for efficient operation.

Applications Software

There is a wide variety of applications software programs available for the microcomputer. More is on the way and, in fact, the software explosion is just beginning. Prices will come down and quality will go up. There are a number of general application program types which are particularly important to planning and management. These include:

1. The electronic spreadsheet
2. The database management system
3. The project scheduler
4. The graphics generator
5. The telecommunications packages
6. The statistical package
7. The word processor
8. The integrated package which contains some of the program types listed above all operating within a common framework

1. The Electronic Spreadsheet

The electronic spreadsheet is a computerized version of a two-dimensional worksheet of rows and columns. It is the single most important tool available to planners and managers. It will be extensively covered in successive chapters. Current popular programs include Lotus 1-2-3 for IBM-type personal computers, Multiplan and Supercalc for a variety of machines, and Jazz and Excel for the Apple Macintosh.

2. The Database Management System

Database management systems computerize record-keeping activities, including storing data, querying a file to find a particular piece of information, and statistically analyzing a data file. With the increasing interest in database management in planning and public management, these programs become increasingly important. There is a variety of database programs available. One of the most widely used is dBASE II or dBASE III PLUS, and this package will be discussed in a chapter on database systems in this book.

3. The Project Scheduler

The allocation of resources to a complex project has also been computerized. The available project scheduler programs permit the allocation of resources to the different steps in a project using PERT (Project Evaluation and Review Technique) and Gantt charts.

Krueckeberg and Silvers (1974) discuss the use of PERT and CPM (Critical Path Method) for urban planning management. The currently available programs, such as Harvard Total Project Manager or Superproject, are potentially useful to planners and public sector managers for complex projects. The use of such programs for smaller tasks is unnecessary but is extremely helpful for larger jobs.

4. The Graphics Generator

One of the emerging areas of microcomputer applications is the development of graphics to support verbal and written presentations. There are a number of microcomputer-based packages which can generate bar charts, pie charts and a number of other visual aids for presentation purposes. Also, some multi-purpose packages, such as the Lotus 1-2-3 electronic spreadsheet, have graphics capacities built in.

The Apple Macintosh, introduced in 1984, is a revolutionary computer which utilizes graphics as a central organizing device. Graphics are used to carry out general operating system functions such as running a program or copying disks as well as permitting superior graphic capacity to be included in various printed outputs. The Macintosh uses "icons" — graphic representations of items and activities — rather than words to assist the user. Essentially, the user can treat the computer screen as an automated desktop. By manipulating a mechanical mouse on a desktop, the user can point to various functions on the screen, produce a wide variety of graphics, or call up a word processor or electronic spreadsheet. The Macintosh was designed to permit easy transfer of data among different programs, permitting a level of integration difficult to achieve on other machines.

The impact of the Macintosh is greater than the actual number of computers sold. It is generally believed that the graphics framework developed for the Macintosh will become widely available on other machines. Windows, an icon-based operating system, is an attempt by Microsoft to develop an integrated environment for the already-existing IBM family of machines and clones. In Windows, different areas of the screen will display alternative user options such as a word processor, an electronic spreadsheet, or a business graphics program. Digital Research has brought out GEM (Graphics Environment Manager), which has an interface similar to the Apple Macintosh. At another level, IBM has introduced Topview which, although not based in graphics, does permit easy transfer among different programs.

5. The Telecommunications Packages

One of the increasingly important developments in microcomputer utilization is the use of telecommunications. There are a number of areas in which communications over telephone lines to other systems will become more and more convenient and necessary. These communications would include the following:

1. Querying national databases such as those run by Control Data Corporation, containing demographic information, bibliographic references useful in urban planning and management, and the like.
2. Communicating with national information services such as Compuserve, The Source, etc. which contain a wide range of activities, including computer-specific user forums, useful programs, and electronic mail service among members.
3. Sending and receiving electronic mail to other professionals. Such electronic mail can instantly be transferred from user to user employing a national electronic mail service such as MCI Mail. Such electronic mail services will permit a user to both send and receive messages, reports and possibly even graphics, to others on the system. A user can also send messages to those not on the system by having the message printed at a city near the recipient and mailed from that location. Some of these electronic mail services permit international telex messages to be sent and received. This means that the professional can communicate from a microcomputer at home or at the office to anywhere in the world which has a telex station.

A microcomputer set up for telecommunications needs a modem, a device which converts electronic bits of information into audio signals which can be sent over telephone lines. Such modems are relatively inexpensive when designed to transmit at low speeds, but become significantly more expensive at higher transmission rates. At a higher level of integration, microcomputers can also be "networked," meaning that they can be connected together with high-speed cables. Such a system is sometimes referred to as a "local area network," or LAN, and permits the sharing of programs and data among connected machines. The increasing use of multiple microcomputers in the same office is prompting the move toward LAN's.

6. The Statistical Package

One of the most widely available programs on larger mainframe computers in universities and research centers is the statistical package. Many graduate and undergraduate programs in a wide variety of disciplines have used these mainframe packages, such as SPSS or SAS. In urban planning and management applied statistics are often important analytic tools. Both SPSS and SAS, among others, are available for microcomputers, albeit with varying degrees of success. Fridlund (1986) found widely varying capacity and usefulness in his examination of five packages. The availability of statistical packages on micros will greatly increase the potential for using statistics in planning and management situations. While it is relatively common for universities and research organizations to have access to statistical packages, the typical public sector computing system, perhaps in a county administration building, will not. The advent of widely available micro-based packages will provide a great opportunity to strengthen planning and policy analysis. Urban planners and managers can build statistical models and undertake survey research analysis using inferential statistics.

7. The Word Processor

One of the most obvious uses of the microcomputer is word processing. The more powerful word processing programs can handle large files, do a wide variety of editing tasks including deletions, moves, and insertions, and contain spelling checkers and even grammatical checkers. There is a wide variety of software packages available, and an even wider variety of instructional books and videotapes available explaining this software.

8. Integrated Packages

An integrated package is one which contains a number of different sub-programs. A current good example is Symphony, developed by Lotus Development Corporation, the creator of Lotus 1-2-3. Symphony contains spreadsheet, database, word processing, telecommunications and graphics capacity, all working in a coordinated fashion. The advantage of an integrated package is that a variety of tasks can be performed on a set of data without having to use different programs.

Potentially, an urban planner could call up a national database containing particular demographic information on his or her community and "download" (transfer from the database to the personal computer) the relevant information into an integrated package such as Symphony. The planner could then analyze the demographic data in an electronic spreadsheet format, save it in a database on the microcomputer for further work, and write a report using the word processing portion of the package. The tables generated by the spreadsheet could be integrated with the written report, adding any graphics which might be required.

The disadvantage of such a system is that these integrated packages are extremely complex to design and often will contain a very large number of instructions. Lotus 1-2-3, a very successful electronic spreadsheet, is still selling very well in spite of the introduction of Symphony by Lotus Development Corporation. Lotus 1-2-3 performs its electronic spreadsheet functions well, and is still preferred by many because the instruction set is reasonably sized.

There is every expectation that a large number of integrated packages will emerge in the next decade. The continual growth in the size of the microcomputer in speed and memory capacity will create an environment within which programmers can develop very large programs which do a great many things. For example, Symphony may require a minimum of 320K of memory but any serious application will need 512K or more. Framework, another integrated package, requires 384K to operate at a minimum. It will not be unreasonable to expect many emerging packages to require a million bytes of memory to operate and to be extremely complex.

This general discussion of the various kinds of general packages available for use in planning and management is important to the discussion of specific developments in urban planning and management software. The rapid technological changes occurring will impact the specific applications available in planning and management. The next section discusses current applications of microcomputers (as of the mid-1980's) in planning and management. It is at best a fuzzy snapshot of what in future years will move far beyond the current situation.

Current Utilization of Microcomputers in Planning

It is difficult to assess the actual extent of microcomputer applications in planning because of the widely dispersed use of these machines in public and private environments. However, there are two indicators of the increasing use of microcomputers in planning practice and research — the increasing number of existing planning-specific packages available from different sources, and the growing use of microcomputers in planning situations.

There is a wide variety of planning packages available, particularly in the transportation and the planning information system areas. A number of software packages which address local planning problems, such as fiscal impact analysis and zoning and site design issues, are also being developed. A recent transportation software listing cites 45 different models under the general title of "transportation planning" (U.S. Department of Transportation, 1985). These software packages include both the traditional regionally focused network-based transit and highway models and locally specific traffic impact analysis models. The PRC Voorhees MicroTRIPS package, for example, can simulate a highway and transit network and do travel demand forecasting, loading the network by using a variety of traffic assignment techniques. The vendor claims over 50 installations worldwide. This package, and other similar ones such as those by COMSIS Corporation and Roger Creighton Associates, are scaled-down versions of the larger mainframe computer models such as the Urban Transportation Planning System, developed and sponsored by the U.S. Department of Transportation.

A number of traffic impact models have also been developed. These models assess the traffic impacts of proposed housing and commercial developments on the surrounding roadway system. One package, the Quick Response System, developed by COMSIS Corporation, was funded with federal dollars and is in the public domain. Over 100 copies of this package have been purchased by various organizations, providing many local agencies with powerful but relatively inexpensive analytic capacity. There is good evidence that the package is being used. For example, the Quick Response System has been used in Las Cruces, New Mexico, to examine alternative comprehensive plans, in Portland, Oregon, to analyze alternative uses of vacant tract, and in Clackamas County, Oregon, to examine a 400-acre change in zoning classification (Spanovich, 1984).

While transportation is clearly a leader in the amount of application software available, there are two other areas in which planning-focused software is beginning to emerge — the development of planning information systems and fiscal impact analysis models. The term "planning information systems" is a broad one, and is meant here to refer to the establishment of a database containing a number of different sets of data which can be integrated and manipulated for planning purposes. One example of a land management system which has been implemented on microcomputers is the New Haven, Connecticut Land Use Information System (LUIS). Operating since August, 1984, this system contains detailed information on 26,000 parcels (Kops, Hall, Goetze and Canto, 1986).

On a more generic level, a number of mapping programs have been made available for the microcomputer. While not specifically information systems which are designed to manipulate land-based data, these geographically based display systems are powerful graphic tools. Essentially, these mapping programs predominantly do "choropleth" or "conformant" mapping, in which the coordinates of predefined unit areas, such as census tracts, are mapped to a computer screen, printer, or plotter (Carter, 1984). Color or black/white patterns can be used to differentiate the areas mapped in terms of a selected variable. If the mapped variable is census tract median income for a city, then high income tracts might be colored green and lower income tracts red. There are several of these packages available (Wiggins, 1986). Interestingly, there are also vendors who have coded the geographic coordinates of state, county, census tract, and zip code boundaries, and these can be purchased for use with the mapping programs.

Development impact analysis has also moved to the microcomputer. The Bureau of Economic and Business Research of the University of Florida has developed both a fiscal impact model (Fishkind, Sipe, and Milliman, 1983) and a capital needs assessment model (Milliman, Sipe, and Hopkins, 1983). On another level, Kendig (1984) has developed a computerized method which analyzes zoning ordinances for consistency in site requirements. Stockman (1984) has outlined the wide variety of software packages which were discussed or exhibited at the 1984 annual conference of the American Planning Association.

Unfortunately, while the number of microcomputer-based packages is increasing steadily, it is difficult to determine the extent of microcomputer utilization in planning at this time. Recent surveys of computer utilization have only limited usefulness because micros are only now finding their way into planning practice. One recent survey by Hysom and Ruth (1984) confirms this observation, as does Stockman (1984) in his assessment of the presentations of the 1984 American Planning Association annual meetings. Hysom and Ruth suggest that many planning agencies are considering the purchase of microcomputers, usually in conjunction with already existing mainframe systems. Microcomputers are considered to be just one element of an overall computing system, with the eventual goal of creating local area networks (LAN's) which would connect all computer systems allowing the rapid exchange of information (Davis, 1982; Saal, 1983).

The survey by Hysom and Ruth was taken in 1983 and, according to the researchers, at a time when the typical reference point for microcomputer capacity was an Apple II with 64K bytes (characters) of memory. The responses do not reflect either the 1985-1986 microcomputers which typically contain one-quarter to one-half million bytes of memory or future technology when the desktop computer will be as powerful as current generation minicomputers.

Two Examples of Microcomputer Applications

Two different examples of the use of the microcomputer in planning practice and research will be presented to show the potential of the machines. Obviously, space limitations do not allow an extensive treatment of the two cases, but the presentation should be useful in highlighting alternatives.

The first example is drawn from an extensive transit study which used a number of different commercially available packages and original programming in a systematic fashion. The advantage of using different programs is the simple fact that often no single package is totally able to do all tasks equally well. In this transit study (Pucher and Brail, 1984), data on approximately 100 transit routes were entered into VisiFile, a straightforward file manager in which the computer screen can be made to look like a paper form. The ease of data entry permitted relatively unsophisticated computer users to enter large amounts of information quickly into labeled fields: the process was very much like filling in the blanks on a questionnaire. In turn, the data were transferred from VisiFile data files into VisiCalc and eventually, when available, into Lotus 1-2-3. These are both electronic spreadsheets, and both permitted exploration and analysis of the transit route data. Since the project involved the use of a simulation model to shift service levels on the transit routes, a program in the BASIC programming language was written to do the calculations. It was also possible to use Lotus 1-2-3 to do the simulation, but the process was cumbersome and not as flexible as the BASIC program.

The BASIC model could read in data from Lotus 1-2-3 and output the simulation results, involving transit route changes, back to

Lotus 1-2-3. The simulation output was then analyzed and graphs made for inclusion in the project report using the Lotus 1-2-3 software. Limited exploratory statistical analysis was required and performed using a microcomputer-based package. The data could just as easily have been transferred, or "uploaded," to a mainframe statistical package, such as SPSS (Statistical Package for the Social Sciences), for analysis. With a modem, which permits communication between a microcomputer and another computer over telephone lines, the microcomputer could be used as a terminal to the mainframe (Jordan, 1983). Or, the transit route data could have been updated and maintained over time for future analysis by using either Lotus 1-2-3 or a file manager.

The important point is that no centralized computer facility was used for the project. The entire process was done on commonly available microcomputers with software tools which were unavailable on the mainframe computer at this time. More importantly, under tight project deadlines there was **no queue** for the mainframe and no concern if the mainframe "went down" (stopped running). Since there was more than one microcomputer available, there was redundancy in the system. If one needed repairs, although none did, there were others. Since the micros were always "on-line," the staff could assume that any machine would be usable whenever needed. The project came in at budget and on time, in part because project management was able to reduce the uncertainties of dealing with a central computing environment, and because the microcomputer software available was easily mastered by relatively unsophisticated users.

As a second example, let us construct a simple land use planning scenario to illustrate how local analysis and decision-making can be enhanced through the use of the microcomputer. A housing development and adjacent shopping center have been proposed for a tract adjacent to a major arterial highway. The local planners are interested in examining the impacts of the development on the municipal budget, on the local transportation system, and on environmental quality. They decide to use their microcomputer.

First, an electronic spreadsheet is constructed of the costs and revenues associated with the proposed development. This spreadsheet uses the techniques outlined in Burchell and Listokin, *The Fiscal Impact Handbook* (1978), to establish the expected costs and revenues from the project. (Or, the BASIC program of a fiscal impact model found in Chapter 7 of this book could be adapted. Also, an existing model, such as the one by Fishkind, Sipe and Milliman (1983), could be used.)

The transportation impacts are analyzed by the Quick Response System program, discussed earlier and available from the Transportation Systems Center. Trip generation rates from the expected development are calculated, distributed in various directions, and assigned to particular highway links. The effects of additional traffic created by the proposed development on the highway system can be evaluated in terms of the amount of increased congestion and the potential roadway improvements which might alleviate the situation.

Typically, a locality has a capital improvement program which contains proposed transportation projects. Federal regulations require a transportation improvement program (TIP) if federal dollars are involved. Such improvements are obvious candidates to be entered into a computerized database for easy display, analysis and updating. If a local TIP has been put into a file manager or database management program, then the current programmed expenditures can be examined to see if the roadway improvements implied by the development either are already in the program or can be added. Depending on the sophistication of the database management program used, expenditures and federal, state, local or private contributions may be juggled from year to year to fit new projects in if there is room.

Also, the air quality impacts of the proposed development can be evaluated using one of several package programs. For example, ROADWAY AQ is a spreadsheet template which will calculate carbon monoxide, hydrocarbon and oxides of nitrogen emissions from the transportation activity which is caused by development (U.S. Department of Transportation, 1985).

Finally, by use of a mapping program, any of a range of estimated impacts of the proposed development can be displayed in color on a computer screen or printed out. For example, carbon monoxide concentrations can be calculated for a set of zones set up around the development.

Issues in Hardware and Software Selection

There are four issues which the planner and manager will face in hardware and software selection. The planner or manager must necessarily realize that hardware and software choices are interdependent. A particular software product may run on only one kind of microcomputer. On the other side, only certain microcomputers are powerful enough to handle particular applications. Here are the four issues:

1. The rapid evolution of microtechnology
2. The availability of "off-the-shelf" software
3. The viability and costs of custom-designed software
4. The selection of a particular package for a task

These four topics can provide a frame of reference which can shed some light on the process of software selection.

The Rapid Evolution of Technology

The earlier chapter on hardware discussed how quickly technology has evolved in the period since 1977. This development of microtechnology means that currently powerful machines will become obsolete at some future time. This means that the user will either have to upgrade or buy a new machine. Owning a machine with a large base of installed users will more likely ensure that upgrade components will be available. The general recommendation is that expressed in the earlier chapter on hardware — buy a more powerful machine than is needed for the immediate job, and buy a popular one that is upgradable. Machines with open architecture and available slots or plugs for plug-in components will probably have upgrade components produced by a variety of sources. Already there are speed-up kits available for the IBM PC's and clones which use the 8088 chip, replacing this slower chip with the faster 80286 chip. However, even the Apple Macintosh with no slots is upgradable by the dealer, often by simply replacing the motherboard or other components. The best test for a machine's potential upgrade capacity is empirical — are there upgrade kits available already, or is there a company tradition of making upgrades available for older products?

Availability of Software

In general, the analyst should seldom commission a custom programming application if commercial software is available. An individual programming effort is usually expensive and time-consuming. The available commercial packages will usually be more than adequate for the task. The electronic spreadsheet program, such as Lotus 1-2-3, Supercalc, or Multiplan, is the single most important planning and management tool. In the next chapter, the electronic spreadsheet will be discussed in detail with a number of examples from urban planning analysis. It is often much easier to develop an electronic spreadsheet model than to write a program in a programming language such as BASIC, Pascal, C or Modula-2. This point will be reinforced and discussed further in succeeding chapters. Also, the advent of project scheduling, statistical analysis and database manipulation software provides additional reasons why commercially available software is often a preferred option to writing a custom program.

The Viability and Costs of Custom Software

Specially designed software for a particular situation is sometimes the only option available. For example, a community might wish to develop a special program to assess developers for a portion of off-site improvements. An electronic spreadsheet program is not appropriate and no existing package is available from any vendor. Or, perhaps a commercial package is available from a software development firm but it is too expensive for a license. Or, while the cost of a single license for one machine is reasonable, there are six microcomputers in the office requiring six copies of the program: this single-license approach can be very expensive.

Unfortunately, the limited number of potential purchasers in a smaller profession such as urban planning or public management will not attract the serious concern of specialized software developers: potential profits are meager. Assuming that the custom programming effort goes forward, then caution and patience are advised. The writing of custom software, either by staff within the agency or by consultants from outside, requires patience and a serious commitment to testing the program. The process of error-checking can be extremely time-consuming. Initially, the program has to be "debugged" to make it run satisfactorily from beginning to end. This process can be extremely tedious in itself. However, there is a second level of error-checking in which various combinations of data are entered into the model to determine model behavior. It is not uncommon to find errors in program logic which may show up only under some relatively unlikely combination of input variables. It is important that a number of error checks be run on any custom programming effort to ensure to the greatest degree possible that the program is sound.

Selecting a Particular Package

By "commercial" package we are referring to computer programs which are sold outright or licensed to a purchaser by a vendor. At the broadest level there are the general types of programs, such as electronic spreadsheets or database programs, which have already been discussed. At a more narrow level there are the specialized programs in urban planning and management, such as the urban transportation planning models. At both levels, there are often at least several packages available from which one can choose. Below are some general common sense rules for selection among competing packages.

First, choose only among packages which work on your hardware as currently configured or on a future system which you know is absolutely guaranteed to work with the selected package. There are severe incompatibility problems between computers from different manufacturers and even among machines of the same manufacturer. Assume that you own an IBM Personal Computer. Even if the package claims that it will work with an IBM PC there are still questions to be answered. The IBM PC can contain any number of different video display cards, many of which are incompatible with each other. Software designed to work with one card may not work on yours if you have a different video card. Also, different printers use different software controls to direct the printing. Compatibility is also an issue with printers.

One of the major stumbling blocks to the use of some packages is memory. Programs are becoming increasingly memory-hungry, as we have already discussed. Also, the minimum requirement memory which is sometimes listed for a package is often not adequate at all. A program such as Lotus 1-2-3 (Version 2.0) which lists a requirement minimum of 256K of random access memory can do very little with this memory. Lotus 1-2-3 is much better run with at least 512K of memory so that a reasonable size problem can be entered.

Many complex systems require a large-capacity hard disk storage device to run effectively. If your current computer has no hard disk, make certain that the one purchased will in fact work efficiently with the software selected. Hard disks vary widely in speed of data access and technical specifications.

Second, determine the general reputation of the product from colleagues, computer stores, and publications. Most major products have been reviewed in trade publications and have developed a reputation among knowledgeable individuals. The specialized software in planning and management is a more difficult matter. There are, for example, several transportation planning packages which purport to do much the same thing. Determining which to use is difficult unless the user can contact colleagues who have used the different packages. In this situation, the user has to depend on the general experience of the program authors and the firm which is selling the package. Over time product reviews will begin to emerge in the planning and management fields which will provide additional information. For example, the *Journal of the American Planning Association* is publishing reviews on planning software. The first of these was on mapping packages (Wiggins, 1986).

Third, after narrowing the field to compatible products with strong reputations, pick a product which has enough capacity for the intended jobs to which the program will be put. This requires an extensive assessment of the size of the problems expected to be encountered in the course of work activities. As an example, consider the development of a database of all land use parcels in a community. Assuming that one would want to have 50 items (or, in database terms, fields) of information on each of 20,000 parcels (or records), then at a minimum the database would have to be able to handle a million pieces of information. In the succeeding chapter on databases we shall examine this issue in more detail, but the point is clear in this context — choose a system of adequate size.

Fourth, even if capacity is sufficient, be sure that the program possesses the appropriate features for efficient operation. In the land use parcel example there will be the need to ask the database questions about the number and the nature of the land uses within the community. Different database programs permit different kinds of questions, with the more complex ones permitting a broad range of queries which would not be available in the simpler ones.

Fifth, determine how well the program fits with other programs with which it will have to interact. There are two levels on which the interaction can occur. Any selected program should be able to share information with other programs and to use the same equipment. In general, sharing information means that data files stored on disk can be understood by a number of different selected programs, each of which has been chosen to perform a particular task. For example, it may be important to take the output from an electronic spreadsheet and put it into a database program. Since different programs store data on disk differently, there must be provision in available software to permit the reading of files from the other program. File incompatibility among programs is a serious problem at this time, although there are standardized methods by which data can be transferred. Even if the situation should improve over the next decade, the issue will still be there, defining, at times, the choice or rejection of a piece of software.

Programs also need to be able to use the same hardware. Since many micros support a number of different video formats, printers, and storage devices, care must be taken that a selected set of programs will be hardware compatible as a group. Should one need a special graphics card, then all programs using the same machine will have to be able to use the same card.

Sixth, be sure that the program possesses a high effectiveness-cost ratio. The program's power and user-friendliness should be high relative to the cost of the package. This means that some expensive programs are worth it in spite of the cost. Correspondingly, there are inexpensive programs, such as PC-CALC, PC-FILE and PC-WRITE, each of which costs under a hundred dollars, which are extremely good values. These three are sometimes called "shareware," and were developed by small groups of individuals to be shared at modest costs among users.

These six levels of program analysis — computer compatibility, reputation, capacity, features, program compatibility, and effectiveness-cost ratio — are basic to the selection process. One seldom makes a selection in a vacuum. There are any number of individuals and groups available for advice, as long as you remember to ask. These six rules, coupled with common sense and shared information, will go a long way toward making hardware and software choices easier.

Future Directions in Software Development

There are a number of evolutions in software design occurring which will be important to the easier use of microcomputers in future years. In general, these developments will make it easier to handle the more complex integrated packages which are being developed to do a wide range of tasks within a common framework. There are three particular evolutionary developments which will have substantial impacts on the urban planning and management fields. First, microcomputers will become easier to use because of graphic aids. As suggested earlier, more and more programs are using icons to represent different computer activities. For example, the screen might contain a number of images, such as a file folder representing a database, a telephone representing a telecommunications option, and a matrix of rows and columns representing an electronic spreadsheet. The initial widely touted computer sporting this icon-based system is the Apple Macintosh.

There is a second area in which micros will become easier to use. Microcomputers will become better able to exchange data among different programs and different computer systems. Currently, many programs store data on disk differently. Thus, a Lotus 1-2-3 worksheet stored on disk is not directly usable by another spreadsheet program or a word processing package. There are file conversion routines which many software packages contain, but file conversion is a separate step and is not always available. The potential development of standardized data storage formats would permit a greater flexibility for the user and a better chance of sharing work with other machines and other users.

Finally, there is the last software development issue — the increasing size and complexity of commercially available software. This issue has already been discussed in the context of the increasing size and speed of future hardware. However, it is not only general purpose computer software that will become more powerful: special purpose software will also emerge and become increasingly able to perform complex urban planning and management tasks.

One of the often missed elements in the current microtechnological boom is the development of a new generation of programmers who possess both profession-specific skills as well as computer programming abilities. Already there is evidence that the introduction of microcomputers into large corporations has affected the capacity and interest of staff professionals to do computer programming and manipulation. Staff who began with manipulating simple spreadsheet models have moved both to more complex models and to original programming in languages such as BASIC, Pascal or C when spreadsheets were not useful. The current and future training of urban planning and management professionals in computer skills will have an effect on the development of those specialized tools useful in planning and management.

Conclusion

There is little doubt that both microcomputer hardware and software are evolving rapidly. The clear message is that the potential user in a planning or management position will have to stay flexible and understand these shifts. It is also true, however, that fundamental knowledge of a limited number of microcomputer tools will provide the professional with powerful capacity to do his or her work. The first and perhaps most important tool for the planner or manager is the electronic spreadsheet, discussed in the next chapter.

Suggested Further Readings

Klosterman, Richard E. 1986. "An Assessment of Three Microcomputer Software Packages for Planning Analysis," *Journal of the American Planning Association* 52:2 (Spring): 199-202.

Kops, Daniel W., Jr., Lawrence Hall, Jr., Rolf Goetze, and Gerardo Canto. 1986. *Managing Municipal Information Needs Using Microcomputers.* Planning Advisory Service Number 393. Chicago, Illinois: American Planning Association.

Lima, Robert J. 1984. *Planning Software Survey.* Planning Advisory Service Number 388. Chicago, Illinois: American Planning Association.

Ottensmann, John R. 1984. *Using Personal Computers in Public Agencies.* New York: John Wiley and Sons.

Standefer, Norman R. and James Rider. 1983. "The Politics of Automating the Planning Office," *Planning* 49:6 (June): 18-21.

U.S. Department of Transportation. 1985. *Microcomputers in Transportation Software and Source Book, February 1985.* Prepared by the Methods Division, Urban Mass Transportation Administration. Washington: U.S. Department of Transportation.

Whited, William. 1982. *Using Microcomputers in Urban Planning.* Planning Advisory Service Report Number 372. Chicago, Illinois: American Planning Association.

4

Introduction to Electronic Spreadsheets

Introduction

One of the most important software packages for the microcomputer is the "electronic spreadsheet." The electronic spreadsheet is particularly appropriate for urban planning and management applications because of its ability to handle two-dimensional tables for modeling and financial analysis applications. The first package developed for the micro which attained wide popularity was VisiCalc. This electronic spreadsheet was originally developed for the Apple II microcomputer in the 1978-79 period. It has been reported that VisiCalc legitimized the Apple II as a business machine rather than as a toy for games or electronic hobbyists. Successive improvements to the electronic spreadsheet format with the introduction of Lotus 1-2-3, Jazz, and others have made this software tool an important tool for professional use.

There is one curious thing about an electronic spreadsheet. We could spend a great number of pages describing exactly what an electronic spreadsheet is and what it does, but you would not know its full power without using the package. To fully understand the concept and the operation you must spend time with it. The discussions in this chapter will utilize Lotus 1-2-3 because of its wide popularity at the time of this writing. Ideally, the reader should have access to a spreadsheet package on a microcomputer. There are many packages available at this point for a wide variety of computers. Even the most inexpensive micro generally has a spreadsheet available, a tribute to the power of the concept. However, even if you do not have access to a spreadsheet program on a microcomputer, it is still possible to obtain a working knowledge of concepts and applications from this chapter.

The Concept

Seven items define the conceptual base of the spreadsheet.

1. A series of rows and columns of data is always on the screen. This series is really a matrix, or array, of cells.
2. Each cell can be individually addressed with data entered or erased.
3. The cells can contain any of three kinds of items:
    a. Numeric data
    b. Labels — alphanumeric strings of characters
    c. Cell referents (locations of other cells) which often contain equations
4. The numeric data in the cells can be algebraically manipulated and the output of these calculations placed in another cell.
5. There is a **command line** somewhere on the screen which is a menu of task options in the program.
6. This command line is **hierarchical** in structure. This means that a selection of a task from the menu will often bring up another menu with specific extensions of the selected item.
7. A wide variety of operations can be performed from the command line including retrieving or saving a file on disk, moving data around the spreadsheet, formatting the data, or printing out a piece of the spreadsheet.

While VisiCalc was the first popular spreadsheet, there have been important new developments in spreadsheet design. We shall concentrate our efforts on Lotus 1-2-3, a powerful and widely used package. Lotus 1-2-3 represents the combination of spreadsheet, graphic displays and database management within an integrated framework which has become a standard in the industry. Lotus 1-2-3 is very close to VisiCalc in structure and choice of commands and was designed specifically this way. Most spreadsheet programs look reasonably alike, so learning one will quickly enable one to learn another.

Some interesting evolutions in spreadsheet design must be understood against hardware restrictions. The original VisiCalc program was relatively compact in memory utilization because it was designed for 8-bit machines. You may remember from Chapter 2 that an 8-bit processor like the Apple II 6502 or the CP/M Z80 can directly address only 64K of memory. There are ways to trick an 8-bit microprocessor and address 128K or 192K in 64K segments such as is found on the

Apple IIe, but this technique was not widely used in the 1978-79 period. The designers of VisiCalc had to design a program which would fit within 64K of addressable memory of the Apple II 8-bit processor.

The electronic spreadsheet program is generally designed to be loaded into memory all at once, with all commands immediately available. This means that any spreadsheet instruction can be immediately executed from memory without continual disk access to program instructions. VisiCalc, as the original 8-bit spreadsheet for a 64K Apple II system, was about 30K in size. This means that 34K is available for workspace for spreadsheet data, labels and formulas. Not only is the program always in memory in an electronic spreadsheet, but the worksheet is also. This means that all the data, formulas, and labels for a particular spreadsheet application are in memory along with the program. Electronic spreadsheets, as outlined in the chapter on software, are extremely memory-hungry since everything is resident at the same time.

The Lotus 1-2-3 program itself requires over 100K or more, depending on the version being used. The program was designed to be run on the IBM family of machines, or clones, which utilize the Intel 8088 and related microprocessors. Lotus 1-2-3 requires about four times the amount of memory of the earlier VisiCalc. Also, since Lotus 1-2-3 uses "help" files located on the disk, the program disk must be located in a drive at all times. This means that at least two drives are required for the system — one for the program and one for the data disk.

This discussion points to the need to balance software needs with hardware requirements. Lotus 1-2-3 does more than VisiCalc because of built-in graphics and data management capacity. However, Lotus 1-2-3 also requires more hardware and more memory. As the price of memory continues to fall and microprocessors become more powerful, software will consume more space and perform more functions. In its most recent form (Version 2), Lotus 1-2-3 is only possible in a machine which contains at least 256K or more of memory. This suggests the following "law" of software development — **application programs will expand in size to fill the capacity of the machine available.** Program designers write their creations to current and emerging technology.

A Simple Population Projection Example

The first example of an electronic spreadsheet is a population projection model using a variety of projection methods. In Exhibit 4-1 a blank Lotus 1-2-3 spreadsheet is shown as it would appear on the screen. Note its simplicity. In the top left hand corner is "A1:" which tells us on which cell the cursor is located. Just below is a list of commands — Worksheet, Range, etc., which are operations which the program can perform. This command structure will be discussed in more detail subsequently. The blank area is the matrix of cells within which the user will work. The rows are numbered down the left-hand side of the screen, while the columns are given letter designations. Hence the cell in the upper left-hand corner of the matrix is designated "A1." The cell immediately to the right is labeled "B1."

Exhibit 4-1

A Blank Lotus 1-2-3 Worksheet

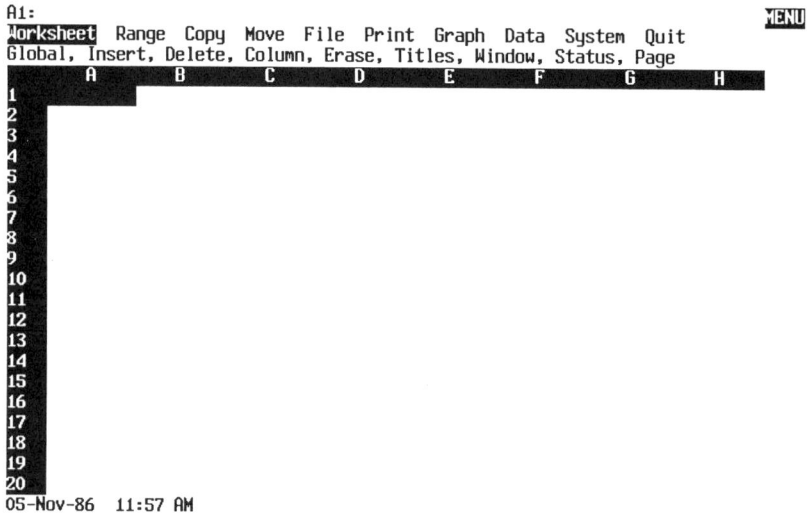

The advantage of using both letters and numbers to designate a particular cell can be seen in the following example. If one were to add the contents of cell A1 to the contents of cell B1 and divide by C2, the algebra would look like this:

$$(A1 + B1) / C2 \quad (/ \text{ means divide})$$

This notation can be called "cell algebra" since it is specific to particular cells. If one attempted to designate both rows and columns with numbers, as would occur in standard matrix algebra notation, then the row value would have to be differentiable from the column value. Microsoft Corporation tried this approach in an electronic spreadsheet called Multiplan in which the upper left-hand corner is called R1C1, for row 1 and column 1. While conceptually more in tune with mathematical notation, the Multiplan approach can become unnecessarily complex and difficult to read. The same equation shown above would be:

$$(R1C1 + R1C2) / R2C3$$

Essentially, R1C1 (Row 1, Column 1), is a different and more cumbersome label for cell A1. Correspondingly, R1C2 and R2C3 are the same as B1 and C2. Most spreadsheets have followed the letter and number labeling found in VisiCalc and Lotus 1-2-3 — A1, B1, etc. — and it will be used here. Unfortunately, the more complex equations in applied model building such as those found in urban planning analysis do not easily lend themselves to a cell algebra approach. On balance, however, this system is the best of current choices.

The matrix on the screen as seen in Exhibit 4-1 shows 20 rows and eight columns, A through H. Do not be misled. The matrix is much bigger than the area displayed on the screen. A Lotus 1-2-3 worksheet in Version 2.0 can contain 8,192 rows and 256 columns. By contrast, in the earlier VisiCalc the matrix was 254 rows down by 63 columns wide. However, the available memory for the spreadsheet in the computer will often fill up before the matrix has information in every cell. As has been emphasized, spreadsheet programs are very memory-hungry if the user wants to build large applications.

The potential of the electronic spreadsheet is great for the kinds of analysis done in urban planning and management. Let us explore some of this potential with a simple example which projects population for four communities — Alpha, Beta, Gamma, and Delta — in Athens County. In the process of discussing this example, we will show how linear projection techniques can be used in an electronic spreadsheet. The basic information on the four communities is shown in Exhibit 4-2 as it would appear on the computer screen with row and column designations indicated. Population information is available for 1960, 1970 and 1980 for the four communities. Note in the upper left-hand corner "A1: 'REGIONAL POPULATION PROJECTION MODEL - VERSION 1." This indicates that the cursor is on cell A1 in which is located the long label beginning "REGIONAL...." The spreadsheet projects population to 1990 and 2000 using the linear model.

Exhibit 4-2

Regional Population Projection Model, Version 1

A1: 'REGIONAL POPULATION PROJECTION MODEL - VERSION 1   READY

	A	B	C	D
1	REGIONAL POPULATION PROJECTION MODEL - VERSION 1			
2		POPULATION	POPULATION	POPULATION
3	MUNICIPALITY	1960	1970	1980
4	---------	---------	---------	---------
5	ALPHA	3100	3400	3500
6	BETA	12800	15700	17800
7	GAMMA	14000	21900	33000
8	DELTA	1700	2000	2200
9				
10		31600	43000	56500
11				
12		AVERAGE	LINEAR MODEL	LINEAR MODEL
13	MUNICIPALITY	CHANGE	PROJECTED 1990	PROJECTED 2000
14	---------	---------	---------	---------
15	ALPHA	200	3700	3900
16	BETA	2500	20300	22800
17	GAMMA	9500	42500	52000
18	DELTA	250	2450	2700
19				
20		12450	68950	81400

20-Jan-87   12:10 PM

Introduction to the Population Projection Spreadsheet

This spreadsheet shown in Exhibit 4-2 is essentially what would be seen on screen, or on the printed page without the row and column designations. The conceptual breakthrough of spreadsheet design is found in what is **behind** the entries in the cells. The Cell Listing of the spreadsheet is found in Exhibit 4-3. This listing shows the mathematics which produces the projections of population found in Exhibit 4-2. The listing is the product of a separate program called Spreadsheet Auditor which produces a range of reports on a spreadsheet. This particular listing shows the contents of each cell. An examination of this cell listing is important to understanding how a spreadsheet works. Essentially, the spreadsheet concept involves two levels of presentation. There is the spreadsheet "appearance," as is found on the screen in Exhibit 4-2. And there is the spreadsheet "reality," the equations and general structure behind the appearance, as is shown in Exhibit 4-3.

The linear model spreadsheet in Exhibit 4-2 is split into two tables, one below the other. This spreadsheet design principle is used here because it permits more on a single screen and permits cell list-

Introduction to Electronic Spreadsheets 55

ings to fit on the page without complications. However, the **vertical** structures of spreadsheets presented subsequently are also easier to navigate than comparable horizontal structures.

Exhibit 4-3

Cell Listing

Regional Population Projection Model, Version 1

	A	B	C	D
1	'REGIONAL POPULATION PROJECTION MODEL - VERSION 1			
2		^POPULATION	^POPULATION	^POPULATION
3	'MUNICIPALITY	^1960	^1970	^1980
4	'---------------	'---------------	'---------------	'----------
5	'ALPHA	3100	3400	3500
6	'BETA	12800	15700	17800
7	'GAMMA	14000	21900	33000
8	'DELTA	1700	2000	2200
9	'---------------	'---------------	'---------------	'----------
10		@SUM(B5..B8)	@SUM(C5..C8)	@SUM(D5..D8)
11				
12		^AVERAGE CHG	^LINEAR MODEL	^LINEAR MODEL
13	'MUNICIPALITY	^1960-80	^PROJECTED 1990	^PROJECTED 2000
14	'---------------	'---------------	'---------------	'----------
15	'ALPHA	(D5-B5)/2	(D5+(1*B15))	(D5+(2*B15))
16	'BETA	(D6-B6)/2	(D6+(1*B16))	(D6+(2*B16))
17	'GAMMA	(D7-B7)/2	(D7+(1*B17))	(D7+(2*B17))
18	'DELTA	(D8-B8)/2	(D8+(1*B18))	(D8+(2*B18))
19		'---------------	'---------------	'----------
20			@SUM(C15..C18)	@SUM(D15..D18)
21				
22				

In the top table the first column (A) contains the names of the towns. In columns B, C, and D are the community populations for 1960 through 1980. In the second table, column B contains the first formula in which the average change in population between 1960 and 1980 is calculated. Alpha grew from 3100 in 1960 to 3500 in 1980, an increase of 400. The average change **per decade** for Alpha over the 1960 to 1980 period for Alpha is 200 (400 divided by 2 decades, 1960-1970 and 1970-1980). The number 200, the average change 1960-80 for Alpha, is found in cell B15 of the spreadsheet.

The cell listing in Exhibit 4-3 is a matrix of the numbers, labels and equations which lie behind the spreadsheet. The cell listing is in a row and column format identical to the spreadsheet itself. While the number 200 is what is reported out on the printed report or would be seen on the computer screen, the Cell Listing shows the equation behind the number in cell B15:

$$(D5-B5) / 2$$

This equation is an example of cell algebra. It means that the contents of cell B5 (Alpha's 1960 population) are subtracted from D5 (Alpha's 1980 population) and this difference divided by 2. This equation calculates the average change in population per decade for Alpha. Note that B16 contains the same equation except that "6's" replace "5's." In cells B17 and B18, the "6's" are replaced with "7's" and "8's," respectively.

Besides equations, the Cell Listing also contains numbers and labels. Note that cell A1 contains a long label, REGIONAL POPULATION PROJECTION MODEL - VERSION 1. The label in A1 is preceded by a single quote to indicate that it is a label. Other labels, such as AVERAGE CHG in cell B12, have a "^" in front: in Lotus 1-2-3 this character means that the label should be centered within the column. Cell B10 contains @SUM(B5..B8), a built-in function which adds all numbers in cells B5 to B8. All spreadsheets contain a wide variety of built-in functions such as averages, sums, net present value, and many others. Columns C and D in the bottom table contain the projected populations for 1990 and 2000.

The Linear Model

In a linear model the assumed growth is a straight line, as shown in Exhibit 4-4. Assuming a community with a population of 10,000 in 1980 grows by an average amount of 4,000 each year, a linear model indicates that over a 10-year period the community will grow to 50,000 in 1990.

The simple linear model can be represented by:

$$V(T+N) = V(T) + (N * AVGCHG) \quad \text{Note: * means multiply}$$

where:

V(T+N),V(T)	Projected variable at time T+N and T
AVGCHG	The average change in past time periods
N	The number of time periods into the future for the projection

Exhibit 4-4

The Linear Model

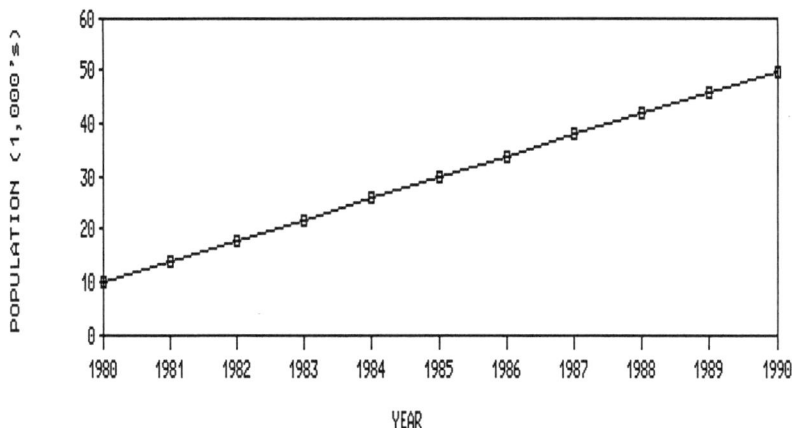

Essentially, the model takes the average change of past periods and applies it to future time periods. Since T is considered the current time for which data are available, V(T) is the 1980 population for the different communities. In the example in Exhibit 4-2 and 4-3, V(T) for Alpha is 3500. Since population data are available by decade, the time period is a decade also. For the year 1990 N is one, a single decade projection. Hence:

$$V(T+1) = V(T) + (1 * AVGCHG)$$

For Alpha:

$$\text{Population}_{1990} = \text{Population}_{1980} + (1 * \text{AvgChange}_{1960-80})$$

$$3700 = 3500 + (1 * 200)$$

In cell algebra notation, cell C15 would contain:

$$(D5+(1*B15))$$

For the year 2000, N would become 2. Alpha's 2000 projection would be:

$$\text{Population}_{2000} = \text{Population}_{1980} + (2*\text{AvgChange}_{1960-80})$$

$$3900 = 3500 + (2 * 200)$$

Cell D15 would contain:

$$(D5 + (2 * B15))$$

Each of the four communities has had its population projected with a linear model. It is clear once again from the cell listing that linear model equations have a similar structure. Each cell has its own equation referring specifically to the particular cells required: this is the cell algebra discussed earlier.

While it is true that each cell has a unique equation, one of the essential components of an electronic spreadsheet is the ability to easily replicate equations which have a similar structure. It is possible to directly type in the linear model equations in columns C and D in the bottom table for the four cities. It is much faster and more accurate for the program to simply copy the equations, changing the appropriate row or column designations when necessary. For example, the user would enter the equation for cell C15 and D15 initially, but then would use a copy command to generate C16 through C18 and D16 through D18.

While copying an equation for four cities may seem trivial, picture the boredom, potential errors, and time necessary to do similar equations for 100 cities. Electronic spreadsheets, of necessity, require a replicate function to make the peculiar cell-specific algebra workable.

The Command Structure of an Electronic Spreadsheet

The electronic spreadsheet will contain a command line somewhere on the spreadsheet which presents options for manipulating, retrieving, storing, and printing worksheets which have been created. As an example of the kinds of commands a typical spreadsheet will contain, Exhibit 4-5 contains a brief summary of the Lotus 1-2-3 command structure. In Lotus 1-2-3, there are 10 general sets of commands each of which in turn encompasses sets of more specific instructions. The WORKSHEET commands perform general operations such as inserting or deleting columns or rows in a worksheet, or changing the width of a column. RANGE commands operate on selected parts of the spreadsheet, such as formatting the data in terms of number of decimal places or with dollar signs. The COPY command replicates numbers, labels, and formulas across the spreadsheet. This is a very necessary and powerful tool when dealing with cell-specific algebra.

The MOVE command will transfer data, labels, or equations to different locations in the spreadsheet. FILE commands control the access to worksheets stored on disk. Files can be saved and retrieved from disk, as well as being combined or taken apart. The PRINT commands output the worksheets to a variety of printers and plotters. The GRAPH commands set up worksheet data to be displayed as charts both on the screen and on printers and plotters. Finally, the DATA commands permit limited database-type manipulation of the spreadsheet, including sorting and querying the database. The DATA command also contains two wonderful additions which first appear in Version 2 — matrix manipulation, including inversion and multiplication, and multiple regression analysis.

There are a great many tasks which a spreadsheet can accomplish. This short introduction to the command structure of one successful spreadsheet program shows the typical kinds of activities which can be done. A spreadsheet is easily generated, manipulated, printed out or saved on disk. One of the primary difficulties is the need to use cell algebra and the complications which arise as a result.

A Second Example

In the first example a relatively simple linear model was presented. In this expanded example, the four communities in Athens County will have their populations projected by four alternative models. The spreadsheet for this example is shown in Exhibit 4-6.

This spreadsheet is more complex than the earlier linear model spreadsheet in Exhibit 4-2. To simplify the presentation, 1990 is the only projection year. The different municipal-level models shown in Exhibit 4-6 include: (1) the linear model, (2) the exponential model, (3) the modified exponential model, and (4) a simple multiplier model using persons per household and projected households. A regional constrained model is presented as an overlay to the projection methods presented, where the projections for each community are adjusted to match an exogenous regional total.

These models represent a broad variety of options for projecting any kind of data. Broader discussions of the alternative methods of projecting population can be found in Krueckeberg and Silvers (1974).

Exhibit 4-5

Lotus 1-2-3 Worksheet Commands

The following commands are in the Version 2 of the Lotus 1-2-3 electronic spreadsheet program. The Command line is evoked by the "/" key.

- WORKSHEET (These commands perform general operations.)

Global	Performs command for entire worksheet.
Insert	Inserts a row or column.
Delete	Deletes a row or column.
Column	Sets a column width.
Erase	Clears out the entire worksheet.
Titles	Sets up horizontal or vertical titles.
Window	The screen can be divided into two areas each of which contains a different section of the worksheet.
Status	Provides information on available memory, etc.
Page	Sets a page break in the worksheet.

- RANGE (These commands operate on a portion of the worksheet.)

Format	Permits the cell values or labels to be displayed in a variety of ways — with a particular number of decimal places, as a percent, with dollar signs, etc.
Label-Prefix	The label can be right or left justified, or centered.
Erase	A portion of the worksheet can be erased.
Name	A worksheet range can be given a name.
Justify	Permits paragraphs to be created in a worksheet using sets of columns.
Protect	A range of cells can be protected so that they cannot be changed without being unprotected.
Unprotect	Permits a range of cells to be unprotected so they can be changed.
Input	Permits data to be entered into unprotected cells in range.

Exhibit 4-5, continued

Value   Converts formulas to values for a given range.
Transpose   Tranposes a column into a row or a row into a column.

- COPY (Copies data, labels or formulas across cells. Note the problem of absolute versus relative addressing of formulas.)

- MOVE (Moves data, labels or formulas across cells.)

- FILE (These commands save a worksheet to disk under a DOS name, retrieve a worksheet from disk into memory so it can worked on, and do various other file operations. Note that worksheets can be combined, and portions of worksheets can be extracted for use alone.)

Retrieve   Brings a file from disk into memory so it can be worked on.
Save   Puts a worksheet in memory onto disk using a name of 8 characters or less. For example, one might store a file called "HIGHWAY." On the disk directory it will be called "HIGHWAY.WK1," indicating that it is a special Lotus worksheet file.
Combine   Two files can be put together. Note that this process must be done with care so that one file does not simply write data over another.
Xtract   A portion of a file can be taken out for use by itself. Care must be taken that one understand the difference between extracting formulas (tricky) and only data.
Erase   Eliminates a worksheet from disk.
List   Lists names of files on disk.
Import   Copies a print file (in ASCII format) produced by a wordprocessor or similar program into the worksheet.
Directory   Permits a file directory to be changed.

- PRINT (These commands will print the worksheet in memory onto a printer or disk.)

Exhibit 4-5, continued

- GRAPH (Permits data in a spreadsheet to be displayed on the computer screen as graphics — line, bar and pie charts. Requires that the IBM PC or compatible have the standard graphics card installed. These graphics can be printed on a dot-matrix printer, on a laser printer, or with a plotter.)

Type	Sets type of graph to be displayed.
X-range	Sets the X-axis data range.
A-F range	Sets up to 6 different ranges which can be graphed at the same time on the Y-axis.
Reset	Resets all settings to default values.
View	Shows the graph on the computer screen.
Save	Saves a picture to disk under the selected name.
Options	Calls up commands to create titles, legends, etc. on the graph.
Name	Gives a name to current graph settings.
Quit	Quits out of the Graph commands.

- DATA (Puts data into table format or rearranges data.)

Fill	Fills a sequence of numbers into a range of cells.
Table	Creates a data table which permits the testing of various values in formulas — a type of sensitivity analysis.
Sort	Sorts rows of data based on the values of data into one (primary sort field) or two (primary and secondary sort fields). Treats the worksheet data as a relational database.
Query	Permits the worksheet acting as a database to be asked questions about the values in the cells. This is an awkward procedure which is generally more easily done in a regular database program.
Distribution	Calculates a frequency distribution.
Matrix	Can multiply or take the inverse of a matrix up to 90 by 90 cells.

Exhibit 4-5, continued

Regression   Performs multiple regression analysis.
Parse   Converts a column of long labels into several columns for use as a worksheet.

- SYSTEM (Permits the operating system to be accessed while inside Lotus 1-2-3.)

- QUIT (Leaves Lotus 1-2-3.)

The linear model has already been presented above. The exponential, modified exponential and multiplier models will be discussed next.

The Exponential Model

The exponential model is a compound growth rate formulation. In general notation:

$$V(T+N) = V(T) * (1 + R)^N$$

where:

$V(T), V(T+N)$ Variable at time T and T+N

R   The average percent change in population over past time periods T-1, T-2, etc.

The average percent change over past time periods is calculated as shown:

$$R = [((V(T)-V(T-1)/V(T-1)) + ((V(T-1)-(V(T-2)/V(T-2)) + ...] / p$$

where:

p   The number of time period differences over which the average is taken.

There is a graphic representation of an exponential model in

Exhibit 4-6

Regional Population Projection Model, Version 2

TABLE 1 - BASIC STATISTICS

CITY	POPULATION 1960	POPULATION 1970	POPULATION 1980	NUMBER OF HOUSEHOLDS 1980	PERSONS/ DWELLINGUNIT 1980
ALPHA	3100	3400	3500	1000	3.50
BETA	12800	15700	17800	6000	2.97
GAMMA	14000	21900	33000	14000	2.36
DELTA	1700	2000	2200	700	3.14
	31600	43000	56500	21700	

TABLE 2 - CALCULATED AND PROJECTED VALUES

CITY	AVERAGE CHANGE 1960-80	PROJECTED PERSONS/DU 1990	PROJECTED HOUSEHOLDS 1990
ALPHA	200	3.15	1100
BETA	2500	2.67	5900
GAMMA	9500	2.12	17000
DELTA	250	2.83	780
			24780

TABLE 3 - MODEL PARAMETERS

CONSTRAINED 1990 POPULATION TOTAL	45000
EXPONENTIAL GROWTH RATE (R) OF GAMMA	0.5356
CARRYING CAPACITY (K) OF DELTA	2500
MODIFIED EXP. RATIO (V) OF DELTA	0.6125

TABLE 4 - PROJECTED 1990 POPULATION USING VARIOUS MODELS

CITY	POPULATION PROJECTIONS		CHOICE		CHOICE
	PERSON/DU	LINEAR	NUMBER	MODEL	CONSTRAINED
ALPHA	3465	3700	3700	LINEAR	2298
BETA	15753	20300	15753	PERS/DU	9785
GAMMA	36064	42500	50674	EXPONENTIAL	31477
DELTA	2206	2450	2316	MODIFIED EXP	1439
	57489	68950	72443		45000

Exhibit 4-7 using sample data. The base value of population, 10,000, is projected to grow with a rate of change (R) of 20 percent each year. The community will grow from 10,000 in 1980 to approximately 70,000 in 1990, a hefty increase in size.

Exhibit 4-7

The Exponential Model

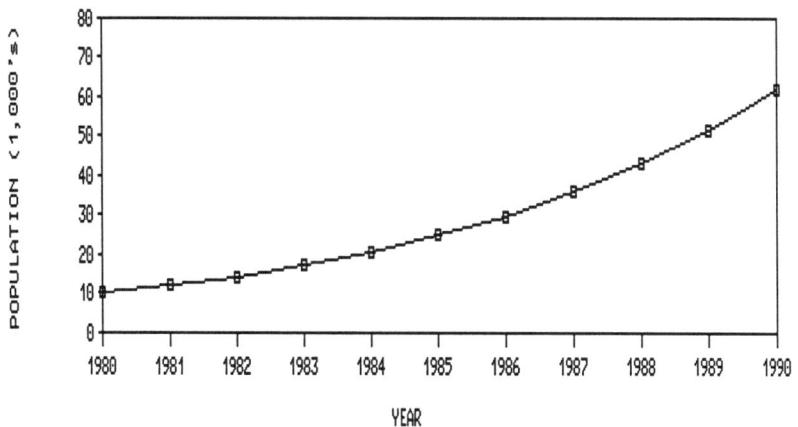

In our example from Alpha County, the calculation of R in each of the four communities would be based on the following equation:

$$R = [((POP_{80}-POP_{70})/POP_{70}) + ((POP_{70}-POP_{60})/POP_{60})] / 2$$

There are several population projections to 1990 for the four communities in Exhibit 4-6. Table 4 contains the projection values. The first column (PERSONS/DU) lists the 1990 projected values from the multiplier model. The second column (LINEAR) shows the results from the linear model, derived directly from the earlier spreadsheet. Finally, there is a choice of models used depending on the assumed population changes in the four communities. The different model selections for each city are listed in the MODEL column, and the projected 1990 values shown in the NUMBER column.

Population change in Gamma appears to follow the exponential model pattern. The community had absolute increases in the 1970-80 period (11,100) larger than the 1960-70 period (7,900). The growth rates in these two time periods were similar — 56.43 percent (7,900 /

14,000) during the 1960-1970 period and 50.68 percent ((33,000 - 21,900) / 21,900) from 1970 to 1980. The average percent growth over the two decades was 53.56 percent ((56.43 + 50.68)/ 2). The exponential growth rate (R) of Gamma in Table 3 is shown as 53.56 percent.

The extensive cell listing of this more complex projection model in shown in Exhibit 4-8. As can be seen, the equation which calculates the R value in Cell E31 is:

$$(((D10-C10)/C10) + ((C10-B10)/B10)) / 2$$

Clearly one must count parentheses to ensure that they match. This equation will work for any variable for which a historical change rate is desired. The value of p in this calculation is 2, the number of time period differences in the data.

In Cell D43 the exponential model is calculated:

$$+D10 * (1 + E31)$$

multiplying the 1980 population of Gamma by 1+R.

The Modified Exponential Model

While it was decided to use an exponential model for Gamma, the modified exponential will be used for the town of Delta. The modified exponential model looks like the graphic in Exhibit 4-9.

In this example, the population of 10,000 in 1980 is assumed to top out at 25,000, a growth ceiling. Basically, the model assumes a lid or ceiling, K, to the potential upper limit of the projecting variable, V. Such a modified exponential model is fashionable in these days of "carrying capacity" concepts where, for example, population growth might be restricted to the amount which can be supported by the available community infrastructure.

The modified exponential model has the following structure:

$$V(T+N) = K - [((K - V(T)) * (U)^N]$$

where:

$V(T+N), V(T)$ The variable V at time T, T+N

K   Upper limit of V

U   Unused capacity ratio

and:

$$U = [((K-V(T))/(K-V(T-1))) + ((K-V(T-1))/(K-V(T-2))) + \ldots] / p$$

The unused capacity ratio, U, is based on historical data. Basically, the ratio indicates how quickly the projecting variable is approaching the ceiling. The higher the value of U the slower the variable is approaching the limit, K. In Exhibit 4-9 two different equations have been projected with U equal to .4 and .9. Both reach the population ceiling of 25,000, but at different rates.

While the equations for U and the projecting variable V look complicated, they are really straightforward. Their use in Exhibit 4-6 requires a number of entries. In Cell E32 is the carrying capacity K for Delta of 2,500. The unused capacity ratio, U, is in Cell E33 as shown in Exhibit 4-8:

$$(((E32-D11)/(E32-C11)) + ((E32-C11)/(E32-B11))) / 2$$

The equation is complex and, in fact, could be broken up into a number of simpler equations if thought necessary. It follows the general structure of the equation for U, assuming p, the number of intervals, is two. The equation which calculates the 1990 population of Delta is in Cell D44:

$$+E32 - ((E32-D11) * (E33^\wedge 1))$$

A Simple Multiplier Model

An extremely simple but often useful model uses a multiplier approach. The community Beta has been projected to 1990 with a multiplier model using a persons per dwelling unit estimate and projected 1990 households:

$$\text{Population}_{1990} = \text{Persons/Dwelling Unit} * \text{Dwelling Units}_{1990}$$

This model was run for all four communities as shown in Table 4. It has also been selected as the model of choice for Beta. The model

68 Introduction to Electronic Spreadsheets

Exhibit 4-8

Cell Listing
Regional Population Projection Model, Version 2

	A	B	C	D	E	F
1	'REGIONAL POPULATION PROJECTION MODEL - VERSION 2					
2						
3	'TABLE 1 - BASIC STATISTICS					
4					^NUMBER OF	^PERSONS/
5		^POPULATION	^POPULATION	^POPULATION	^HOUSEHOLDS	^DWELLINGUNIT
6	'CITY	^1960	^1970	^1980	^1980	^1980
7	'-----	'-----------	'-----------	'----------	'-----------	'---------
8	'ALPHA	3100	3400	3500	1000	(D8/E8)
9	'BETA	12800	15700	17800	6000	(D9/E9)
10	'GAMMA	14000	21900	33000	14000	(D10/E10)
11	'DELTA	1700	2000	2200	700	(D11/E11)
12	'-----	'-----------	'-----------	'----------	'-----------	'---------
13		@SUM(B8..B11)	@SUM(C8..C11)	@SUM(D8..D11)	@SUM(E8..E11)	
14						
15	'TABLE 2 - CALCULATED AND PROJECTED VALUES					
16						
17		^AVERAGE	^PROJECTED	^PROJECTED		
18		^CHANGE	^PERSONS/DU	^HOUSEHOLDS		
19	'CITY	^1960-80	^1990	^1990		
20	'-----	'-----------	'-----------	'----------		
21	'ALPHA	(D8-B8)/2	(F8*0.9)	1100		
22	'BETA	(D9-B9)/2	(F9*0.9)	5900		
23	'GAMMA	(D10-B10)/2	(F10*0.9)	17000		
24	'DELTA	(D11-B11)/2	(F11*0.9)	780		
25	'-----	'-----------	'-----------	'----------		
26				@SUM(D21..D24)		
27						
28	'TABLE 3 - MODEL PARAMETERS					
29						
30	'CONSTRAINED 1990 POPULATION TOTAL				45000	
31	'EXPONENTIAL GROWTH RATE (R) OF GAMMA				(((D10-C10)/C10)+((C10-B10)/B10))/2	
32	'CARRYING CAPACITY				2500	
33	'MODIFIED EXP. RATIO (V) OF DELTA				(((E32-D11)/(E32-C11))+((E32-C11)/(E32-B11)))/2	

Introduction to Electronic Spreadsheets 69

Exhibit 4-8, continued

	A	B	C	D	E	F
34						
35	'TABLE 4 - PROJECTED 1990 POPULATION USING VARIOUS MODELS					
36						
37		'---------- POPULATION PROJECTIONS ----------				
38				'-------- CHOICE ---------		^CHOICE
39	'CITY	^PERSON/DU	^LINEAR	^NUMBER	^MODEL	^CONSTRAINED
40	'-----	'----------	'----------	'----------	'----------	'----------
41	'ALPHA	(D21*C21)	(D8+((1 *B21)))	(D8+((1*B21))	'LINEAR	+D41*($E$30/$D$46)
42	'BETA	(D22*C22)	(D9+((1 *B22)))	(D22*C22)	'PERS/DU	+D42*($E$30/$D$46)
43	'GAMMA	(D23*C23)	(D10+((1 *B23)))	+D10*(1+E31)	'EXPONENTIAL	+D43*($E$30/$D$46)
44	'DELTA	(D24*C24)	(D11+((1 *B24)))	+E32-((E32-D11)*(E33^1))	'MODIFIED EXP.	+D44*($E$30/$D$46)
45	'-----	'----------	'----------	'----------	'----------	'----------
46		@SUM(B41..B44)	@SUM(C41..C44)	@SUM(D41..D44)		@SUM(F41..F44)

Exhibit 4-9

The Modified Exponential Model

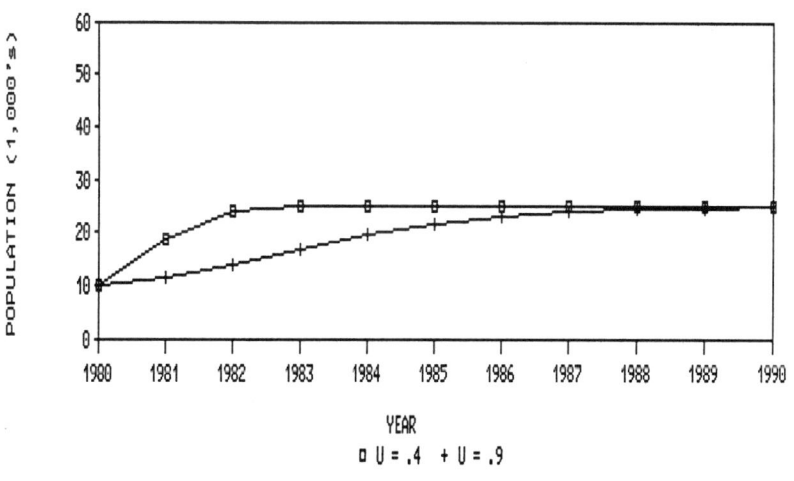

calculates the average persons per household for 1980 in Table 1, and projects this to 1990 in Table 2. It has been assumed that there will be a reduction in persons per household in 1990 to 90 percent of the 1980 values as shown in Exhibit 4-6. Also, there is the need to project 1990 households by some method. In this example, these projected households have been directly entered into Table 2 without using a model. The projected population is calculated by multiplying the projected persons per household by the projected number of households. The necessary calculations can be seen by examining the cell listing (Exhibit 4-8) in cells B41-B44.

A Constrained Regional Model

The four communities have each had their populations projected to 1990 by different models. The total regional population of these four communities is 72,443 using the choice models in Table 4. However, what if other analysis indicates that the total regional population should be no more than 45,000? The constrained regional population total of 45,000 and the corresponding reductions in the projected populations of each of the four communities is shown in Table 4. The cell listing (Exhibit 4-8) shows the calculation of the constrained model in cells F41-F44, and introduces a new concept — **absolute versus relative addressing**.

The concept of cell-specific algebra and relative addressing has already been introduced. For example, the calculation of the average change in population (Cell B21) for Alpha in Exhibit 4-8 shows the same equation — (D8-B8)/2 — repeated below with different row numbers in Cells B22 through B24. One can copy the equation in Cell B21 to Cells B22 to B24, using the relative addressing concept. The program will automatically change the row number as it copies the equation to the cells. However, what happens if a constant is being used, an absolute cell reference? Table 4 contains the constrained population projection values under the heading CHOICE CONSTRAINED. Cell F41 contains the following:

+D41 * ($E$30 / $D$46)

The dollar signs mark an absolute cell reference in Lotus 1-2-3. This means that regardless of where an equation is copied, the absolute reference will stay the same. Thus, $E$30 and $D$46 are the same in all cells, F42 through F44. The equation takes the value of the projected population in the Column D and multiplies it by the ratio of the constrained regional value (Cell E30) to the unconstrained total (Cell D46). This ratio approach is one way of adjusting population to a constrained total, and is a useful way of introducing the absolute addressing concept.

A Perspective on the Population Problem

The population projection techniques demonstrated for Athens County show the potential of electronic spreadsheet programs to do simple modeling. The model structures developed can be used in a wide variety of situations. For example, the exponential model is, in reality, a compound interest formulation and can be used in such situations. It is not uncommon to develop an operating budget for an agency and multiply through by an inflation factor to reflect future expected costs. Often, the rate R is not calculated, but estimated based on historical patterns and judgment.

The one important characteristic of a spreadsheet not discussed so far is its "what-if" capacity. Lotus 1-2-3 and similar programs are able to trace any change in any cell through all subsequent cells dependent on that cell. **Change a cell and all cells dependent on it change**. For example, in Exhibit 4-6 the constrained regional total is 45,000. Should one decide, based on new information, to increase this estimate to 60,000, then the Column F constrained values would change. The constrained value is built directly into the calculation as has been shown, and any change entered into the spreadsheet in cell E30, the constrained 1990 population, will automatically affect the individual community values in the Choice Constrained column.

The power of this automatic recalculation feature is very useful for doing alternative scenarios. Different population projection assumptions can be made and tested. If operating budgets are being developed, different assumptions about an inflation factor can be made or dollars can be easily switched among categories. This powerful concept is directly dependent on the cell algebra structure of a spreadsheet program.

Conclusion

Spreadsheets are a powerful addition to a planner, analyst or manager. In fact, such a wide variety of activities can be done with a spreadsheet program that it may well serve as the primary piece of software in a planning or public management organization. Emerging developments in easing the use of spreadsheet programs will make this software even more accessible. The developers of Lotus 1-2-3 have introduced HAL (Human Language Interface). HAL is a program which permits natural language commands to be used in instructing Lotus 1-2-3 about what operations to perform (Warner, 1986). The barriers which sometimes make a complex program inaccessible to novices are coming down.

In the next chapter a number of planning and management applications will be presented. While programs may be easier to use in coming years, there is still the need to know how to apply these tools to professional experience.

Suggested Further Readings

Foot, David. 1981. *Operational Urban Models: An Introduction.* New York: Methuen.

Krueckeberg, Donald A. and Arthur Silvers. 1974. *Urban Planning Analysis: Methods and Models.* New York: John Wiley & Sons.

Oppenheim, Norbert. 1980. *Applied Models in Urban and Regional Analysis.* Englewood Cliffs, New Jersey: Prentice-Hall.

Sawicki, David S. 1985. "Microcomputer Applications in Planning," *Journal of the American Planning Association* 51:2 (Spring): 209-215.

5

Modeling with Electronic Spreadsheets

Introduction

In the last chapter, the electronic spreadsheet was introduced. In this chapter, the discussion will be extended to demonstrate how the spreadsheet can be used in modeling employment trends, land use development and transportation networks, and in fiscal analysis. A number of models will be presented illustrating a variety of spreadsheet concepts. The models will be broken into two categories — models of urban development and models which assist the urban management process. The reader is warned that some prior knowledge of the models will be very helpful. However, even if the reader is unfamiliar with the topics, the presentation and spreadsheet illustrations should be useful. Also, the models are relatively simple examples of sometimes rather complex operations. It is hoped that their presentation will show the range of possibilities available in spreadsheet design.

One important concept — structured spreadsheet design — will be introduced in the latter part of the chapter. It represents a series of steps which will assist in developing legible and organized spreadsheets. The chapter will conclude with a general discussion of the spreadsheet in planning and management.

Modeling Urban and Regional Development

There are many urban and regional areas in which spreadsheet models are appropriate. A typical planning analysis text, such as the one by Krueckeberg and Silvers (1974) or Oppenheim (1980), contains the four areas in which projection models are built — employment and income, population, land use development, and transportation system implications. As Exhibit 5-1 shows, these four areas constitute a framework which takes broader demographic and economic trends and reduces them to site and zone specific land use and transportation impacts.

There is a general distinction in the delineation of model outputs between aggregate and allocation models. Aggregate models predict totals for larger geographic areas while allocation models calculate the portions of a total to smaller sub-areas. Typically, the regional analyst will predict population and employment data at the municipal or county levels, while the urban modeler will allocate these totals to sub-municipal areas, such as census tracts and planning districts, and develop projections of land use and transportation impacts.

Exhibit 5-1

An Urban Modeling Framework

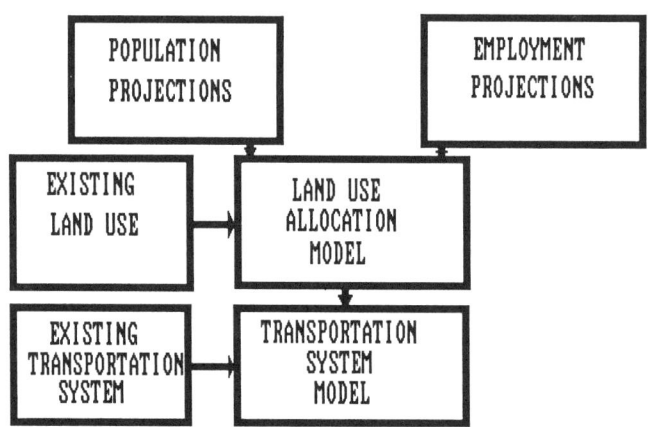

In Chapter Four, simple aggregate population projection models for municipalities were presented. This chapter will carry the model-building process further by examining a series of models. Two allocation models will be presented. The first is a residential location model which uses a simple allocation method to distribute population to zones within an urban area. Based on the work of Hansen as presented by Krueckeberg and Silvers (1974), the model demonstrates

Modeling with Electronic Spreadsheets 75

how to break up an equation into parts in a spreadsheet, and demonstrates a way of presenting the information.

Second, the Lowry model of urban development will be presented. This ingenious model projects both service sector employment and residential household location within zones of a city. This model is particularly useful to present because it uses two-dimensional matrices in its calculations and because the model iterates, or cycles, in order to reach a solution.

These two "land use" models, in fact, project sub-area populations and, in the case of Lowry, employment. The Hansen-based model assumes that aggregate population projection figures are available, while Lowry assumes sub-area basic employment figures are determinable. Following these two models, an employment projection model will be examined, using concepts from shiftshare and location quotient analysis. Ideally, regional employment projections are input to land use models, but the size of the employment projection spreadsheet mandated that it be placed at this point in the chapter.

The final urban model presented will be derived from transportation planning analysis. The classic approach to transportation planning models has involved the four steps of trip generation, trip distribution, modal split, and traffic assignment. In this spreadsheet example, the generation, distribution, and assignment phases will be put into spreadsheet form. This application will show how it is possible to handle complex modeling in a spreadsheet format. Its presentation will also raise the issue surrounding the use of a spreadsheet program at the boundary of potential application. It is not at all clear that a spreadsheet is appropriate in certain situations. In this example as well as the earlier ones the problem will be kept small in scale. Only 5 zones will be handled in the transportation model, while actual problems may easily contain 50 or 100 zones.

A Population Allocation Model

The Concept

A straightforward model of residential location has been outlined by Krueckeberg and Silvers (1974) based on the work of Hansen (1959). Essentially, the model allocates population to zones within a region. In our case, the zones can be thought of as planning areas within a municipality. We have simplified and altered the model to allocate population based on the relative attractiveness of competing areas. The model will be applied to the growth in the community of Beta for the 1980-90 period.

The population allocation model formulation uses a straightforward proportional approach. A summation sign is represented by the sigma (Σ) followed by the subscript over which the summation will take place. In the following equation

$$POPCHG_I = TOTPOPCHG * (ATT_I / \Sigma_I\, ATT_I)$$

where:

POPCHG$_I$ The projected population change in Zone I over some time period

TOTPOPCHG   The total population change in the region over the time period

ATT$_I$ The attractiveness score of Zone I

This version of the residential allocation model calculates an attractiveness score for each zone's potential development. In this example, the attractiveness index is somewhat arbitrarily constructed out of three variables — the amount of vacant, residentially zoned land, the capacity of local roadways, and the availability of water and sewer. In the Krueckeberg and Silvers version, based on Hansen, the variables include vacant land and accessibility to employment. The selection of variables to be used to create an attractiveness index could be determined by either reasoned judgment or through statistics. For example, regression analysis could be done on possible candidates and the most important contributors used.

The Spreadsheet

In Exhibit 5-2 the spreadsheet is presented. Note that the 1980 and 1990 populations of Beta are drawn from the population projection spreadsheet presented in Chapter 4. Each of the individual scales for vacant land, roadway capacity or sewer and water capacity ranges from 0 to 10, where 10 is the highest ranking and 0 the lowest. The roadway and water/sewer scores for each zone are developed from "reasoned judgment." For example, in Table 1, Zone 1 has very good

Exhibit 5-2

Population Allocation Model

BETA MUNICIPALITY

TABLE 1 - BASIC STATISTICS

ZONE	POPULATION 1980	RESIDENTIALLY ZONED VACANT ACRES (1980)	LOCAL ROADWAY CAPACITY 1980 SCALE 1-10	SEWER & WATER CAPACITY 1980 SCALE 1-10
1	4500	200	8	5
2	6300	4300	5	4
3	7000	500	3	9
TOTAL	17800	5000	16	18

TABLE 2 - CALCULATION OF EXPECTED GROWTH, 1980-90

PROJECTED 1990 POPULATION (FROM LINEAR MODEL IN CHAPTER 4)	20300
1980 POPULATION	17800
PROJECTED GROWTH, 1980-90	2500

TABLE 3 - WEIGHTS OF PREDICTOR VARIABLES

VARIABLE	WEIGHT
RESIDENTIALLY ZONED VACANT ACRES	2
LOCAL ROADWAY CAPACITY 1980	1
SEWER & WATER CAPACITY 1980	1

TABLE 4 - PROJECTED ZONAL ALLOCATIONS, 1990

ZONE	WEIGHTED ATTRACTIVENESS SCORE	ATTRACTIVENESS PROPORTION	PROJECTED ZONAL GROWTH 1980-90	TOTAL PROJECTED POPULATION 1990
1	0.86	0.21	536	5036
2	2.25	0.56	1409	7709
3	0.89	0.22	555	7555
TOTAL	4.00	1.00	2500	20300

local road capacity and receives a score of "8." On the other hand, Zone 3 has relatively poor roads and receives a "3." The combined attractiveness score weights the different factors and sums across all factors to produce the combined attractiveness for each zone as below:

$$ATT_I = \Sigma_K[W_K * (SCORE_{I,K} / \Sigma_I SCORE_{I,K})]$$

where:

W_K The weight applied to the factor K

$SCORE_{I,K}$ The score given to factor K in Zone I

Each of the factors, such as vacant land, sewer and water availability, or accessibility, can be weighted differently. For example, studies might show that the amount of vacant land in a zone might be three times as important as sewer and water availability in predicting population distributions. The weights for the factors are shown in Table 3 of the spreadsheet. The weighted attractiveness score (ATT_I) for each zone is shown in Table 4. This is a summation of three factors. The weighted attractiveness score for Zone 1 is shown in cell B37 of the Cell Listing (Exhibit 5-3):

($D$27*(C11/$C$15))+($D$28*(D11/$D$15))+($D$29*(E11/$E$15))

The weighted attractiveness score for Zone 1 in Table 4 is .86. The equation represents the summation of three factors, each weighted by the values in cells D27 to D29. For the first factor in the equation, the amount of vacant land in Zone 1 (C11) is divided by the total amount of land available (C15), and multiplied by a weight, cell D27. The result is added to the D11/D15 and E11/E15 modified by the weights in D28 and D29. In Lotus 1-2-3 the "$" in the equation, such as $D$27, means that this cell is treated as a constant when replicating formulas. Other spreadsheet programs may handle the distinction between absolute and relative addressing differently, but the general principle is the same.

Table 4 (column C) contains the ratio of the zonal weighted attractiveness to the total weighted attractiveness of all zones. These column values are proportions which represent the shares each zone will receive of total expected population growth of 2,500. Column D contains the population growth each zone is expected to receive. The

Modeling with Electronic Spreadsheets 79

Exhibit 5-3

Cell Listing, Population Allocation Model

	A	B	C	D	E
1	'POPULATION ALLOCATION MODEL				
2					
3	'BETA MUNICIPALITY				
4					
5	'TABLE 1 - BASIC STATISTICS				
6					
7			^RESIDENTIALLY	^LOCAL ROADWAY	^SEWER & WATER
8		^POPULATION	^ZONED VACANT	^CAPACITY 1980	^CAPACITY 1980
9	'ZONE	^1980	^ACRES (1980)	^SCALE 1-10	^SCALE 1-10
10	'------	'--------------	'--------------	'--------------	'--------------
11	^1	4500	200	8	5
12	^2	6300	4300	5	4
13	^3	7000	500	3	9
14	'------	'--------------	'--------------	'--------------	'--------------
15	"TOTAL	@SUM(B11..B13)	@SUM(C11..C13)	@SUM(D11..D13)	@SUM(E11..E13)
16					
17	'TABLE 2 - CALCULATION OF EXPECTED GROWTH, 1980-90				
18					
19	'PROJECTED 1990 POPULATION			20300	
20	' (FROM LINEAR MODEL IN CHAPTER 4)				
21	'1980 POPULATION			+B15	
22	'PROJECTED GROWTH, 1980-90			+D19-D21	
23					
24	'TABLE 3 - WEIGHTS OF PREDICTOR VARIABLES				
25					
26		^VARIABLE		"WEIGHT	
27	'RESIDENTIALLY ZONED VACANT ACRES			2	
28	'LOCAL ROADWAY CAPACITY 1980			1	
29	'SEWER & WATER CAPACITY 1980			1	
30					
31	'TABLE 4 -PROJECTED ZONAL ALLOCATIONS, 1990				
32					
33		^WEIGHTED		^PROJECTED	^TOTAL
34		^ATTRACTIVENESS	^ATTRACTIVENESS	^ZONAL GROWTH	^PROJECTED
35	'ZONE	^SCORE	^PROPORTION	^1980-90	'POPULATION 1990
36	'------	'--------------	'--------------	'--------------	'--------------
37	^1	($D$27*(C11/$C$15))+($D$28*(D11/$D$15))+($D$29*(E11/$E$15))	+B37/$B$41	+C37*$D$22	+B11+D37

Exhibit 5-3, continued

	A	B	C	D	E
38	^2	($D$27*(C12/$C$15))+($D$28*(D12/$D$15))+($D$29*(E12/$E$15))	+B38/$B$41	+C38*$D$22	+B12+D38
39	^3	($D$27*(C13/$C$15))+($D$28*(D13/$D$15))+($D$29*(E13/$E$15))	+B39/$B$41	+C39*$D$22	+B13+D39
40	!------	!--------------	!---------------	!--------------	!--------------
41	"TOTAL	@SUM(B37..B39)	@SUM(C37..C39)	@SUM(D37..D39)	@SUM(E37..E39)

model formulation presented here is a "constrained" version, meaning the total population allocated to the three zones is fixed before the calculations are done. The output of this example is population projections to 1990 for the 3 zones in Beta. The model could be extended to additional time periods, and could be run under a variety of assumptions. The model could also be used for any kind of situation in which a fixed total has to be allocated to a number of zones within some defined region.

Alternatives Analysis

One of the powerful potentials of a spreadsheet is the easy generation of alternatives. For example, what if there are questions about the weights of the different factors in this example of the population allocation model? It is easy enough to run alternatives and ascertain the effects on the output. In such an alternatives analysis approach, the planner could create a set of upper and lower boundaries to various assumptions about factor weights and run the spreadsheet model. In doing so the analyst would create an envelope within which the projected zonal populations should be found. This testing of alternatives is easily done in an electronic spreadsheet. Care must be taken, however, to structure the alternatives developed so that the number of different spreadsheets calculated is kept reasonable.

The Lowry Model of a Metropolis

The Concept

This second example of a land use model is considerably more complex than the population allocation model. In particular, the

Lowry model also has an iterative component. In other words, the model carries out the same calculations repeatedly until a solution is reached. This iterative feature presents difficulties for the user. To maintain a complete record, the user should record all calculations sequentially in the spreadsheet. Yet, the generation of successive sets of iterative output not only takes up considerable space in the spreadsheet but also takes a great deal of time to set up. However, the use of appropriate spreadsheet techniques can mitigate the problems created by iterative models.

The structure of the Lowry model has been described in numerous texts and papers (Goldner, 1971; Garin, 1966; Foot, 1981; Batty, 1976). The spreadsheet is shown in Exhibit 5-4. There is the fundamental distinction between basic and service sectors in the economy. Basic workers are employed in industry, commercial, and office facilities whose location selections are based on considerations other than locally required access. For example, an auto manufacturing plant selects a site based on a series of considerations such as market access, availability of labor, materials and transportation, and management predispositions.

On the other hand, service workers are employed in firms which derive income from proximity to basic industry. For example, many shops, restaurants and office activities depend on a nearby population for business. The Lowry model uses this distinction between basic and service sectors to generate a population distribution within an urban area.

There are two major inputs needed for the Lowry model — the location and size of the basic industries within the region, and a generalized transportation system which can provide travel times among zones within the region. The basic workers located in the basic firms need to live somewhere.

$$BASHH_J = \Sigma_I [(BASWRK_I * ACCESS1_{I,J}) * HHMULT]$$

where:

$BASHH_J$ Number of basic workers who are living in households in Zone J

$BASWRK_I$ Number of basic workers with jobs in Zone I

Exhibit 5-4

The Lowry Model of Urban Development

LOWRY MODEL OF URBAN DEVELOPMENT

This model uses exogenously determined locations
  of basic employment to project the location
  of residences and non-basic employment

TABLE 1 - LOCATION OF BASIC EMPLOYEES

ZONE	1	2	3	4	5	6	TOTAL
	100	300	400	50	200	1,000	2,050

TABLE 2 - TIME-DISTANCE MATRIX

ZONE	1	2	3	4	5	6
1	8	12	15	20	22	21
2	12	6	7	12	20	18
3	15	7	5	8	10	12
4	20	12	8	7	10	20
5	22	20	10	10	8	12
6	21	18	12	20	12	6

TABLE 3 - FRICTION FACTOR MATRIX, WORKER TO RESIDENCES

***** USING FRICTION FACTOR EXPONENT   0.8 = EXP1

ZONE	1	2	3	4	5	6	TOTAL
1	0.19	0.14	0.11	0.09	0.08	0.09	0.70
2	0.14	0.24	0.21	0.14	0.09	0.10	0.91
3	0.11	0.21	0.28	0.19	0.16	0.14	1.09
4	0.09	0.14	0.19	0.21	0.16	0.09	0.88
5	0.08	0.09	0.16	0.16	0.19	0.14	0.82
6	0.09	0.10	0.14	0.09	0.14	0.24	0.79

TABLE 4 - PROBABILITY MATRIX OF WORKPLACE-TO-HOUSEHOLD ACCESSIBILITIES

ZONE	1	2	3	4	5	6	TOTAL
1	0.27	0.19	0.16	0.13	0.12	0.12	1.00
2	0.15	0.26	0.23	0.15	0.10	0.11	1.00
3	0.11	0.19	0.25	0.17	0.15	0.13	1.00
4	0.10	0.16	0.22	0.24	0.18	0.10	1.00
5	0.10	0.11	0.19	0.19	0.23	0.17	1.00
6	0.11	0.13	0.17	0.12	0.17	0.30	1.00

Exhibit 5-4, continued

TABLE 5 - DISTRIBUTION OF BASIC SECTOR WORKERS TO RESIDENCES

POPULATION-TO-EMPLOYMENT RATIO   2.5

ZONE	1	2	3	4	5	6	TOTAL
WORKERS	251	331	410	294	329	436	2,050
POPULATN	627	827	1,025	734	822	1,090	5,125

TABLE 6 - FRICTION FACTOR MATRIX, HOUSEHOLDS TO SERVICE ESTABLISHMENTS

****** USING FRICTION FACTOR EXPONENT   0.8 = EXP2

ZONE	1	2	3	4	5	6	TOTAL
1	0.19	0.14	0.11	0.09	0.08	0.09	0.70
2	0.14	0.24	0.21	0.14	0.09	0.10	0.91
3	0.11	0.21	0.28	0.19	0.16	0.14	1.09
4	0.09	0.14	0.19	0.21	0.16	0.09	0.88
5	0.08	0.09	0.16	0.16	0.19	0.14	0.82
6	0.09	0.10	0.14	0.09	0.14	0.24	0.79

TABLE 7 - PROBABILITY MATRIX OF HOUSEHOLD-TO-SERVICE ACCESSIBILITIES

ZONE	1	2	3	4	5	6	TOTAL
1	0.27	0.19	0.16	0.13	0.12	0.12	1.00
2	0.15	0.26	0.23	0.15	0.10	0.11	1.00
3	0.11	0.19	0.25	0.17	0.15	0.13	1.00
4	0.10	0.16	0.22	0.24	0.18	0.10	1.00
5	0.10	0.11	0.19	0.19	0.23	0.17	1.00
6	0.11	0.13	0.17	0.12	0.17	0.30	1.00

TABLE 8 - DISTRIBUTION OF SERVICE WORKERS TO ESTABLISHMENT
          SUPPORTED BY BASIC HOUSEHOLDS

****** POPULATION-SERVING RATIO   0.2

ZONE	1	2	3	4	5	6	TOTAL
WORKERS	136	176	212	169	164	168	1,025

****

Exhibit 5-4, continued

```
TABLE 9 - SUMMARY TABLE

ZONE            1       2       3       4       5       6     TOTAL
------------------------------------------------------------------
BASIC WKR     100     300     400      50     200   1,000   2,050
BASIC POP     627     827   1,025     734     822   1,090   5,125

ROUND 1
SERV WKR      136     176     212     169     164     168   1,025
SERV POP      346     448     535     432     406     396   2,563

ROUND 2
SERV WKR       69      90     107      87      81      78     513
SERV POP      174     225     268     217     202     195   1,281

ROUND 3
SERV WKR       35      45      54      43      40      39     256
SERV POP       87     113     134     108     101      98     641

ROUND 4
SERV WKR       17      23      27      22      20      20     128
SERV POP       43      56      67      54      51      49     320

ROUND 5
SERV WKR        9      11      13      11      10      10      64
SERV POP       22      28      34      27      25      24     160
------------------------------------------------------------------
TOTAL
WORKERS       367     645     813     381     515   1,314   4,036
POPULATN    1,299   1,698   2,063   1,572   1,607   1,852  10,090
```

ACCESS1$_{I,J}$ Proportion of workers employed in Zone I who will live in Zone J distributed by interzonal accessibilities

HHMULT   The household multiplier which converts workers into households

In this equation the basic sector workers (BASWRK) are distributed to households (BASHH) by a transportation network represented by an accessibility matrix (ACCESS1). The household multiplier (HHMULT) converts workers to families.

The households with basic workers require services, such as shops, restaurants, etc. These service workers employed in these shops are located in zones according to the following equation:

$$\text{SERVWRK}_J = \Sigma_I [(\text{BASHH}_I * \text{ACCESS2}_{I,J}) * \text{SERVMULT}]$$

where:

SERVWRK$_J$ — Number of service workers employed in Zone J establishments

ACCESS2$_{I,J}$ — The proportion of all workers who will work in Zone J to satisfy the needs of residents of Zone I distributed by interzonal accessibilities

SERVMULT — The multiplier which calculates the number of service workers required per person in the household

In this equation, the service workers (SERVWRK) distribute themselves in shops and other commercial activities based on the service facilities' access (ACCESS2) to the basic households (BASHH). The service multiplier (SERVMULT) translates the household numbers into the number of service employees required to serve them.

However, the service workers themselves need households. Therefore:

$$\text{SERVHH}_J = \Sigma_I [(\text{SERVWKR}_I * \text{ACCESS1}_{I,J}) * \text{HHMULT}]$$

where:

SERVHH$_J$ — The number of service workers who will reside with their households in Zone J

This equation is structurally the same as the first equation which distributed basic households, except that service households are the output. This equation is iterative. The households of service workers located in a zone through this equation will in turn need services themselves. The two equations which produce the zonal location of service workers (SERVWRK) and their households (SERVHH) work in tandem. Under reasonable assumptions, each iteration locating service workers and service households will produce smaller and smaller numbers. The spreadsheet in Exhibit 5-4 shows this iteration process at work in Table 9.

There are two accessibility equations, one which handles the likelihood of a worker living in a particular zone, and one which estimates the likelihood of a household member traveling from home to seek services and goods in another zone. Both equations generate probability matrices. The ACCESS1 matrix handles the journey from work to home. The equation is a form of a gravity model using friction factors. First, a friction factor is calculated for each I,J zonal interchange as a function of time. This particular formulation uses a power function, in which the value of time is raised to a power (Black, 1981).

$$FF_{I,J} = 1 / TIME_{I,J}^{EXP}$$

where:

$FF_{I,J}$ Friction factor between zones I and J

$TIME_{I,J}$ The travel time between zones I and J

EXP   An exponent applied to the time-distance value

These friction factors are a measure of the impacts on travel behavior created by distance. The essential question is how far a worker is likely to travel from home to work. It is assumed for a group of workers that more will live closer than farther away. There are many ways in which one can formulate a friction factor equation, and the literature on the relationship of travel times to friction factors is great (Stopher and Meyburg, 1975; Black, 1981). These friction factors can be converted in probabilities by the following equation:

$$ACCESS1_{I,J} = FF_{I,J} / [\Sigma_J FF_{I,J}]$$

Essentially, the probabilities are being treated as proportions of a whole. If there is a .4 probability that someone working in Zone 5 will live in Zone 12, then 40 of 100 workers in Zone 5 would be expected to live in Zone 12. The ACCESS1 equation describes the relationship between job and home, while a similarly structured ACCESS2 equation would describe the relationship between household location and service worker location.

The Spreadsheet

The spreadsheet of the Lowry model was presented in Exhibit 5-4. Exhibit 5-5 contains the extensive cell listing of the model. The spreadsheet is designed vertically, as have been the earlier ones. It is easier to have the user move down a spreadsheet than across in Lotus 1-2-3, and this seems a reasonably comfortable way to structure a complex spreadsheet design. Also, the cell listing from Spreadsheet Auditor has been shortened by eliminating the labels in rows 1 to 6, and by using a shorthand way of showing copied equations. In many situations, a cell equation is copied from some earlier one which has the same structure. The COPY command in Lotus 1-2-3, or similar commands in other spreadsheets, is used for equation replication, adjusting the relative cell references appropriately. The cell listing in Exhibit 5-5 contains this shorthand notation, the first example of which is seen in rows 32 through 37. The equation in cell B32

$$(1/(B18^\wedge \$F\$28))$$

is the original of the entire matrix in Table 3. Each other cell in the matrix is a mirror of cell B32 except for the relative address. Each is marked "!B32." This means that cell C32, directly to the right of B32, is really:

$$(1/(C18^\wedge \$F\$28))$$

which is appropriate, since it is a friction factor equation described in the previous section.

Table 1 in Exhibit 5-4 shows one of the exogenous inputs, the number of basic employees in the 6 different zones of the example. The model requires that this information be supplied for the model to run. For this example, sample data were entered. Table 2 is the time-distance matrix for the employee to household trip. This matrix contains travel time values between zones in the city. In a typical transportation study these values would reflect actual driving times. However, in the Lowry model these times, as minutes of travel, are relative accessibility values which reflect the assumed desirability of each zone for household location by basic sector workers. Sample values have been entered in this table.

Table 3 calculates the friction factor matrix, following the equation presented above. The cell listing (Exhibit 5-5) shows the equation. The exponent of the power function is in cell F28. Table 4 simply divides the cell friction factor values by the row totals of the factor. Table 5 calculates the first round of basic household distributions (BASHH) which is divided into 2 steps. Starting in cell B58, the number of workers who have decided to live in the 6 zones are calculated. For Zone 1 the equation in cell B58 is:

Exhibit 5-5
Cell Listing, The Lowry Model

	A	B	C	D	E	F	G	H
7	'TABLE 1 - LOCATION OF BASIC EMPLOYEES							
8								
9	'ZONE	1	2	3	4	5	6	"TOTAL
10	'--------	'------	'------	'------	'------	'------	'------	'------
11	1	100	300	400	50	200	1000	@SUM(B11..G11)
12								
13								
14	'TABLE 2 - TIME-DISTANCE MATRIX							
15								
16	'ZONE	1	2	3	4	5	6	
17	'--------	'------	'------	'------	'------	'------	'------	
18	1	8	12	15	20	22	21	
19	2	12	6	7	12	20	18	
20	3	15	7	5	8	10	12	
21	4	20	12	8	7	10	20	
22	5	22	20	10	10	8	12	
23	6	21	18	12	20	12	6	
24								
25								
26	'TABLE 3 - FRICTION FACTOR MATRIX, WORKER TO RESIDENCE							
27								
28	'***** USING FRICTION FACTOR EXPONENT OF					0.8	'= EXP1	
29								
30	'ZONE	1	2	3	4	5	6	"TOTAL
31	'--------	'------	'------	'------	'------	'------	'------	'------
32	1	(1/(B18)^$F$28)	![B32]	![B32]	![B32]	![B32]	![B32]	![H11]
33	2	![B32]	![B32]	![B32]	![B32]	![B32]	![B32]	![H11]
34	3	![B32]	![B32]	![B32]	![B32]	![B32]	![B32]	![H11]
35	4	![B32]	![B32]	![B32]	![B32]	![B32]	![B32]	![H11]
36	5	![B32]	![B32]	![B32]	![B32]	![B32]	![B32]	![H11]
37	6	![B32]	![B32]	![B32]	![B32]	![B32]	![B32]	![H11]
38								
39								
40	'TABLE 4 - PROBABILITY MATRIX OF WORKPLACE-TO-HOUSEHOLD ACCESSIBILITIES							
41								
42	'ZONE	1	2	3	4	5	6	"TOTAL
43	'--------	'------	'------	'------	'------	'------	'------	'------
44	1	+B32/$H32	![B44]	![B44]	![B44]	![B44]	![B44]	![H11]
45	2	![B44]	![B44]	![B44]	![B44]	![B44]	![B44]	![H11]
46	3	![B44]	![B44]	![B44]	![B44]	![B44]	![B44]	![H11]
47	4	![B44]	![B44]	![B44]	![B44]	![B44]	![B44]	![H11]
48	5	![B44]	![B44]	![B44]	![B44]	![B44]	![B44]	![H11]
49	6	![B44]	![B44]	![B44]	![B44]	![B44]	![B44]	![H11]

Modeling with Electronic Spreadsheets 89

Exhibit 5-5, continued

	A	B	C	D	E	F	G	H
50								
51								
52	'TABLE 5 - DISTRIBUTION OF BASIC SECTOR WORKERS TO RESIDENCES							
53								
54	'POPULATION TO EMPLOYMENT RATIO>			2.5				
55								
56	'ZONE	1	2	3	4	5	6	"TOTAL
57	!--------	!------	!------	!------	!------	!------	!------	!------
58	'WORKERS	(B44*$B$11)+(B45*$C$11)+(B46*$D$11)+(B47*$E$11)+(B48*$F$11)+(B49*$G$11)	![B58]	![B58]	![B58]	![B58]	![B58]	![H11]
59								
60	'POPULATN	+B58*$E$54	![B60]	![B60]	![B60]	![B60]	![B60]	![H11]
61								
62								
63	'TABLE 6 - FRICTION FACTOR MATRIX, HOUSEHOLDS TO SERVICE ESTABLISHMENTS							
64								
65	'****** USING FRICTION FACTOR EXPONENT OF			0.8		'= EXP2		
66								
67	'ZONE	1	2	3	4	5	6	"TOTAL
68	!--------	!------	!------	!------	!------	!------	!------	!------
69	1	(1/(B18^$F$65))	![B69]	![B69]	![B69]	![B69]	![B69]	![H11]
70	2	![B69]	![B69]	![B69]	![B69]	![B69]	![B69]	![H11]
71	3	![B69]	![B69]	![B69]	![B69]	![B69]	![B69]	![H11]
72	4	![B69]	![B69]	![B69]	![B69]	![B69]	![B69]	![H11]
73	5	![B69]	![B69]	![B69]	![B69]	![B69]	![B69]	![H11]
74	6	![B69]	![B69]	![B69]	![B69]	![B69]	![B69]	![H11]
75								
76								

90   *Modeling with Electronic Spreadsheets*

Exhibit 5-5, continued

	A	B	C	D	E	F	G	H
77	'TABLE 7 - PROBABILITY MATRIX OF HOUSEHOLD-TO-SERVICE ACCESSIBILITIES							
78								
79	'ZONE	1	2	3	4	5	6	"TOTAL
80	!--------	!------	!------	!------	!------	!------	!------	!------
81	1	![B44]	![B44]	![B44]	![B44]	![B44]	![B44]	![H11]
82	2	![B44]	![B44]	![B44]	![B44]	![B44]	![B44]	![H11]
83	3	![B44]	![B44]	![B44]	![B44]	![B44]	![B44]	![H11]
84	4	![B44]	![B44]	![B44]	![B44]	![B44]	![B44]	![H11]
85	5	![B44]	![B44]	![B44]	![B44]	![B44]	![B44]	![H11]
86	6	![B44]	![B44]	![B44]	![B44]	![B44]	![B44]	![H11]
87								
88								
89	'TABLE 8 - DISTRIBUTION OF SERVICE WORKERS TO ESTABLISHMENTS							
90		' SUPPORTED BY BASIC HOUSEHOLDS						
91								
92	'****** POPULATION-SERVING RATIO			0.2				
93								
94	'ZONE	1	2	3	4	5	6	"TOTAL
95	!--------	!------	!------	!------	!------	!------	!------	!------
96	'WORKERS	((B81*$B$60)+(B82*$C$60)+(B83*$D$60)+(B84*$E$60)+(B85*$F$60)+(B86*$G$60))*$E$92	![B96]	![B96]	![B96]	![B96]	![B96]	![H11]
97								
98	!********	!******	!******	!******	!******	!******	!******	!******
99								
100	'TABLE 9 - SUMMARY TABLE							
101								
102	'ZONE	1	2	3	4	5	6	"TOTAL
103	!--------	!------	!------	!------	!------	!------	!------	!------
104	'BASIC WKR	+B11	![B104]	![B104]	![B104]	![B104]	![B104]	![H11]
105	'BASIC POP	+B60	![B105]	![B105]	![B105]	![B105]	![B105]	![H11]
106								
107	'ROUND 1							
108	'SERV WKR	+B96	![B108]	![B108]	![B108]	![B108]	![B108]	![H11]

Exhibit 5-5, continued

	A	B	C	D	E	F	G	H
109	'SERV POP	((B$44*$B108)+(B$45*$C108)+(B$46*$D108)+(B$47*$E108)+(B$48*$F108)+(B$49*$G108))*$E$54	![B109]	![B109]	![B109]	![B109]	![B109]	![H11]
110								
111	'ROUND 2							
112	'SERV WKR	((B$81*$B109)+(B$82*$C109)+(B$83*$D109)+(B$84*$E109)+(B$85*$F109)+(B$86*$G109))*$E$92	![B112]	![B112]	![B112]	![B112]	![B112]	![H11]
113	'SERV POP	![B109]	![B109]	![B109]	![B109]	![B109]	![B109]	![H11]
114								
115	'ROUND 3							
116	'SERV WKR	![B112]	![B112]	![B112]	![B112]	![B112]	![B112]	![H11]
117	'SERV POP	![B109]	![B109]	![B109]	![B109]	![B109]	![B109]	![H11]
118								
119	'ROUND 4							
120	'SERV WKR	![B112]	![B112]	![B112]	![B112]	![B112]	![B112]	![H11]
121	'SERV POP	![B109]	![B109]	![B109]	![B109]	![B109]	![B109]	![H11]
122								
123	'ROUND 5							
124	'SERV WKR	![B112]	![B112]	![B112]	![B112]	![B112]	![B112]	![H11]
125	'SERV POP	![B109]	![B109]	![B109]	![B109]	![B109]	![B109]	![H11]
126								
127	!--------	!-------	!-------	!-------	!-------	!-------	!-------	!-------
127	!--------	!-------	!-------	!-------	!-------	!-------	!-------	!-------
128	'TOTAL							
129	'WORKERS	+B104+B108+B112+B116+B120+B124	![B129]	![B129]	![B129]	![B129]	![B129]	![H11]
130	'POPULATN	![B129]	![B129]	![B129]	![B129]	![B129]	![B129]	![H11]

(B44*$B$11) + (B45*$C$11) + (B46*$D$11) +
(B47*$E$11) + (B48*$F$11) + (B49*$G$11)

This equation performs a matrix algebra operation, adding together a set of multiplicative values. Cell B44 contains the probability of a worker with a job in Zone 1 living in Zone 1. When multiplied by the number of workers in Zone 1 (B11), the result is the total number of Zone 1 workers who will live in Zone 1. Cell B45 is the probability of a Zone 2 worker living in Zone 1, and when multiplied by C11, yields total workers from Zone 2 with a residence in Zone 1. The equation sums across all sending zones to give the grand total of workers living in Zone 1. This cell algebra equation is similar in structure to the BASHH equation, except that the household multiplier is calculated separately in row 60.

Once constructed for Zone 1, the equation can be copied into the other zones. The dollar signs make the references to the zonal worker cells constant, permitting the copying of the equation. Hence, $B$11 will still be the same regardless of the cell into which it will be copied. The reader should carefully follow the equation structure as one which will appear in matrix models. The basic population — the total number of people who have a basic worker in the household — is calculated in row 60. It is assumed that household size is 2.5 per worker. Hence the number of workers in a zone is multiplied by 2.5 (cell E54).

Table 6 contains the friction factor calculations for the household to service establishments. The exponent used in this power function is in cell F65. Table 7 contains the probability matrix of visits between households and establishments. These two tables are identical in structure to Tables 3 and 4. In Table 8 the number of service workers needed to support the demand by the households visiting the different zones to go shopping, do personal business, or the like, are calculated. The equations which generate the number of zonal service workers needed in row 96 are similar to the ones in row 58 except that each cell is multiplied by the population-serving ratio found in cell E92. This ratio converts the households seeking services into the number of workers needed on a per capita basis.

Table 9 is the summary table which lists the basic workers and population as well as the round-by-round calculations of the service workers and population. A perusal of the cell listing of the table starting in row 100 shows the complexity of the equations needed to do the round-by-round calculations. However, once each equation for the first cell is set up the rest can be copied using the relative addressing capacity of the Lotus 1-2-3 program. However, note that the equation in cell 109 is:

((B$44*$B108) + (B$45*$C108) + (B$46*$D108) + (B$47*$E108) + (B$48*$F108) + (B$49*$G108)) * $E$54

This is a typical matrix manipulation equation in cell algebra. The Round 1 service population follows the SERVHH equation above. The number of Round 1 service workers (SERVWKR) in cell B108 is multiplied by the probability of a worker with a job in Zone 1 living in Zone 1 (ACCESS1) in cell B44. This value is added to the service workers from all the other zones who will live in Zone 1. Thus, the number of service workers in Zone 2 (cell C108) is multiplied by cell B45, the probability that a worker with employment in Zone 2 will live in Zone 1. Essentially, we are multiplying a row vector (the distribution of service workers) by a column vector (the probability that a worker will live in a particular zone). The result of the vector multiplication is multiplied by the constant in cell E54 — the population-to-employment ratio which converts workers into household populations.

There is a distinction between holding a row constant in an equation as in B$44, holding a column constant as in $B108, and holding both row and column constant as with $E$54. The decision as to what is held constant depends on how the equation is to copied into other cells. We choose the appropriate dollar sign utilization to copy equations properly, and this process may require some experimentation. The basic rule is to **minimize entering complex equations directly in the spreadsheet to avoid error.** In this example, the equation in cell 109 will copy directly into the rest of row 109. However, more importantly, the equation in cell 109 can be copied to all the rounds of service population in Table 9 as shown by the clones of cell 109 in the cell listing. The reader is invited to follow how the equation in cell 109 will produce the appropriate equations in the other cells.

Examining the spreadsheet itself in Exhibit 5-4 shows the round-by-round reduction in numbers which is the expected result of the model multiplier effect. At the bottom of Table 9 are the results of running the model after 5 rounds, total workers and population by zone. The Lowry model is a simple representation of a city. One could add a number of modifications to the model, introducing a number of service worker categories or land use constraints on development in certain zones. Such modifications would increase complexity but could be handled in a spreadsheet context if care were taken in design.

An Employment Projection Model

The Concept

The urban planner or policy analyst often needs to project employment trends as well as population. A number of employment projection techniques have been developed which are useful in a spreadsheet context. We shall examine two options — shiftshare analysis and base-export theory — as potential alternatives. It should be clear that this text can only highlight the complexities of these two approaches and that the reader is directed to any of several sources for more information. Landis (1985) has presented a spreadsheet model of shiftshare and shown how to develop alternative scenarios of future developments. Krueckeberg and Silvers (1974, 1986) have developed the concepts of shiftshare and base-export theory in detail. Brown (1969), James and Hughes (1973), and Greenberg (1972) have analyzed alternative shiftshare models.

In the shiftshare approach, employment trends are analyzed by comparing different components of change. The percent employment change in a local economy over time is the summation of: (1) aggregate percent change in employment in all industries in the nation, $E\%_N$, (2) the difference between this aggregate percent change in the industry nationwide, $E\%_{I,N}$, and total aggregate percent change, $E\%_N$, and (3) the difference between local percent change in an industry, $E\%_{I,K}$, and national industrial percent change, $E\%_{I,N}$. The shiftshare model is a simple mathematical identity. If one examines the equation below, it is obvious that right side reduces to the left using basic algebra.

$$E\%_{I,K} = E\%_N + (E\%_{I,N} - E\%_N) + (E\%_{I,K} - E\%_{I,N})$$

where:

$E\%_{I,K}$ Percent employment change in industry I in region K

$E\%_N$ Percent total national employment change in all industries over some period

$E\%_{I,N}$ Percent employment change in industry I in the nation

The three components of the shiftshare model have labels:

$E\%_N$	Aggregate percent share
$E\%_{I,N} - E\%_N$	Proportional or industrial percent shift
$E\%_{I,K} - E\%_{I,N}$	Differential or regional percent shift

By analyzing these three components of change, conclusions can be drawn about the local economy on an industry-by-industry basis. This is best seen by analyzing an actual example.

The Spreadsheet

The spreadsheet which projects employment to 1990 for Smiley County in Exhibit 5-6 follows the vertical model outlined earlier, dividing the calculations into a series of tables. Also, the shortened cell listing, which "clones" the original equation by referencing the cell from which it came, is used.

Table 1 presents the 1980 and 1984 employment by one-digit SIC (Standard Industrial Classification) codes for the United States and for Smiley County, a fictional area with data loosely based on a real county in the eastern part of the United States. The national data were taken from the *Employment and Earnings* series of the Bureau of Labor Statistics. The percent change columns are straightforward equations, as shown in the cell listing (Exhibit 5-7).

Table 2 contains the industrial and regional shifts. Recall that the industrial shift is a measure of how much better or worse an industry is doing nationwide relative to the nation in aggregate. The equation, as found in cell B30, is

$$(C10/B10) - (\$C\$20/\$B\$20)$$

which subtracts the national ratio of 1984 to 1980 employment from the industry-specific ratio.

The regional shift is a measure of how much better or worse a particular industry does in the local economy, or the county in this case, than in the nation as a whole. The equation in cell D30 shows this comparison, subtracting the industry ratio of 1984 to 1980 employment from the county ratio. The IF statement in columns C and E of Table 2 will enter a "+" if the value in the column to the left is positive, and a "-" if the value is negative. There are very clear winners

Exhibit 5-6

Regional Employment Model

REGIONAL EMPLOYMENT MODEL

TABLE 1 - 1984 EMPLOYMENT IN NATION AND SMILEY COUNTY (THOUSANDS)

	NATION			SMILEY COUNTY		
SECTOR	1980	1984	PCTCHG	1980	1984	PCTCHG
AGRICULTURE	3,529	3,321	-0.059	0.4	0.4	0.000
MINING	979	957	-0.022	0.7	0.6	-0.143
CONSTRUCTION	6,215	6,665	0.072	8.7	8.5	-0.023
MANUFACTURING	21,942	20,995	-0.043	85.4	78.9	-0.076
TRANSPORT/UTL	6,525	7,358	0.128	21.4	21.2	-0.009
WHOLESALE TRD	3,920	4,212	0.074	22.3	27.5	0.233
RETAIL TRADE	16,270	17,767	0.092	44.0	46.0	0.045
FIN/INS/RE	5,993	6,750	0.126	10.7	12.2	0.140
SERVICES	33,929	36,980	0.090	37.5	45.8	0.221
TOTAL	99,302	105,005	0.057	231.1	241.1	0.043

AGGREGATE NATIONAL CHANGE RATE 1980-84   0.057

TABLE 2 - THE COMPONENTS OF SHIFT-SHARE, 1980-84

SECTOR	INDUSTRIAL or PROPORTIONAL SHIFT		REGIONAL or DIFFERENTIAL SHIFT	
AGRICULTURE	-0.116	-	0.059	+
MINING	-0.080	-	-0.120	-
CONSTRUCTION	0.015	+	-0.095	-
MANUFACTURING	-0.101	-	-0.033	-
TRANSPORT/UTL	0.070	+	-0.137	-
WHOLESALE TRD	0.017	+	0.159	+
RETAIL TRADE	0.035	+	-0.047	-
FIN/INS/RE	0.069	+	0.014	+
SERVICES	0.032	+	0.131	+

TABLE 3 - 1990 EMPLOYMENT PROJECTION — CONSTANT SHARE MODEL

SECTOR	EMP 1984	PROJECTD ANNUAL % 1984-90	CONSTANT SHARE MODEL	PROJECTD INDUSTRY SHIFT
AGRICULTURE	0.4	4.41%	0.5	0.004
MINING	0.6	2.23%	0.7	0.003
CONSTRUCTION	8.5	3.44%	10.4	0.058
MANUFACTURING	78.9	1.24%	85.0	0.182

Exhibit 5-6, Continued

TRANSPORT/UTL	21.2	2.04%	23.9	0.082
WHOLESALE TRD	27.5	2.24%	31.4	0.118
RETAIL TRADE	46.0	2.30%	52.7	0.203
FIN/INS/RE	12.2	2.80%	14.4	0.066
SERVICES	45.8	3.18%	55.3	0.285
TOTAL	241.1		274.3	

TABLE 4 - 1990 EMPLOYMENT PROJECTION – CONSTANT SHIFT MODEL

SECTOR	EMP 1984	PROJECTD INDUSTRY SHIFT	REGIONAL SHIFT 1980-84	CONSTANT SHIFT MODEL
AGRICULTURE	0.4	0.004	0.059	0.4
MINING	0.6	0.003	-0.120	0.5
CONSTRUCTION	8.5	0.058	-0.095	8.2
MANUFACTURING	78.9	0.182	-0.033	90.7
TRANSPORT/UTL	21.2	0.082	-0.137	20.0
WHOLESALE TRD	27.5	0.118	0.159	35.1
RETAIL TRADE	46.0	0.203	-0.047	53.2
FIN/INS/RE	12.2	0.066	0.014	13.2
SERVICES	45.8	0.285	0.131	64.9
TOTAL	241.1			286.2

TABLE 5 - ESTIMATION OF 1984 BASIC EMPLOYMENT USING LOCATION QUOTIENTS

SECTOR	EMP 1984	LOCAL LQ	MODEL 1 BASIC EMP 1984	OBERS LQ LIMITS	MODEL 2 BASIC EMP 1984
AGRICULTURE	0.4	0.052	0.0	ALL	0.4
MINING	0.6	0.273	0.0	ALL	0.6
CONSTRUCTION	8.5	0.555	0.0	NEVER	0.0
MANUFACTURING	78.9	1.637	30.7	ALL	78.9
TRANSPORT/UTL	21.2	1.255	4.3	1.2	0.9
WHOLESALE TRD	27.5	2.844	17.8	1.1	16.9
RETAIL TRADE	46.0	1.128	5.2	1.1	1.1
FIN/INS/RE	12.2	0.787	0.0	1.1	0.0
SERVICES	45.8	0.539	0.0	1.2	0.0
TOTAL	241.1		58.0		98.8

TABLE 6 - 1984 EMPLOYMENT MULTIPLIERS

----- MODEL 1 -----		----- MODEL 2 -----	
BASIC	58	BASIC	99
NON-BASIC	183	NON-BASIC	142
MULTIPLIER	3.154	MULTIPLIER	1.440

Exhibit 5-6, continued

TABLE 7 - PROJECTED 1990 BASIC EMPLOYMENT

SECTOR	PROJECTD ANNUAL % 1984-90	MODEL 1 BASIC 1984	MODEL 1 BASIC 1990	MODEL 2 BASIC 1984	MODEL 2 BASIC 1990
AGRICULTURE	0.044	0.0	0.0	0.4	0.5
MINING	0.022	0.0	0.0	0.6	0.7
CONSTRUCTION	0.034	0.0	0.0	0.0	0.0
MANUFACTURING	0.012	30.7	33.0	78.9	85.0
TRANSPORT/UTL	0.020	4.3	4.9	0.9	0.0
WHOLESALE TRD	0.022	17.8	20.4	16.9	19.3
RETAIL TRADE	0.023	5.2	6.0	1.1	0.0
FIN/INS/RE	0.028	0.0	0.0	0.0	0.0
SERVICES	0.032	0.0	0.0	0.0	0.0

TABLE 8 - SUMMARY OF LOCATION QUOTIENT TOTAL EMPLOYMENT

	MODEL 1 1984	MODEL 1 1990	MODEL 2 1984	MODEL 2 1990
BASIC	58.0	64.2	98.8	105.4
NON-BASIC	183.1	202.6	142.3	151.8
TOTAL	241.1	266.9	241.1	257.2

TABLE 9 - EMPLOYMENT PROJECTIONS BY LOCATION QUOTIENT MODELS

SECTOR	MODEL 1 BASIC	MODEL 1 NON BASIC	MODEL 1 TOTAL	MODEL 2 BASIC	MODEL 2 NON BASIC	MODEL 2 TOTAL
AGRICULTURE	0.0	0.4	0.4	0.5	0.0	0.5
MINING	0.0	0.7	0.7	0.7	0.0	0.7
CONSTRUCTION	0.0	9.4	9.4	0.0	9.1	9.1
MANUFACTURING	33.0	53.4	86.4	85.0	0.0	85.0
TRANSPORT/UTL	4.9	18.7	23.6	0.0	21.6	21.6
WHOLESALE TRD	20.4	10.7	31.1	19.3	11.3	30.6
RETAIL TRADE	6.0	45.2	51.1	0.0	47.9	47.9
FIN/INS/RE	0.0	13.5	13.5	0.0	13.0	13.0
SERVICES	0.0	50.7	50.7	0.0	48.9	48.9
TOTAL	64.2	202.6	266.9	105.4	151.8	257.2

Exhibit 5-6, continued

TABLE 10 - SUMMARY OF THE FOUR EMPLOYMENT PROJECTIONS TO 1990

		1990			
		CONSTANT	CONSTANT	LQ	
SECTOR	1984	SHARE	SHIFT	MODEL 1	MODEL 2
AGRICULTURE	0.4	0.5	0.4	0.4	0.5
MINING	0.6	0.7	0.5	0.7	0.7
CONSTRUCTION	8.5	10.4	8.2	9.4	9.1
MANUFACTURING	78.9	85.0	90.7	86.4	85.0
TRANSPORT/UTL	21.2	23.9	20.0	23.6	21.6
WHOLESALE TRD	27.5	31.4	35.1	31.1	30.6
RETAIL TRADE	46.0	52.7	53.2	51.1	47.9
FIN/INS/RE	12.2	14.4	13.2	13.5	13.0
SERVICES	45.8	55.3	64.9	50.7	48.9
TOTAL	241.1	274.3	286.2	266.9	257.2

and losers in Smiley County. Agriculture, wholesale trade, finance, real estate and insurance, and services have positive regional shifts, indicating that these industries do better in the county than in the nation. Mining, construction, transportation, and retail trade do worse.

While there is concern among researchers (Brown, 1969; Greenberg, 1972) about the stability of components of the shiftshare model over time, it can be used for projection with caution. The model could be set up for projection in a number of ways (Landis, 1985; Krueckeberg and Silvers, 1974, 1986). We have selected two approaches found in the literature. The first is a version of the constant share approach. National projections of industrial change in employment are assumed to be accurate for local areas. This is called the "Super Ingrow" model. Essentially, the percent change in jobs projected to occur nationally in the 1984-1990 period is applied to the local economy (Krueckeberg and Silvers, 1986).

$$E_{I,K,1990} = (1 + E\%_{I,N,1984-90})^T * E_{I,K,1984}$$

where:

$E_{I,K,1990}$ Projected employment to 1990

T   Number of years between current and projected year — T = 6 for the 1984-1990 period

$E\%_{I,N,1984-90}$ The projected annual employment percent change in a national industry between the years 1984 and 1990

$E_{I,K,1984}$ Employment in industry I in the local economy K in 1984

This is a form of the exponential model discussed in Chapter 4. A modified version of this Super Ingrow model will be used in this example, with state-specific projections used in place of national projections. Table 3 contains the first projection using a constant share model. As used here, a set of industry-specific projections of employment changes between 1984 and 1990 is used. These are taken from OBERS projections for the State of New Jersey and are assumed to be appropriate for Smiley County. Other projection sets may be more appropriate, and are available from such sources as the U.S. Bureau of Labor Statistics. Ideally, these projections should be done with more detailed industrial classifications. Such a change could be done as a logical extension of the presentation here. Cell D46 contains the exponential equation found in the constant share model, transforming an annual change into a six-year period. This version of the constant share model assumes that the county employment will grow proportionally to the statewide projected growth estimates. A projected industry shift is estimated from this projection data and is used in the next table.

Table 4 develops our second projection effort — the constant shift model. This model takes the projected industry shift from Table 3 and adds in the historical regional shift from 1980 to 1984 (Krueckeberg and Silvers, 1986). The equation in cell E64 shows how to construct a constant shift model:

$$+B64 * (1+C64+D64)$$

Cell C64 contains the projected industry shift in the 1984 to 1990 period, and D64 the 1980-84 historical regional shift. The equation takes the 1984 agricultural employment and multiplies it by the growth rate (1+C64+D64). This particular spreadsheet repeats information in the different tables for legibility. Note that cell B64 contains the cell reference B46, and B46 refers to cell F10 — 1980 agricultural employment in Smiley County. A single change in cell F10 will be automatically carried through all subsequent cells which either directly or indirectly contain a reference to F10. An error in input at the outset can be easily and accurately rectified.

This employment model can be extended by introducing an alternative projection approach using location quotients and a base-service multiplier. Essentially, the location quotient approach states that an industry is either basic or nonbasic. A basic industry is one which exports goods and services beyond the local economy, while a nonbasic industry services local needs. An automobile manufacturing facility is basic in that it will export its product all over the nation. The local supermarket is nonbasic, serving local clients. Suffice it to say that there are serious criticisms of the location requirements approach and its companion, the minimum requirements approach (Krueckeberg and Silvers, 1986).

In simple terms, the location quotient is a ratio of proportions:

$$LQ_{I,K} = (E_{I,K}/E_{TOT,K}) / (E_{I,N}/E_{TOT,N})$$

where:

$LQ_{I,K}$ The location quotient for industry I in region K

$E_{I,K}$ The employment in industry I in region K

$E_{TOT,K}$ The employment in region K for all industries

$E_{I,N}$ The employment in industry I in the nation

$E_{TOT,N}$ The employment in the nation for all industries

If the location quotient is greater than one, this means that there is a higher ratio of industry employment to total employment in the local economy than in the nation. This would suggest that the number of workers in this industry in excess of the national proportion must be involved in producing goods or services for export outside the region. Correspondingly, a location quotient less than one means that there are fewer workers proportionally in the industry in the local area than in the nation. All of these local workers would be assumed to be nonbasic.

Exhibit 5-7
Cell Listing, Regional Employment Model

	A	B	C	D	E	F	G
1	'REGIONAL EMPLOYMENT MODEL						
2							
3							
4	'TABLE 1 - 1984 EMPLOYMENT IN NATION AND SMILEY COUNTY						
5							
6		' NATION			' SMILEY COUNTY		
7		!--------	!--------	!--------	!--------	!--------	!------
8	'SECTOR	"1980	"1984	"PCTCHG	"1980	"1984	"PCTCHG
9	!------------	!--------	!--------	!--------	!--------	!--------	!------
10	'AGRICULTURE	3529	3321	(C10-B10)/B10	0.4	0.4	![D10]
11	'MINING		957	![D10]	0.7	0.6	![D10]
12	'CONSTRUCTION	6215	6665	![D10]	8.7	8.5	![D10]
13	'MANUFACTURING	21942	20995	![D10]	85.4	78.9	![D10]
14	'TRANSPORT/UTL	6525	7358	![D10]	21.4	21.2	![D10]
15	'WHOLESALE TRD	3920	4212	![D10]	22.3	27.5	![D10]
16	'RETAIL TRADE	16270	17767	![D10]	44	46	![D10]
17	'FIN/INS/RE	5993	6750	![D10]	10.7	12.2	![D10]
18	'SERVICES	28587+5342	32214+4766	![D10]	37.5	45.8	![D10]
19							
20	"TOTAL	@SUM(B10..B18)	![B20]	![D10]	![B20]	![B20]	![D10]
21							
22	'AGGREGATE NATIONAL CHANGE RATE 1980-84				((C20/B20)-1)		
23							

Exhibit 5-7, Continued

	A	B	C	D	E	F	G
24	'TABLE 2 - THE COMPONENTS OF SHIFTSHARE, 1980-84						
25							
26		"INDUSTRI AL or		"REGIONAL or			
27		"PROPORTI ONAL		"DIFFEREN TIAL			
28	'SECTOR	"SHIFT		"SHIFT			
29	'----------	'--------	'--------	'--------	'--------	'--------	'------
30	'AGRICULTURE	(C10/B10) -($C$20/$ B$20)	@IF(B30>0 ," +"," -")	(F10/E10) -(C10/B10)	! [C30]		
31	'MINING	! [B30]	! [C30]	! [D30]	! [C30]		
32	'CONSTRUCTION	! [B30]	! [C30]	! [D30]	! [C30]		
33	'MANUFACTURIN G	! [B30]	! [C30]	! [D30]	! [C30]		
34	'TRANSPORT/UT L	! [B30]	! [C30]	! [D30]	! [C30]		
35	'WHOLESALE TR D	! [B30]	! [C30]	! [D30]	! [C30]		
36	'RETAIL TRADE	! [B30]	! [C30]	! [D30]	! [C30]		
37	'FIN/INS/RE	! [B30]	! [C30]	! [D30]	! [C30]		
38	'SERVICES	! [B30]	! [C30]	! [D30]	! [C30]		
39							
40	'TABLE 3 - 1990 EMPLOYMENT PROJECTION - CONSTANT SHARE MODEL						
41							
42			"PROJECTD	"CONSTANT	"PROJECTD		
43		"EMP	'ANNUAL %	"SHARE	"INDUSTRY		
44	'SECTOR	"1984	"1984-90	"MODEL	"SHIFT		
45	'----------	'--------	'--------	'--------	'--------		
46	'AGRICULTURE	+F10	0.0441	(B46*(1+C 46)^6)	(D46-B46) /($D$56-$ B$56)		
47	'MINING	! [B46]	0.0223	! [D46]	! [E46]		
48	'CONSTRUCTION	! [B46]	0.0344	! [D46]	! [E46]		
49	'MANUFACTURIN G	! [B46]	0.0124	! [D46]	! [E46]		
50	'TRANSPORT/UT L	! [B46]	0.0204	! [D46]	! [E46]		
51	'WHOLESALE TR D	! [B46]	0.0224	! [D46]	! [E46]		
52	'RETAIL TRADE	! [B46]	0.023	! [D46]	! [E46]		
53	'FIN/INS/RE	! [B46]	0.028	! [D46]	! [E46]		
54	'SERVICES	! [B46]	0.0318	! [D46]	! [E46]		
55							
56	"TOTAL	! [B20]		! [B20]			

Modeling with Electronic Spreadsheets

Exhibit 5-7, Continued

	A	B	C	D	E	F	G
58	'TABLE 4 - 1990 EMPLOYMENT PROJECTION - CONSTANT SHIFT MODEL						
59							
60			"PROJECTD	"REGIONAL	"CONSTANT		
61		"EMP	"INDUSTRY	"SHIFT	"SHIFT		
62	'SECTOR	"1984	"SHIFT	"1980-84	"MODEL		
63	'------------	'--------	'--------	'--------	'--------		
64	'AGRICULTURE	+B46	+E46	+D30	+B64*(1+C64+D64)		
65	'MINING	![B64]	![C64]	![D64]	![E64]		
66	'CONSTRUCTION	![B64]	![C64]	![D64]	![E64]		
67	'MANUFACTURING	![B64]	![C64]	![D64]	![E64]		
68	'TRANSPORT/UTL	![B64]	![C64]	![D64]	![E64]		
69	'WHOLESALE TRD	![B64]	![C64]	![D64]	![E64]		
70	'RETAIL TRADE	![B64]	![C64]	![D64]	![E64]		
71	'FIN/INS/RE	![B64]	![C64]	![D64]	![E64]		
72	'SERVICES	![B64]	![C64]	![D64]	![E64]		
73							
74	"TOTAL	![B20]			![B20]		
75							
76	'TABLE 5 - ESTIMATION OF 1984 BASIC EMPLOYMENT USING LOCATION QUOTIENTS						
77							
78				"MODEL 1	"OBERS	"MODEL 2	
79		"EMP	"LOCAL	"BASIC	"LQ	"BASIC	
80	'SECTOR	"1984	^LQ	"EMP 1984	"LIMITS	"EMP 1984	
81	'------------	'--------	'--------	'--------	'--------	'--------	
82	'AGRICULTURE	![B64]	(B82/$B$92)/(C10/$C$20)	0	"ALL	+B82	
83	'MINING	![B64]	![C82]	0	"ALL	![F82]	
84	'CONSTRUCTION	![B64]	![C82]	0	"NEVER	0	
85	'MANUFACTURING	![B64]	![C82]	+B85-($B$92*(C13/$C$20))	"ALL	![F82]	
86	'TRANSPORT/UTL	![B64]	![C82]	![D85]	1.2	+B86-($B$92*((C14/$C$20)*E86))	
87	'WHOLESALE TRD	![B64]	![C82]	![D85]	1.1	![F86]	
88	'RETAIL TRADE	![B64]	![C82]	![D85]	1.1	![F86]	
89	'FIN/INS/RE	![B64]	![C82]	0	1.1	0	
90	'SERVICES	![B64]	![C82]	0	1.2	0	
91							
92	"TOTAL	![B20]		![B20]		![B20]	

Modeling with Electronic Spreadsheets

Exhibit 5-7, Continued

	A	B	C	D	E	F	G
93							
94	'TABLE 6 - 1984 EMPLOYMENT MULTIPLIERS						
95							
96	'------ MODEL 1 ------			'------ MODEL 2 ---			
97	'BASIC	+D92		'BASIC		+F92	
98	'NON-BASIC	+B92-B97		'NON-BASIC		+B92-F97	
99	'MULTIPLIER	+B98/B97		'MULTIPLIER		! [B99]	
100							
101	'TABLE 7 - PROJECTED 1990 BASIC EMPLOYMENT						
102							
103		"PROJECTD	'------ MODEL 1 ----		'------ MODEL 2 ---		
104		"ANNUAL	'------ BASIC -----		'------ BASIC -----		
105	'SECTOR	"% 1984-90	"1984	"1990	"1984	"1990	
106	'------------	'------------	'------------	'------------	'------------	'------------	'-------
107	'AGRICULTURE	+C46	+D82	0	! [C107]	+E107*(1+B107)^6	
108	'MINING	! [B107]	! [C107]	+C108*(1+B108)^6	! [C107]	! [F107]	
109	'CONSTRUCTION	! [B107]	! [C107]	0	! [C107]	0	
110	'MANUFACTURING	! [B107]	! [C107]	! [D108]	! [C107]	! [F107]	
111	'TRANSPORT/UTL	! [B107]	! [C107]	! [D108]	! [C107]	0	
112	'WHOLESALE TRD	! [B107]	! [C107]	! [D108]	! [C107]	! [F107]	
113	'RETAIL TRADE	! [B107]	! [C107]	! [D108]	! [C107]	0	
114	'FIN/INS/RE	! [B107]	! [C107]	0	! [C107]	0	
115	'SERVICES	! [B107]	! [C107]	0	! [C107]	0	
116							
117	'TABLE 8 - SUMMARY OF LOCATION QUOTIENT TOTAL EMPLOYMENT						
118							
119		'------ MODEL 1 ----			'------ MODEL 2 ---		
120		"1984	"1990		"1984	"1990	
121	'------------	'------------	'------------	'------------	'------------	'------------	'-------
122	'BASIC	@SUM(C107..C115)	! [B122]		@SUM(E107..E115)	! [E122]	
123	'NON-BASIC	+B98	+C122*B99		! [C107]	+F122*F99	
124	'TOTAL	@SUM(B122..B123)	! [B124]		! [B124]	! [B124]	

106   *Modeling with Electronic Spreadsheets*

Exhibit 5-7, Continued

	A	B	C	D	E	F	G
125							
126	'TABLE 9 - EMPLOYMENT PROJECTIONS BY LOCATION QUOTIENT MODELS						
127		'----- MODEL 1 ---			'----- MODEL 2 ---		
128			"NON			"NON	
129	'SECTOR	"BASIC	"BASIC	"TOTAL	"BASIC	"BASIC	"TOTAL
130	'----------	'--------	'--------	'--------	'--------	'--------	'------
131	'AGRICULTURE	+D107	(B82-D82)*($C$123/$B$123)	@SUM(B131..C131)	+F107	(B82-F82)*($F$123/$E$123)	![D131]
132	'MINING	![B131]	![C131]	![D131]	![E131]	![F131]	![D131]
133	'CONSTRUCTION	![B131]	![C131]	![D131]	![E131]	![F131]	![D131]
134	'MANUFACTURING	![B131]	![C131]	![D131]	![E131]	![F131]	![D131]
135	'TRANSPORT/UTL	![B131]	![C131]	![D131]	![E131]	![F131]	![D131]
136	'WHOLESALE TRD	![B131]	![C131]	![D131]	![E131]	![F131]	![D131]
137	'RETAIL TRADE	![B131]	![C131]	![D131]	![E131]	![F131]	![D131]
138	'FIN/INS/RE	![B131]	![C131]	![D131]	![E131]	![F131]	![D131]
139	'SERVICES	![B131]	![C131]	![D131]	![E131]	![F131]	![D131]
140							
141	'TOTAL	![B20]	![B20]	![B20]	![B20]	![B20]	![B20]
142							
143	'TABLE 10 - SUMMARY OF THE FOUR EMPLOYMENT PROJECTIONS TO 1990						
144							
145				'---------- 1990 --------			
146				"CONSTANT	"CONSTANT	"----- LQ -------	
147	'SECTOR	"1984	"SHARE	"SHIFT	"MODEL 1	"MODEL 2	
148	'----------	'--------	'--------	'--------	'--------	'--------	
149	'AGRICULTURE	+B82	+D46	+E64	+D131	+G131	
150	'MINING	![B149]	![C149]	![D149]	![E149]	![F149]	
151	'CONSTRUCTION	![B149]	![C149]	![D149]	![E149]	![F149]	
152	'MANUFACTURING	![B149]	![C149]	![D149]	![E149]	![F149]	
153	'TRANSPORT/UTL	![B149]	![C149]	![D149]	![E149]	![F149]	
154	'WHOLESALE TRD	![B149]	![C149]	![D149]	![E149]	![F149]	
155	'RETAIL TRADE	![B149]	![C149]	![D149]	![E149]	![F149]	
156	'FIN/INS/RE	![B149]	![C149]	![D149]	![E149]	![F149]	
157	'SERVICES	![B149]	![C149]	![D149]	![E149]	![F149]	
158							
159	'TOTAL	![B20]	![B20]	![B20]	![B20]	![B20]	

Some research has indicated that it is more reasonable to assume that location quotients may have values greater than 1 before an industry is declared to have an export component. OBERS, the employment projection series of the Bureau of Economic Analysis in the U.S. Department of Commerce, has developed a set of location quotients for various industrial categories different from unity. Moreover, sometimes OBERS will characterize either all or none of employment in some industries as basic. This approach is included below.

Table 5 calculates basic employment in Smiley County using two different location quotient approaches. The local location quotient equation shown in cell C82 is the ratio of local to national proportions of agricultural employment to total employment. Model 1 is the traditional approach. An industry will only have basic employment when the location quotient exceeds 1. If the value for an industry is greater than 1, then the equation in cell D85 is used:

$$+B85 - (\$B\$92 * (C13/\$C\$20))$$

Basic employment is equal to total employment (B85) minus the amount of employment needed to satisfy the nonbasic requirements — total county employment ($B$92) multiplied by the national proportion of industry to total employment (C13/$C$20).

Model 2 uses the OBERS approach. The OBERS LQ LIMITS column contains the location quotient requirements for determining basic employment. For example, in OBERS agriculture is always basic while construction is never basic. Cell F86 contains the equation to calculate basic employment and is similar to cell D85 discussed above, except that the nonbasic portion is multiplied by the OBERS ratio (cell E86). This additional element in the equation is needed to account for the fact that the location quotient is not always exactly 1.

Table 6 calculates the basic/nonbasic multiplier — the ratio of nonbasic to basic workers in the two models. Note the differences between the two estimates. Table 7 projects basic employment to 1990 using the growth rates in the constant share model taken from the New Jersey OBERS series. Table 8 calculates 1990 employment by carrying basic employment from Table 7 and by using the 1984 basic/nonbasic multiplier to generate 1990 nonbasic employment. Cell C123 contains the multiplier equation, +C122*B99.

Table 9 breaks out the location quotient projections into industry categories. A simple ratio approach is used. Cell C131 contains the industry specific nonbasic employment equation:

(B82-D82) * ($C$123/$B$123)

The nonbasic employment in 1984 (B82-D82) is multiplied by the ratio of total 1990 nonbasic to total 1984 nonbasic, thereby attaching the overall growth ratio to each industry.

Table 10 summarizes the four projections. Three projections have reasonably close total values, although the methodology does differ among them. Of course, the same growth rates applied to the constant share model are used in the location quotient models as well. However, the basic/nonbasic multiplier differs greatly between Model 1 and Model 2, yet the projections are similiar. Clearly, there is potential for experimentation here. The reader may disagree with the assumptions in this example and wish to change it. The advantage of a spreadsheet approach is that model structure and data are easily changed if thought appropriate. One can truly construct one's own image of the "better" employment projection model: the basics are highly flexible.

An Urban Transportation Planning Model

The Concept

In this example we will introduce both a transportation planning application and a spreadsheet example which creates and uses three interrelated models. Traditionally, transportation planning has been the most active sub-field in the use of computerized techniques to do analysis. The commercial availability of computers in the 1950's led to the development of a number of regional transportation planning models which heavily relied on extensive numerical processing. Creighton (1970) has chronicled the early development of these models. Others (Stopher and Meyburg, 1975; Dickey, et al., 1975) have presented a broad view of the field.

The transportation planning process is often divided into a series of four steps:

1. Trip generation
2. Trip distribution
3. Modal split
4. Traffic assignment

These four tasks are surrounded by two others. Trip generation calculations require some knowledge of land use patterns. Also, an evaluation phase is a necessary component of a planning activity. The central output of this process is future traffic loadings on roadways within the study area. These expected traffic volume estimates are the product of the traffic assignment phase of the analysis. However, the preceding three steps in the process — generation, distribution, modal split — must be carried out first.

In the trip generation phase, expected future land use developments within the study area are converted into trips. There already exists a wide body of literature which examines the traffic-generating capacity of a wide variety of land use activities. For example, a typical single-family home is expected to generate about 10 automobile movements a day entering and leaving the driveway. Also, a fast food restaurant, such as McDonald's, is estimated to have about 550 vehicles a day entering and leaving the facility per 1,000 square feet of gross floor area. These estimates are derived from a series of studies on land use activities at different sites. The single best source of these trip generation rates is *Trip Generation* (Institute of Transportation Engineers, 1983). In this handbook, the results of numerous studies are cataloged and typical average values developed for the different land use categories contained. Such a handbook on trip generation rates can provide only generalized values which may or may not be appropriate for a particular situation.

The trip distribution phase allocates the trips generated by a particular zone within the study area to all the other zones in the study area as well as outside the area. Usually, this distribution is done by trip purpose. Each trip allocated is said to have two ends — the starting point and the finishing location. The Quick Response System (QRS), developed under federal contract (Sosslau, et al., 1978), has received wide attention by local transportation planners as a low-cost manual technique for doing transportation impact and corridor work. The U. S. Department of Transportation (1984) has developed a computerized version of the QRS model which has proved useful in planning applications (Spanovich, 1984). In the Quick Response System three trip purposes are used — home-based work, home-based non-work, and non-home-based. Home-based work trips are those which have an origin or destination at home and, obviously, have the other end of the trip at a work location. Home-based non-work trips are defined similarly, but have as purpose such activities as shopping, social visits, personal business, medical trips and the like. Non-home-based trips are those which have neither end at home. The Quick

Response System distributes trips among zones for these three trip purposes.

Modal split is the division between the different modes of travel. Typically, auto trips are dominant in most urban areas. Also, many applications of a spreadsheet-based transportation model, as will be demonstrated here, involve assessing the local traffic impacts of a proposed development. The impacts generally sought are from auto travel, not public transit operations. A number of these modal split models lend themselves directly to spreadsheet applications. For example, the model outlined in the guide to QRS (Sosslau, et al., 1978: 63-65) is a variant of the gravity model and could be modeled on a spreadsheet.

The traffic assignment phase is the most complicated element of the urban transportation planning process to put on a spreadsheet. In fact, traffic assignment could not be realistically done on a spreadsheet except in the simplest cases. Typical assignment models must perform a variety of steps in order to allocate a traffic volume to a particular link. These include:

1. The development of a highway network which contains links and nodes. Links are the highway sections between intersections, or nodes.
2. The construction of minimum travel time paths through the network.
3. The allocation of trips between zones, an output of the trip distribution phase, to highway links.

The highway network shown in Exhibit 5-8 has all roadway intersections, called nodes, coded numerically. Each link is uniquely identified by the beginning and ending node values. For example, link 104-105 intersects at node 105 with links 105-108, 105-102 and 105-106. This coding method is conventional for larger transportation models because this particular nodal representation permits paths to be built through the network from zone to zone. A particular link's end is correspondingly the beginning of new links connected to this earlier link. This nodal system, however, is overly complex if the paths through the network are to be constructed by visual inspection.

Instead, the links themselves can be numbered as shown in Exhibit 5-9. While one cannot trace a path through the network by nodal connections, the human ability to see patterns and make judgments works well with this system. All potential paths between zone cen-

Exhibit 5-8

Typical Coding of a Highway Network

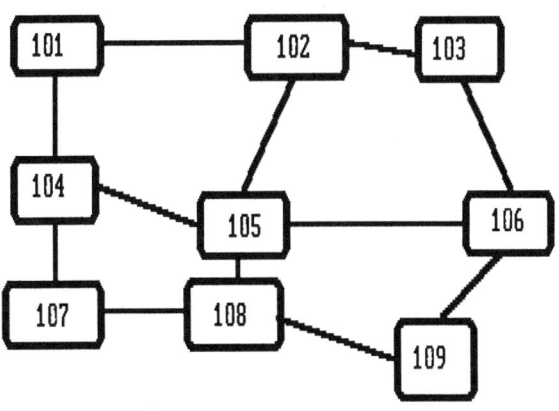

Exhibit 5-9

The Branchbrook Transportation System

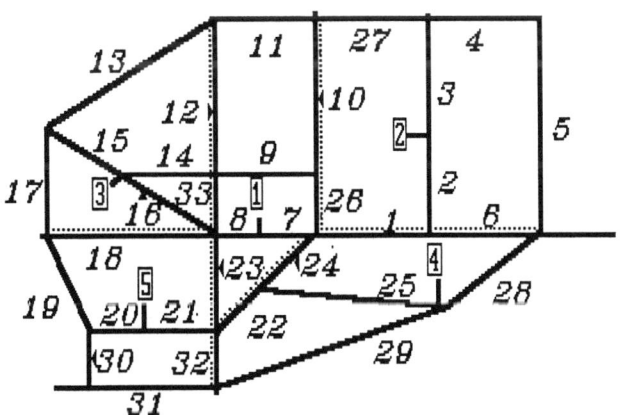

troids can be examined in terms of travel times. Many paths can be quickly disregarded as too long, and a limited set of paths can be selected as potential routes among zones. According to traffic assignment logic, drivers will often take the shortest route between two places in terms of travel time. If alternative paths are approximately the same in travel time, drivers will use these alternatives in roughly equal proportion. The community of Branchbrook is divided into 5 analysis zones. There are 33 links in the roadway system. The centroids of each of the zones 1 through 5 are indicated by a number in a box. The dotted lines mark the zonal boundaries.

The Spreadsheet

An extensive spreadsheet structure has been developed to replicate this urban transportation planning process. The example will utilize three steps of the process — generation, distribution, and assignment. Modal split, which projects the division between auto and transit trips, will not be modeled in this effort. The example presented will involve a five-zone city of Branchbrook with 33 highway links. Each zone is assumed to have one centroid from which all traffic emanates. While this is unrealistic in a five-zone city in which the zones are relatively large, a typical real world transportation study contains 50, 100 or 1,000 relatively small zones. With such a large number of small zones it is perfectly appropriate to consider all traffic emanating from a zone centroid.

The spreadsheet model to do trip generation and distribution is presented in three pieces. Exhibit 5-10 contains the trip generation and distribution phases of the model for Branchbrook. Exhibit 5-11 contains the link travel times, while Exhibit 5-12 contains the traffic assignment phase. The extensive cell listing is found in the Appendix. The model presented is designed to estimate the traffic impacts of proposed residential and non-residential development.

The calculations have been broken into a number of tables, each of which performs particular elements in the analysis. As with earlier models the tables are organized in a vertical fashion. Table 1 contains a table derived from the QRS guide (Sosslau, el al., 1978) which relates the number of person-trips per household (AVG PT/HH) to income level and assumes a distribution of trips among the three trip purposes — home-based work (HBW), home-based non-work (HBNW), and non-home-based (NHB) trips. A typical household in the $10,000 to $15,000 range, using 1970 dollars, is expected to make 18 person-trips per day of which 19 percent would be for the purpose of going to work. Often, trips are estimated to vary by the number of automobiles owned in the household; thus Table 1 could be modified to reflect this approach.

The estimates of auto occupancy rates are given in Table 2. This table converts person-trips into auto trips. Note that these rates are explicitly available and recognizable in the spreadsheet. Like all input variables, they can be easily changed should circumstances dictate.

Table 3 contains the proposed residential development to be analyzed by the model. Note that the user must estimate the income levels of the potential households which are to be located in the six zones. Typically, any proposed residential development would have a proposed mix of residential units — single-family, townhouses, etc. — along with proposed selling prices or rental rates. The analyst could estimate household income from such data. Or, the table could be restructured to use other data. For example, the ITE trip generation report (Institute of Transportation Engineers, 1983) contains rates broken out by type of residential unit. One would have to know how many units of each type were proposed and redo Tables 1 and 3 to use this approach. The information in Tables 1 and 3 is the basis for Table 4, in which person-trips per zone are calculated.

Table 5 divides person-trips by auto occupancy, taking the distribution of trips by trip purposes into account. An examination of the cell listing in the Appendix shows the multiplication of the income-specific person-trips by trip purpose percent. For example, the 406 Zone 1 home-based vehicle work trips (HBW) in cell B49 are calculated by summing the multiplication of the top row in Table 4 — Zone 1 person trips by income — by the HBW percentage of total trips in Table 1, and dividing by the HBW auto occupancy rate in Table 2. Note how the equation is constructed in terms of absolute cell references:

(($B37*C$8)+($C37*C$9)+($D37*C$10)+($E37*C$11)+($F37*C$12))/$B$16

Recall from the discussion in the Lowry model section that the dollar sign can make the column constant, as in $B37, or the row in C$8. Both row and column are constant in $C$16. The decision to hold either the row, column, or both constant is a function of how the equation is to be copied into other cells. One wants to avoid at all cost retyping formulas because of potential errors. In the above equation, cell B37 has the column held constant because the equation will be copied across the rows of the table, and the column should remain the

Exhibit 5-10

The Branchbrook Transportation Planning Study

URBAN TRANSPORTATION PLANNING MODEL

TABLE 1 - RESIDENTIAL TRIP PRODUCTION CHARACTERISTICS

		- % AVG DAILY PT-PURPOSE -		
INCOME	AVG PT/HH	HBW	HBNW	NHB
0-5	6.4	0.22	0.58	0.20
5-10	13.4	0.20	0.57	0.23
10-15	18.0	0.19	0.56	0.25
15-20	19.6	0.18	0.56	0.26
20+	20.5	0.18	0.55	0.27

TABLE 2 - AUTO OCCUPANCY RATES (NO TRANSIT ASSUMED)

HBW	1.37	PASSENGERS PER VEHICLE
HBNW	1.81	
NHB	1.43	

TABLE 3 - PROPOSED RESIDENTIAL DEVELOPMENT

	-------- NO OF HOUSEHOLDS BY ZONE AND INCOME --------					
ZONE	0-5	5-10	10-15	15-20	20+	TOTAL
1	50	20	10	50	60	190
2	20	0	100	0	300	420
3	20	0	120	0	120	260
4	10	40	150	0	230	430
5	10	0	200	0	100	310
TOTAL	110	60	580	50	810	1610

TABLE 4 - PERSON TRIP PRODUCTIONS BY ZONE AND INCOME

	---NO OF PERSONS TRIPS BY ZONE AND INCOME LEVEL---					
ZONE	0-5	5-10	10-15	15-20	20+	TOTAL
1	320	268	180	980	1230	2978
2	128	0	1800	0	6150	8078
3	128	0	2160	0	2460	4748
4	64	536	2700	0	4715	8015
5	64	0	3600	0	2050	5714
TOTAL	704	804	10440	980	16605	29533

Exhibit 5-10, continued

TABLE 5 - VEHICLE TRIP PRODUCTIONS, PROPOSED DEVELOPMENT

- NO OF TRIPS BY PURPOSE, PROPOSED DEVELOPMENT -

	HBW	HBNW	NHB	TOTAL
1	406	1215	553	2174
2	1078	3259	1559	5896
3	643	1925	898	3466
4	1082	3247	1521	5850
5	779	2322	1070	4171
TOTAL	3989	11967	5601	21557

TABLE 6 - NONRESIDENTIAL TRIP ATTRACTION CHARACTERISTICS

CODE	CATEGORY	DAILY TP/ACRE	% PURPOSE HBW	HBNW	NHB
*** RETAIL ***					
SHOP CT	SHOPPING CENTER	889.3	0.05	0.60	0.35
COMMERCL	OTHER COMMERCL	1000.0	0.05	0.60	0.35
*** MANUFACTURING ***					
LT IND	LIGHT INDUSTRIAL	52.4	0.90	0.05	0.05
MANUF	MANUFACTURING	38.9	0.90	0.05	0.05
IND PK	INDUSTRIAL PARK	62.8	0.90	0.05	0.05
*** OFFICE ***					
OFFSMALL	OFFICE<100000SF	137.0	0.20	0.45	0.35
OFFLARGE	OFFICE>100000SF	166.0	0.20	0.45	0.35
*** RESTAURANT ***					
QUALREST	QUALITY	200	0.05	0.70	0.25
OTHREST	OTHER	932	0.05	0.54	0.41
FASTFOOD	FAST FOOD	1825	0.05	0.54	0.41
*** RECREATIONAL ***					
PARK	LOCAL PARK	6.0	0.00	0.90	0.10

TABLE 7 - PROPOSED NONRESIDENTIAL DEVELOPMENT

------- PROPOSED NONRESIDENTIAL ACTIVITY IN ACRES ----

ZONE	SHOP CT	COMMERCL	LT IND	MANUF	IND PK	OFFSMALL
1	3	0	0	0	0	1
2	0	2	0	3	0	0
3	0	0	2	6	10	0
4	2	3	0	2	0	4
5	0	0	2	0	20	0
TOTAL	5	5	4	11	30	5

ZONE	OFFLARGE	QUALREST	OTHREST	FASTFOOD	PARK	TOTAL
1	12	0	0	0	0	16
2	0	0	0	0	10	15
3	0	0	0	0	0	18
4	0	1	0	0	0	12
5	0	0	0	0	0	22
TOTAL	12	1	0	0	10	83

Exhibit 5-10, continued

TABLE 8 - VEHICLE TRIP ATTRACTIONS FROM NONRESIDENTIAL

- VEHICLE TRIP ATTRACTIONS BY LAND USE AND ZONE -

ZONE	SHOP CT	COMMERCL	LT IND	MANUF	IND PK	OFFSMALL
1	2668	0	0	0	0	137
2	0	2000	0	117	0	0
3	0	0	105	233	628	0
4	1779	3000	0	78	0	548
5	0	0	105	0	1256	0
TOTAL	4447	5000	210	428	1884	685

ZONE	OFFLARGE	QUALREST	OTHREST	FASTFOOD	PARK	TOTAL
1	1992	0	0	0	0	25928
2	0	0	0	0	60	23320
3	0	0	0	0	0	21204
4	0	200	0	0	0	20437
5	0	0	0	0	0	15581
TOTAL	1992	200	0	0	60	106471

TABLE 9 - NONRESIDENTIAL TRIP ATTRACTIONS BY PURPOSE AND ZONE

- NO OF NONRESIDENTIAL ATTRACTIONS BY PURPOSE -

ZONE	HBW	HBNW	NHB	TOTAL
1	559	2559	1679	4797
2	205	1260	712	2177
3	870	48	48	966
4	429	3258	1918	5604
5	1225	68	68	1361
TOTAL	3287	7193	4425	14905

TABLE 10 - RESIDENTIAL TRIP ATTRACTIONS BY PURPOSE AND ZONE

```
                    NO. HBNW ATTRACTIONS/HH=     1.0
                    NO. NHB ATTRACTIONS/HH=      0.5
```

ZONE	NO. HH	HBW	HBNW	NHB	TOTAL
1	190	0	190	95	285
2	420	0	420	210	630
3	260	0	260	130	390
4	430	0	430	215	645
5	310	0	310	155	465
TOTAL	1610	0	1610	805	2415

Exhibit 5-10, continued

TABLE 11 - TOTAL TRIP ATTRACTIONS

ZONE	HBW	HBNW	NHB	TOTAL
1	559	2749	1774	5082
2	205	1680	922	2807
3	870	308	178	1356
4	429	3688	2133	6249
5	1225	378	223	1826
TOTAL	3287	8803	5230	17320

TABLE 12 - TOTAL TRIP PRODUCTIONS (FROM TABLE 5)

ZONE	HBW	HBNW	NHB	TOTAL
1	406	1215	553	2174
2	1078	3259	1559	5896
3	643	1925	898	3466
4	1082	3247	1521	5850
5	779	2322	1070	4171
TOTAL	3989	11967	5601	21557

TABLE 13 - (PRODUCTIONS - ATTRACTIONS)

HBW	HBNW	NHB
702	3164	371

TABLE 14 - PRODUCTION/ATTRACTION ADJUSTMENT FACTORS (TP/TA)

	HBW	HBNW	NHB
TOTAL PRODUCTIONS	3989	11967	5601
TOTAL ATTRACTIONS	3287	8803	5230
FACTOR	1.21	1.36	1.07

TABLE 15 - ADJUSTED TRIP PRODUCTIONS AND ATTRACTIONS

ZONE	1	2	3	4	5	TOTAL
HBW PRD	406	1078	643	1082	779	3989
HBW ATT	679	249	1055	520	1486	3989
HBNW PRD	1215	3259	1925	3247	2322	11967
HBNW ATT	3737	2284	419	5013	514	11967
NHB PRD	553	1559	898	1521	1070	5601
NHB ATT	1900	987	191	2285	239	5601

Exhibit 5-10, continued

```
TABLE 16 - TIME-DISTANCE MATRIX
ZONE            1       2       3       4       5
---------------------------------------------------
  1             5      14       7      11      13
  2            14       5      21      15      21
  3             7      21       5      18      14
  4            11      15      18       5      12
  5            13      21      14      12       5
```

***** HOME-BASED WORK (HBW) TRIP DISTRIBUTIONS *****

```
TABLE 17 - HBW F-MATRIX (FRICTION FACTOR MATRIX)
                                EXPONENT=    0.4
ZONE           1       2       3       4       5      TOTAL
-----------------------------------------------------------
  1         0.5253  0.3480  0.4592  0.3832  0.3584   2.0741
  2         0.3480  0.5253  0.2959  0.3385  0.2959   1.8035
  3         0.4592  0.2959  0.5253  0.3147  0.3480   1.9430
  4         0.3832  0.3385  0.3147  0.5253  0.3701   1.9318
  5         0.3584  0.2959  0.3480  0.3701  0.5253   1.8977
```

```
TABLE 18 - HBW TRIP DISTRIBUTIONS (ROUND 1)
ZONE           1       2       3       4       5      TOTAL
-----------------------------------------------------------
  1            87      21     118      49     130      406
  2           197     109     260     147     366     1078
  3           124      29     220      65     205      643
  4           188      61     240     197     397     1082
  5           114      35     173      90     367      779
TOTAL         710     255    1011     548    1466     3989
```

```
TABLE 19 - ADJUSTED ATTRACTIONS (A(J,IT)=A(J,IT-1)*(A(J)/(C(J,I)))
ZONE             1       2       3       4       5
---------------------------------------------------
GENHBW ATT     679     249    1055     520    1486
DISHBW ATT     710     255    1011     548    1466
A(J,IT=1)      649     243    1101     494    1507
```

```
TABLE 20 - HBW TRIP DISTRIBUTION (ROUND 2)
ZONE           1       2       3       4       5      TOTAL
-----------------------------------------------------------
  1            83      21     124      46     132      406
  2           188     107     272     139     372     1078
  3           118      28     229      61     207      643
  4           180      60     251     188     404     1082
  5           109      34     180      86     371      779
TOTAL         679     249    1055     520    1486     3989
```

Exhibit 5-10, continued

***** HOME BASED NON-WORK (HBNW) TRIP DISTRIBUTIONS *****

TABLE 21 - HBNW F-MATRIX (FRICTION FACTOR MATRIX)
                                    EXPONENT=   0.7

ZONE	1	2	3	4	5	TOTAL
1	0.3241	0.1577	0.2561	0.1866	0.1661	1.0906
2	0.1577	0.3241	0.1187	0.1502	0.1187	0.8694
3	0.2561	0.1187	0.3241	0.1322	0.1577	0.9888
4	0.1866	0.1502	0.1322	0.3241	0.1756	0.9688
5	0.1661	0.1187	0.1577	0.1756	0.3241	0.9422

TABLE 22 - HOME BASED NON-WORK (HBNW) TRIP DISTRIBUTIONS (ROUND 1)

ZONE	1	2	3	4	5	TOTAL
1	545	162	48	421	38	1215
2	875	1100	74	1119	91	3259
3	874	248	124	605	74	1925
4	806	396	64	1877	104	3247
5	719	314	77	1020	193	2322
TOTAL	3819	2220	387	5042	500	11967

TABLE 23 - ADJUSTED ATTRACTIONS (A(J,IT)=A(J,IT-1)*(A(J)/(C(J,I)))

ZONE	1	2	3	4	5
GENHBNW AT	3737	2284	419	5013	514
DISHBNW AT	3819	2220	387	5042	500
A(J,IT=1)	3657	2350	454	4985	528

TABLE 24 - HOME BASED NON-WORK (HBNW) TRIP DISTRIBUTIONS (ROUND 2)

ZONE	1	2	3	4	5	TOTAL
1	535	167	53	420	40	1215
2	854	1128	80	1109	93	3264
3	856	255	135	603	76	1925
4	790	409	70	1871	107	3247
5	703	323	83	1014	198	2322
TOTAL	3739	2282	419	5017	514	11972

***** NON HOME BASED (NHB) TRIP DISTRIBUTIONS *****

TABLE 25 - NHB F-MATRIX (FRICTION FACTOR MATRIX)
                                    EXPONENT=   0.7

ZONE	1	2	3	4	5	TOTAL
1	0.3241	0.1577	0.2561	0.1866	0.1661	1.0906
2	0.1577	0.3241	0.1187	0.1502	0.1187	0.8694
3	0.2561	0.1187	0.3241	0.1322	0.1577	0.9888
4	0.1866	0.1502	0.1322	0.3241	0.1756	0.9688
5	0.1661	0.1187	0.1577	0.1756	0.3241	0.9422

Exhibit 5-10, continued

TABLE 26 - NON HOME BASED (NHB) TRIP DISTRIBUTIONS (ROUND 1)

ZONE	1	2	3	4	5	TOTAL
1	265	67	21	183	17	553
2	461	492	35	528	44	1559
3	434	105	55	270	34	898
4	412	172	29	860	49	1521
5	359	133	34	456	88	1070
TOTAL	1930	969	175	2297	231	5601

TABLE 27 - ADJUSTED ATTRACTIONS (A(J,IT)=A(J,IT-1)*(A(J)/(C(J,I))

ZONE	1	2	3	4	5
GENHBNW AT	1900	987	191	2285	239
DISHBNW AT	1930	969	175	2297	231
A(J,IT=1)	1870	1006	209	2273	247

TABLE 28 - NON HOME BASED (NHB) TRIP DISTRIBUTIONS (ROUND 2)

ZONE	1	2	3	4	5	TOTAL
1	261	68	23	183	18	553
2	452	500	38	524	45	1559
3	428	107	60	268	35	898
4	406	176	32	857	50	1521
5	353	136	37	453	91	1070
TOTAL	1900	986	191	2285	239	5601

TABLE 29 — TOTAL TRIPS FROM DISTRIBUTION MODEL

ZONE	1	2	3	4	5	TOTAL
1	880	256	199	649	189	2174
2	1495	1735	390	1773	510	5902
3	1402	390	424	932	318	3466
4	1376	644	353	2915	562	5850
5	1165	492	300	1553	660	4171
TOTAL	6318	3518	1665	7823	2239	21562

same. Correspondingly, the row in cell C8 is held constant because the HBW proportions are to remain the same down the column in Table 5. One has to work at the appropriate uses of absolute addressing, but it is a necessary skill to effective model construction.

At this point, a distinction must be made between trip productions and trip attractions. The output in Table 5 is the number of residentially based trips in each zone broken out by trip purpose. These are considered trip productions. Residences alone are said to produce trips. However, all land uses are attractors. The definition must be carefully understood. A trip from home to the workplace includes two trip ends — beginning and a destination. This is a home-based work trip with one trip production from the zone in which the residence is located, and one attraction attributed to the zone in which the job is located.

However, the accounting system requires that a trip from the job to home be treated in a less intuitive fashion. Even though the worker leaves from work, the job site and zone are assumed to generate a trip attraction. Correspondingly, the home end, even though in this case it is the trip destination, is assumed to have produced the trip.

A trip to and from work from home, therefore, is assumed to generate two home-based work productions in the zone in which the residence is located, and two home-based work attractions in the zone in which the job is located. An examination of Table 5 shows that residences also produce home-based non-work trips and non-home-based trips. Home-based non-work trips — shopping, social, etc. — are handled the same way as work trips in terms of productions and attractions. Non-home based trips, however, are treated conventionally: a zonal production is a trip from the originating zone to somewhere else.

Table 6 contains the residential trip attraction characteristics for a set of land uses selected for this study. Clearly, others could be selected depending on the situation. The attractions are couched in terms of acres of land use. Other measures of the amount of land use activity could also be used — for example, gross area of a facility, number of jobs, etc. The ITE report (Institute of Transportation Engineers, 1983) provided these trip attraction values, while the percent purpose estimates were derived from the Quick Response manual (Sosslau, et al., 1978).

Table 7 contains the amount of proposed nonresidential development in the Branchbrook community. In a traditional traffic impact model the entries in this table would be the proposed new development. However, in the specific example used here, the entries represent the amount of selected land uses needed to balance the amount of residential development entered in Table 3. As will be seen in the trip distribution element of the model, productions and attractions must be equal in the region. Every trip has a single production and a single attraction. Across all trips, then, there must be equality. In this example entries in Table 7 generate the attractions in Table 8 since:

TRIPATTRACTIONS = TRIPS/ACRE * NUMACRES

In Table 9 the nonresidential attractions are summed by zone across trip purposes. The cell listing shows the lengthy equations needed. However, by carefully specifying the use of absolute addressing (the dollar sign), these equations can be copied once entered in the top cell of the column.

Table 10 estimates the number of residential trip attractions which the households in Table 3 would generate. For example, a social visit to a friend's house would be counted as an attraction. The zonal sums from Table 3 are copied into the first column of Table 10 and multiplied by the attractions per household (ATTRACTIONS/HH) for home-base non-work and non-home-based purposes.

Table 11 sums Tables 9 and 10. Table 12 is copied directly from Table 5. Table 13 represents Table 12 minus Table 11, or productions minus attractions summed across all zones. Remember that systemwide productions must exactly equal attractions. In our example we set the amount of nonresidential development in Table 7 to balance relatively closely the amount of residential development established in Table 3. In Table 14 the ratios of productions to attractions are calculated. These are used in Table 15 to make total regional productions exactly equal attractions, as can be seen in the totals column.

The time-distance matrix in Table 16 is an important input to the trip distribution calculations. The structure of this and subsequent matrices must be understood. The rows are the origins of the trips and the columns the destinations. Hence, reading across Table 16 in the topmost row, it is expected to take an average of 14 minutes to travel from Zone 1 to Zone 2, and 11 minutes to go from 1 to 4. This time-distance matrix is "symmetric," in that the value is row 1, column 2 is the same as row 2, column 1. It is assumed that if it takes 14 minutes to go from Zone 1 to 2, that the same roads will be used in the reverse direction and it will take 14 minutes to go from 2 to 1.

Tables 17 to 19 represent the first round of the trip distribution process. Table 17 contains the friction factors calculated based on the time-distances in Table 16. Recall that we introduced the friction factor concept in the Lowry model. This model is of a similar form to the Lowry model, as can be seen from the cell listing in the Appendix. However, the equations in Table 17 are in the form of an IF statement as shown in cell B211:

$$@IF((B198>0),(1/B198\verb|^|\$F\$207)),0)$$

The IF statement will insert the friction factor in cell B211 if the corresponding time-distance value in Table 16 is positive. Should the time-distance value be blank because the data were for less than 5 zones, then the IF statement would set B211 to zero, rather than causing an error by dividing by zero.

The trip distribution model used, a form of the now-familiar gravity model, must iterate to come to a satisfactory solution. In Table 18 the following equation produces trips:

$$TRIPS_{I,J} = PRD_I * [(ATT_J * FF_{I,J}) / \Sigma_J (ATT_J * FF_{I,J})]$$

where:

$TRIPS_{I,J}$ Trips from Zone I to Zone J

PRD_I Trip productions from Zone I

ATT_J Trip attractions to Zone J

$FF_{I,J}$ Friction factor between Zones I and J

In cell B221 the equation reads:

(($B$187*B211*B$188) / (($B211*B$188) + ($C211*$C$188) + ($D211*$D$188) + ($E211*$E$188) + ($F211*$F$188)))

An examination of the cell listing will show that this equation is directly comparable to the general equation above. The absolute cell references are designed to allow the equation to be copied to all cells in Table 18. Table 19 sets up an adjustment equation to equalize the total attractions from the generation and distribution phases. The need for this adjustment centers on the structure of the gravity model, and is beyond our concern here (Black, 1981). Essentially, the trip attractions from the generation phase will not automatically equal the attractions from the distribution phase. The iteration represented by Round 2 as shown in Table 20 is essential. In fact, there may be the need to do 5 to 10 iterations to have the model settle in appropriately, although a two-iteration model seems to work well in this example. Note that the figures in the row labeled TOTAL in Table 20, the attractions from Round 2 of the distribution phase, are exactly equal to the generation attractions (GENHBW ATT) in Table 19. This is the desired result.

Exhibit 5-11

Travel Times in the Branchbrook System

TABLE 30 - LINK TIMES (IN MINUTES)

LINK	TIME(MIN)	LINK	TIME(MIN)
1	6	17	5
2	5	18	6
3	5	19	5
4	6	20	3
5	8	21	3
6	6	22	4
7	3	23	7
8	3	24	3
9	5	25	5
10	10	26	3
11	5	27	5
12	6	28	4
13	8	29	9
14	3	30	3
15	4	31	5
16	4	32	3
		33	4

Tables 21 through Table 28 contain the trip distribution calculations for the home-based non-work and non-home-based purposes. Table 29 sums the trips across all purposes. The output of the distribution model is input to assignment. The travel times in minutes for the 33 links in the Branchbrook transportation system are shown in Exhibit 5-11 as Table 30. These travel times are built directly into a single spreadsheet as can be seen in the cell listing in the Appendix. The listing of the travel times in Exhibit 5-11 is a two column space-saving version of the vertical list actually in the spreadsheet. The vertical list is used in the spreadsheet because of the ease of formula replication.

The assignment model found in Exhibit 5-12 is primitive. The user searches visually for the shortest paths between the centroids of the zones and assigns either all traffic to one path or splits the traffic among competing paths. A total of 1,601 trips is expected to travel between zones 1 and 3. This is the sum of flows from 1 to 3 (199) and 3 to 1 (1,402) as found in Table 29 and also shown at the bottom of Table 32. It is assumed that all trips between the centroids of zones 1 and 3 will take link 8 (see Exhibit 5-9). In Table 31 the value 1 is placed in the 1-3 zonal interchange column for link 8. However, trips are split 60-40 between two alternative paths between centroids — link 16 and links 33-14 — based on travel times (Exhibit 5-11). In Table 31 the values .6 and .4 in the 1-3 interchange for these links reflect this split. Table 32 calculates the trips by link.

A Comparative Cost Model

The model displayed in Exhibit 5-13 shows how a fiscal analysis can be done on two program options. The example used is the determination of which of two computer systems should be purchased by a city to handle its financial affairs. As shown in Exhibit 5-13, the spreadsheet shows the ten-year cost structure of two computer system options. Option 1 is the more capital intensive system costing 1.2 million dollars. This amount is shown in the Capital and Fixed Costs column as being paid in the first two years of the ten-year analysis. Option 2 costs 600,000 dollars paid over two years. Both have fixed consultant retainers of $15,000 and $10,000 in years 3 to 10 in the Capital and Fixed Costs column. Maintenance costs also vary between options in year 1. More importantly, these maintenance costs are inflated yearly. Labor costs assume two classes of workers, differentiated by the hourly wage rate paid. The wage rates for the two classes of workers are also inflated over time. The exact method of inflation will be discussed below. The Total System Costs are the summations of capital, maintenance and labor costs, while the Deflated Systems Costs are calculated using a present value analysis.

This is an example of a structured spreadsheet application with various modules contained in the spreadsheet. Ideally, such a schematic map as shown in Exhibit 5-14 should be included in any documentation on the spreadsheet. In this map there is a variety of components including a description of the nature of the spreadsheet and a separate section of parameters which can be changed in the model. The actual working spreadsheet in Exhibit 5-13 is labeled "COMPARATIVE COST SPREADSHEET" on the map. It is only one of the elements in a structured spreadsheet design.

Exhibit 5-12

Traffic Assignment in the Branchbrook System

TABLE 31 - PATH SELECTION

    Either a single or multiple path can be assigned
    Values of 1 indicate a single path, while less than 1
    indicate a proportional assignment

	ZONAL INTERCHANGES							
LINK	1-1	1-2	1-3	1-4	1-5	2-2	2-3	2-4
1	0	1	0	0	0	0.2	1	0.4
2	0	1	0	0	0	0.5	1	1
3	0	0	0	0	0	0.5	0	0
4	0	0	0	0	0	0.2	0	0
5	0	0	0	0	0	0.2	0	0
6	0	0	0	0	0	0.2	0	0.6
7	0.5	1	0	1	0	0	0.5	0
8	0.5	0	1	0	1	0	0.5	0
9	0.2	0	0	0	0	0	0.5	0
10	0.2	0	0	0	0	0.2	0	0
11	0.2	0	0	0	0	0	0	0
12	0.2	0	0	0	0	0	0	0
13	0	0	0	0	0	0	0	0
14	0	0	0.4	0	0	0	0.5	0
15	0	0	0	0	0	0	0	0
16	0	0	0.6	0	0	0	0.5	0
17	0	0	0	0	0	0	0	0
18	0	0	0	0	0.4	0	0	0
19	0	0	0	0	0.4	0	0	0
20	0	0	0	0	0.4	0	0	0
21	0	0	0	0	0.6	0	0	0
22	0	0	0	0	0	0	0	0
23	0	0	0	0	0.6	0	0	0
24	0	0	0	1	0	0	0	0.4
25	0	0	0	1	0	0	0	0.4
26	0.2	0	0	0	0	0.2	0.5	0
27	0	0	0	0	0	0.2	0	0
28	0	0	0	0	0	0	0	0.6
29	0	0	0	0	0	0	0	0
30	0	0	0	0	0	0	0	0
31	0	0	0	0	0	0	0	0
32	0	0	0	0	0	0	0	0
33	0.2	0	0.4	0	0	0	0	0

Exhibit 5-12, continued

ZONAL INTERCHANGES

LINK	2-5	3-3	3-4	3-5	4-4	4-5	5-5
1	1	0	0	0	0.2	0	0
2	1	0	0	0	0	0	0
3	0	0	0	0	0	0	0
4	0	0	0	0	0	0	0
5	0	0	0	0	0	0	0
6	0	0	0	0	0.2	0	0
7	0.4	0	0.5	0	0	0	0
8	0.4	0	0.5	0	0	0	0
9	0	0	0.5	0	0	0	0
10	0	0	0	0	0	0	0
11	0	0	0	0	0	0	0
12	0	0.2	0	0	0	0	0
13	0	0.2	0	0	0	0	0
14	0	0.33	0.5	0	0	0	0
15	0	0.33	0	0	0	0	0
16	0	0.33	0.5	1	0	0	0
17	0	0.2	0	0	0	0	0
18	0	0.2	0	0.3	0	0	0.2
19	0	0	0	0.3	0	0	0.2
20	0	0	0	0.3	0	0	0.5
21	1	0	0	0.7	0	1	0.5
22	0.6	0	0	0	0.2	0.6	0
23	0.4	0	0	0.7	0	0	0.2
24	0.6	0	1	0	0.2	0	0
25	0	0	1	0	0.33	0.6	0
26	0	0	0.5	0	0	0	0
27	0	0	0	0	0	0	0
28	0	0	0	0	0.33	0	0
29	0	0	0	0	0.33	0.4	0
30	0	0	0	0	0	0	0.2
31	0	0	0	0	0	0	0.2
32	0	0	0	0	0.2	0.4	0.2
33	0	0.2	0	0	0	0	0

Exhibit 5-12, continued

TABLE 32 — LINK VOLUMES

ZONAL INTERCHANGES

LINKS	1-1	1-2	1-3	1-4	1-5	2-2	2-3	2-4
1	0	1751	0	0	0	347	780	967
2	0	1751	0	0	0	867	780	2417
3	0	0	0	0	0	867	0	0
4	0	0	0	0	0	347	0	0
5	0	0	0	0	0	347	0	0
6	0	0	0	0	0	347	0	1450
7	440	1751	0	2026	0	0	390	0
8	440	0	1601	0	1354	0	390	0
9	176	0	0	0	0	0	390	0
10	176	0	0	0	0	347	0	0
11	176	0	0	0	0	0	0	0
12	176	0	0	0	0	0	0	0
13	0	0	0	0	0	0	0	0
14	0	0	640	0	0	0	390	0
15	0	0	0	0	0	0	0	0
16	0	0	961	0	0	0	390	0
17	0	0	0	0	0	0	0	0
18	0	0	0	0	542	0	0	0
19	0	0	0	0	542	0	0	0
20	0	0	0	0	542	0	0	0
21	0	0	0	0	813	0	0	0
22	0	0	0	0	0	0	0	0
23	0	0	0	0	813	0	0	0
24	0	0	0	2026	0	0	0	967
25	0	0	0	2026	0	0	0	967
26	176	0	0	0	0	347	390	0
27	0	0	0	0	0	347	0	0
28	0	0	0	0	0	0	0	1450
29	0	0	0	0	0	0	0	0
30	0	0	0	0	0	0	0	0
31	0	0	0	0	0	0	0	0
32	0	0	0	0	0	0	0	0
33	176	0	640	0	0	0	0	0
TOTAL	880	1751	1601	2026	1354	1735	780	2417

Exhibit 5-12, continued

ZONAL INTERCHANGES

LINKS	2-5	3-3	3-4	3-5	4-4	4-5	5-5	TOTAL VOLUMES
1	1002	0	0	0	583	0	0	5430
2	1002	0	0	0	0	0	0	6817
3	0	0	0	0	0	0	0	867
4	0	0	0	0	0	0	0	347
5	0	0	0	0	0	0	0	347
6	0	0	0	0	583	0	0	2380
7	401	0	643	0	0	0	0	5650
8	401	0	643	0	0	0	0	4829
9	0	0	643	0	0	0	0	1208
10	0	0	0	0	0	0	0	523
11	0	0	0	0	0	0	0	176
12	0	85	0	0	0	0	0	261
13	0	85	0	0	0	0	0	85
14	0	140	643	0	0	0	0	1813
15	0	140	0	0	0	0	0	140
16	0	140	643	618	0	0	0	2751
17	0	85	0	0	0	0	0	85
18	0	85	0	185	0	0	132	944
19	0	0	0	185	0	0	132	859
20	0	0	0	185	0	0	330	1057
21	1002	0	0	433	0	2115	330	4692
22	601	0	0	0	583	1269	0	2453
23	401	0	0	433	0	0	132	1778
24	601	0	1285	0	583	0	0	5462
25	0	0	1285	0	962	1269	0	6508
26	0	0	643	0	0	0	0	1555
27	0	0	0	0	0	0	0	347
28	0	0	0	0	962	0	0	2412
29	0	0	0	0	962	846	0	1808
30	0	0	0	0	0	0	132	132
31	0	0	0	0	0	0	132	132
32	0	0	0	0	583	846	132	1561
33	0	85	0	0	0	0	0	901
TOTAL	1002	424	1285	618	2915	2115	660	

Exhibit 5-13
A Comparative Cost Model Spreadsheet

OPTION 1

YEAR	CAPITAL & FIXED COSTS	MAINT. COSTS	LABOR COSTS			
			CLASS 1		CLASS 2	
			EMPLOYEES	WAGE RT	EMPLOYEES	WAGE RT
1	600,000	30,000	5	7.50	2	15.00
2	600,000	31,500	5	7.95	2	15.90
3	15,000	33,075	5	8.43	2	16.85
4	15,000	34,729	5	8.93	2	17.87
5	15,000	36,465	5	9.47	2	18.94
6	15,000	38,288	5	10.04	2	20.07
7	15,000	40,203	5	10.64	2	21.28
8	15,000	42,213	5	11.28	2	22.55
9	15,000	44,324	5	11.95	2	23.91
10	15,000	46,540	5	12.67	2	25.34

YEAR	TOTAL LABOR COSTS	TOTAL SYSTEM COSTS	DEFLATED SYSTEM COSTS
1	122,850	752,850	752,850
2	130,221	761,721	692,474
3	138,034	186,109	153,809
4	146,316	196,045	147,292
5	155,095	206,560	141,084
6	164,401	217,689	135,168
7	174,265	229,468	129,529
8	184,721	241,934	124,150
9	195,804	255,128	119,019
10	207,552	269,092	114,121
		3,316,597	2,509,496

Exhibit 5-13, continued

OPTION 2

YEAR	CAPITAL & FIXED COSTS	MAINT. COSTS	LABOR COSTS			
			CLASS 1		CLASS 2	
			EMPLOYEES	WAGE RT	EMPLOYEES	WAGE RT
1	300,000	20,000	8	7.50	2	15.00
2	300,000	21,000	8	7.95	2	15.90
3	10,000	22,050	8	8.43	2	16.85
4	10,000	23,153	8	8.93	2	17.87
5	10,000	24,310	8	9.47	2	18.94
6	10,000	25,526	8	10.04	2	20.07
7	10,000	26,802	8	10.64	2	21.28
8	10,000	28,142	8	11.28	2	22.55
9	10,000	29,549	8	11.95	2	23.91
10	10,000	31,027	8	12.67	2	25.34

YEAR	TOTAL LABOR COSTS	TOTAL SYSTEM COSTS	DEFLATED SYSTEM COSTS
1	163,800	483,800	483,800
2	173,628	494,628	449,662
3	184,046	216,096	178,591
4	195,088	228,241	171,481
5	206,794	241,104	164,677
6	219,201	254,727	158,165
7	232,353	269,155	151,931
8	246,295	284,437	145,961
9	261,072	300,621	140,242
10	276,737	317,763	134,763
		3,090,572	2,179,274

Exhibit 5-14
Spreadsheet Map, Comparative Cost Model

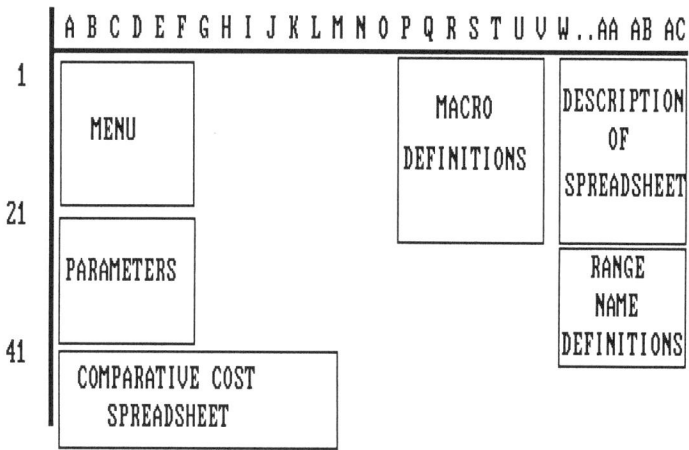

The cell listing of this spreadsheet is found in the Appendix. Exhibit 5-15 contains the menu of macros as found in A1 to F20 according to the map, and the parameter section in which changes can be made in the assumptions. Macros in Lotus 1-2-3 are single key press commands which perform a series of commands on the spreadsheet. On the IBM Personal Computer these macros are evoked by holding down the Alt key while pressing any alphabetic or numeric key. According to the menu, an Alt-S will bring up the spreadsheet located in A41 to J78. Macros can be developed to do any of the wide variety of tasks available in a spreadsheet.

Different spreadsheet programs handle macros in different ways. While the current Lotus 1-2-3 macro environment is difficult to understand and to use, it is clear that macros will become increasingly easier to employ in successive spreadsheet evolutions. Current macro command structures are powerful enough to permit elementary programming, including logical branches and the use of subroutines. This development is an additional reason to learn some programming of a microcomputer-based language.

The macros used in this example are very simple. Essentially, they are used to move around the spreadsheet and to show a graph of the two options. The actual macro instructions are shown in Exhibit 5-16, and found in cells P1 to V23. For example, the macro commands

Exhibit 5-15

Menu and Parameter Sections, Comparative Cost Model

COST ANALYSIS OF TWO PROJECTS, 10 YEAR PERIOD

      MENU OF ALTERNATIVE MACROS

ALT-P	Change parameters, including wage rates, discount rate, etc. and show discounted option totals
ALT-S	Show the spreadsheet
ALT-G	Show graph of discounted values
ALT-M	Returns to macro menu
ALT-N	Go to macro instructions
ALT-D	Go to description of the spreadsheet
ALT-R	Go to range names with descriptions

      PARAMETERS AND COMPARISON OF OPTIONS

WAGE RATE - CLASS 1	7.50	WAGE RATE -
CLASS 2	15.00	
YEARLY WAGE RATE PERCENT INCREASE	0.06	
LENGTH OF WORK WEEK	35	
YEARLY MAINTENANCE INFLATION FACTOR	0.05	
DISCOUNT RATE	0.10	
** PRESENT VALUE OF OPTION 1	2,509,496	
** PRESENT VALUE OF OPTION 2	2,179,274	

for Alt-S are listed vertically under Instructions as {HOME} followed by {GOTO}A41~. This command set initializes the cursor at A1 (the HOME command) and then sends the cursor to cell A41, the beginning of the "OPTIONS" portion of the spreadsheet, shown in Exhibit 5-13. The "~" is used by Lotus 1-2-3 to indicate that the Enter key has been pressed within the macro.

Exhibit 5-16

Macro Listing, Comparative Cost Model

MACROS		Instructions	Description
Alt-G	\G	{GRAPH}	Show graph
		{ESC}	Wait for Return key
Alt-N	\N	{HOME}	Initialize
		{GOTO}P1~	Goto Macro area
Alt-S	\S	{HOME}	Initialize
		{GOTO}A41~	Goto top of spreadsheet
Alt-M	\M	{HOME}	Go to menu
Alt-P	\P	{HOME}	Initialize
		{GOTO}A21~	Goto parameter and cost comparison
Alt-D	\D	{HOME}	Initialize
		{GOTO}W1~	Goto Description
Alt-R	\R	{HOME}	Initialize
		{GOTO}W21~	Goto Range variable description

The description of the spreadsheet purpose and a brief discussion of the formulas are found in cells W1 to AC20. It is possible in Lotus 1-2-3 to label a cell or set of cells with a "range name," permitting the user to refer to a spreadsheet location with a name. The range names used in the formulas and their descriptions are found in cells W21 to AC40. They are shown in Exhibit 5-17.

Structured spreadsheet design includes a serious effort at internal documentation. By including a brief description of what is being done in the spreadsheet itself, lost or ignored documentation is a less serious problem. The spreadsheet is designed so that changes in wage rates, inflation factors, discount rate or work-week length can be made with the resulting changes shown in the present values of the options.

Exhibit 5-17

Description and Range Names, Comparative Cost Model

DESCRIPTION OF COMPARATIVE COST MODEL SPREADSHEET

This spreadsheet compares the cost over 10 years of two alternative projects. Costs can be entered across maintenance, capital, consultant and labor costs. Two classes of workers, with different wage rates, can be entered. The spreadsheet can be easily altered for various assumptions, and graphs displayed. Macros are used to move around the spreadsheet.

This options analysis uses equations to generate the effects of inflationary factors on maintenance costs and wage rates; this equation is the compound interest formula, where:

COST(PERIOD T)=COST(PERIOD 1)*(1+RATE)^T-1

The hat (^) means an exponent, and RATE is the inflation rate.
The DEFLATED SYSTEM COSTS are done using present value analysis, where

PRESENTVALUE=COST(PERIOD T)/(1+RATE)^T-1

DESCRIPTION OF RANGE NAMES

RATE	The discount rate for present value analysis
MAINTPCT	The expected rate of inflation for maintenance
WAGEPCT	The expected rate of inflation for wages
WAGERATE1	Initial wage rate for Class 1 employees
WAGERATE2	Initial wage rate for Class 2 employees
WORKWEEK	The number of hours in the workweek

The project with the lower present value cost would be preferred. One of the macros created for this example — Alt-G — puts an instant graph on the screen, as shown in Exhibit 5-18. The user can make changes in the model assumptions and see immediate graphic results. The cell listing of this model is found in Appendix A. The reader is left to examine the structure of this example.

Exhibit 5-18

Graph of Discounted Values, Comparative Cost Model

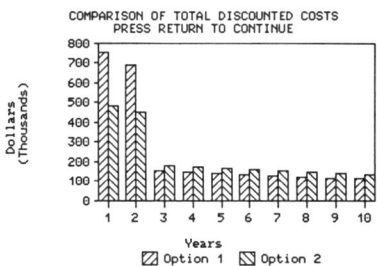

Developing Better Spreadsheets

With the development of complex spreadsheet models, there is a clear need to structure the information presented and document how the calculations were made. In many organizations a number of individuals will be working on the same or similar spreadsheet problems. A common failing among computer programmers is the failure to document how programs work. It is important to develop good spreadsheet habits by documenting thoroughly and designing carefully. A number of recommendations can be made about spreadsheet development.

First, prepare a brief report outlining the purpose of the spreadsheet and explaining how the spreadsheet works. Point out any particularly difficult aspects of the spreadsheet. This report could be contained in the spreadsheet itself.

Second, supply a spreadsheet map such as shown in Exhibit 5-14. This map tells the user where the various elements of the spreadsheet are located. In structured spreadsheet design four kinds of modules can be used — calculations, menu, macro, and descriptor. The heart of the spreadsheet is the **calculations** section where the actual work is carried out. This calculations section can be split into modules itself. For example, the Lowry and transportation planning models were designed in a table format, each table a module fed by earlier tables and supplying output to successive tables.

Another module type, the **menu**, lists the macros used to carry out various operations on the spreadsheet. In complex spreadsheets a macro is essential to efficient use of the spreadsheet. Setting up a menu in turn requires a **macro** module which contains the instructions for each macro contained. Exhibit 5-16 shows a simple macro module. Note that one macro, Alt-M, always returns the user to the menu so that the full set of options can be seen. Finally, there is a clear need for **descriptor** modules about the spreadsheet in general and about range names. Particularly important is a brief description of any complex equations which have been used and citations to appropriate literature.

Third, the calculations section, the central element of the spreadsheet, should be designed for legibility and for ease of change. Headings of the columns and rows should be reasonably intelligible. If an abbreviated label of a variable is used, then somewhere in the spreadsheet there should be a complete description of this label. Before committing to the complete spreadsheet, do a small version to check structure and flexibility. You may want to change the spreadsheet as it develops, often wanting to insert and delete columns and rows. It is much more difficult to insert and delete columns in some designs than in others. Attempt to consider how a newcomer would respond to your design. When in doubt, remember that more legibility rather than less is always preferred.

Equation design requires careful thought. Do not attempt to make any equation too complex. Instead, use smaller equations, creating intermediate steps if necessary. Also, construct formulas which contain variables rather than constants. For example, there is complete flexibility in the Lowry model in changing the exponents used in the time-distance power functions. Also, the parameters module in the comparative cost model allows great flexibility because the equations contain variables, not constants.

These basic recommendations all point to one common theme — legibility of concept and operation. Spreadsheets are powerful additions to planning and public management analysis. They must be used carefully, however, to avoid the "garbage in, garbage out" syndrome.

Conclusion

The focus in this chapter has been to show how a number of different models could be put into a spreadsheet structure. It should be obvious by this point that the electronic spreadsheet is a powerful and flexible tool for the urban planner, analyst or manager. It is highly possible that none of the models discussed in this chapter are directly applicable to your work and aspirations. However, you can gain much knowledge about spreadsheet manipulation by examining the models presented here and in other sources. Ottensmann (1984) presents a simple agency budget example. Page and Sawicki (1984) use a statewide funding allocation as a policy analysis case study. One of the more interesting modeling efforts is found in a simulation of the Klein national macroeconomic model for the United States (Johansson, 1985).

One of the rapidly emerging areas in spreadsheet development is macro creation and use. *Lotus*, the magazine put out by the developers of Lotus 1-2-3, contains a wide range of macro listings. We shall encounter another spreadsheet example in Chapter 8 which uses macros in a powerful way to do file management within an electronic spreadsheet. When one examines these more extensive macro listings carefully, one quickly realizes that such listings have the characteristics of programming languages — loops, branches and the like. The next two chapters will explore programming, a necessary tool for a number of reasons, including the understanding of complex macros.

Suggested Further Readings

Black, John. 1981. *Urban Transport Planning*. Baltimore: Johns Hopkins University Press.

Johansson, Jan-Hendrik. 1985. "Simultaneous Equations with Lotus 1-2-3," *Byte* 10:2 (February): 399-405.

Landis, John D. 1985. "Electronic Spreadsheets in Planning: The Case of Shiftshare Analysis," *Journal of the American Planning Association* 51:2 (Spring): 216-225.

Levine, Ned. 1985. "The Construction of a Population Analysis Program Using a Microcomputer Spreadsheet," *Journal of the American Planning Association* 51:4 (Fall): 496-511.

Ottensmann, John R. 1984. "Analyzing Planning Alternatives Using Electronic Spreadsheets," *Journal of Planning Education and Research* 4:1 (August): 33-42.

Page, G. William, and David S. Sawicki. 1984. "Teaching Computer and Policy Analysis Skills in a Case Study Course," *Journal of Planning Education and Research* 4:1 (August): 43-54.

Sosslau, Arthur, Amin B. Hassam, Maurice M. Carter, and George V. Wickstrom. 1978. *Quick-Response Urban Travel Estimation Techniques and Transferable Parameters: User's Guide*. National Cooperative Highway Research Program Report 187. Washington: Transportation Research Board.

6

Programming: Minimal BASIC

Introduction

While a computer programmer may become deeply involved in the choice of a programming language, the planner or manager has different needs. The programmer is concerned about the power and efficiency of the language. Can he or she write good "code" which will do the assigned task with speed and accuracy? The planner or manager, on the other hand, is not worried about the most efficient way to program a task, but rather about minimizing the amount of resources committed to the task. The purpose of this chapter is to present a limited set of instructions for a programmimg language called BASIC. Among a variety of languages available for micros, BASIC is the most popular. It is provided with virtually every microcomputer sold or is available at a very reasonable cost.

BASIC is a programming language much maligned by computer sophisticates. The primary criticism is that it is unstructured and "sloppy." Critics suggest that BASIC teaches bad programming habits and encourages undisciplined programming habits. These critics have a valid point which should be addressed in discussing BASIC: we will propose a modest response to this issue in a subsequent section.

BASIC, however, is one of the most widely available languages for microcomputers at the present time and will probably continue to be so in the foreseeable future. It is cheap and widely available. Planners or managers who have purchased a micro may find it difficult to justify $300 to $1,000 for another language. The democratization of computing means that the cost must be kept down. BASIC, since it is often free or very reasonably priced, is often the language of choice.

One other option which has emerged in widespread use is Pascal, discussed in a subsequent chapter.

BASIC in its current evolution is also a powerful language. We shall use examples from one state-of-the-art version — the one for the IBM Personal Computer — to illustrate. The IBM BASIC, a version of Microsoft BASIC, has a wide range of commands which allow the programmer to play musical tunes, develop complex graphics routines, format the screen output in a variety of ways, and do relatively complex mathematical routines. BASIC is powerful enough for a wide variety of tasks in planning and management. Clearly, very complex model structures may well require a structured language such as Pascal, or even one of the ancients, such as FORTRAN.

This chapter will introduce BASIC. It will be a "minimal" version which will be presented with examples. There is a clear temptation to call this minimal version "basic BASIC," but we shall refrain from trying to be too cute. The information provided will permit the reader to program adequate BASIC on a wide variety of machines. This chapter will not attempt to present the full set of instructions or to point out sophisticated programming techniques. These tasks are left to the wide range of books currently on the market. What this chapter does is to start the reader on the way toward programming literacy.

Why Programming?

To begin, it is important to spell out why the topic of programming is included in this book. It is perfectly possible to develop one's capacity in building models with electronic spreadsheets without actually learning a programming language. There are those who have argued this position. In fact, it is highly likely that a professional in urban planning and management will never write a serious lengthy program in his or her job. Those arguing this position, however, are missing the point: programming principles are widely used across the whole computing arena. First, it will be recalled that "macros" were introduced in the last chapter. These are, in reality, programming commands which operate in a spreadsheet environment. There are macro commands which "branch" and "loop" — two central concepts in programming. The spreadsheet user who wishes to go beyond the basic spreadsheet environment into macro creation will need to understand programming concepts.

Second, database management systems will be introduced in a succeeding chapter. The particular package demonstrated, dBASE III PLUS, uses the basic "relational" data model as its core concept and, interestingly, contains its own unique programming language. One reason for the popularity of dBASE III PLUS is that one can use it to construct complex database manipulation programs. Once again, the database system user may need to know how to program in order to do the more complex tasks sometimes required.

Third, there are times when a problem requires programming because the spreadsheet or database system option is simply not appropriate. Both complex simulation models and very simple iterative models may well be better done as programs. For example, the classic urban development and transportation planning models are written in a programming language, not as a spreadsheet. One can clearly see the problem with complex models being packed into a spreadsheet format as found in the urban transportation model discussed in the previous chapter. This extensive spreadsheet handled only five zones. Consider the size of the work area if we had been dealing with 50 or 100 zones. Even a simple iterative hill-climbing optimizing model, such as the one developed for a transit simulation study (Pucher and Brail, 1984), was more appropriate as a program than as a spreadsheet.

Finally, you should know how a program works so you can more easily evaluate custom work being done in your organization. The best way to understand what can go wrong and what is a reasonable expectation is to write a program. Conceptualizing, constructing and testing a program is a wonderful way to learn the foibles of human understanding.

The Five Pieces of the Puzzle

Programming is simply the development of a coherent set of instructions telling the computer what to do. As indicated in Chapter 3, the wide variety of languages will range from direct programming in machine or assembly languages to high-level alternatives which look like spoken languages. There are, however, certain elements common to nearly all programming. These are the pieces of the programming puzzle. Knowledge of these elements will permit the novice programmer to understand how programs work, as well as how to program. These five elements of programming practice are:

1. Variable and constant specification
2. Input and output routines
3. Mathematical and logical operations
4. Branching
5. Loops

These five elements represent both programming concepts and operations. In the following sections each topic will be discussed in terms of concept, language and examples.

Variable and Constant Specification

Computer languages use labels to refer to the different items which are to be manipulated within the set of instructions called a program. These labels are either variables or constants. Variable names refer to numeric or alphanumeric data which can be expected to change values in the program. Constants, correspondingly, are not expected to change in the program. These labels in reality refer to locations in memory, and direct reference to the data represented by these memory locations by actual machine address would be cumbersome and unnecessary.

It is much easier to use variable and constant labels. For example, we all know that in the decimal system 2+3=5. However, for illustration purposes we can write a short program to add two numbers together. The program looks like this.

```
NEW
10 A = 2
20 B = 3
30 C = A + B
40 END
```

There are several programming considerations raised in this simple example. First, the word NEW begins the program. In BASIC the word NEW tells the computer to clear all other programs out of internal memory and be ready for a "new" one. You use NEW only at the beginning of writing a new program. Second, notice the use of line numbers — "10," "20," etc. BASIC uses line numbers to organize the programming instructions given by the user. Should you insert a new instruction, say:

```
25 D=6
```

Programming: Minimal BASIC 143

Then the program will look this when listed out:

```
10 A = 2
20 B = 3
25 D = 6
30 C = A + B
40 END
```

Third, and very importantly, when run, the program will begin at the lowest line number and continue mercilessly down the line numbers unless specifically told otherwise. **Make no mistake — a program is linear thinking taken to the ridiculous.** We will discuss "branching" instructions subsequently, which permit the program to go to different locations.

Fourth, the program above demonstrates the use of numeric variables and constants. While "A," "B," "C," and "D" are **numeric variables,** "2" and "3" are **numeric constants.** The computer can store both integer (whole numbers between -32767 and +32767) and real numbers (which can take on virtually any value). Integers are generally designated in BASIC with a % sign following while real numbers have no indicators. Hence, while A% and GREEN% declare the variable as integer, a variable named ACE would indicate that the variable is real. Note that the designation of integer or real "types" of variables is important. Different types are stored in the computer differently. Generally, integer variables take less memory than real variables. For most purposes, real variables are used.

There are also **string variables** and **string constants.** Strings are groups of characters which can be manipulated as a whole. For example:

```
10 V$ = "CITY IS "
20 W$ = "NEW YORK"
30 X$ = V$ + W$
```

In this program V$, W$, and X$ are string variables, while "CITY IS " and "NEW YORK" are string constants. Note that the two strings are added in Line 30, and the output would read what would be expected — "CITY IS NEW YORK." There are very powerful string commands in BASIC. Strings can be examined character by character, taken apart and joined together. In fact, the string manipulation capacity in BASIC exceeds that of many more sophisticated languages like Pascal and FORTRAN.

There are some general rules for using variables names:

1. They must begin with a letter.
2. They generally are limited in character length. For example, only two-character variable names were usable in older Apple II BASIC, but 40 characters are possible in IBM PC BASIC. You could have had names longer than two characters in Apple II BASIC, but the computer would have ignored them.
3. They cannot contain "reserved words," which are program commands like FOR, GOTO, etc.

There is another point to be made about these examples. Programming languages differentiate between equality and replacement. Note in Line 30 of both examples that the answer is to left of the equal sign — C = A + B and X$ = V$ + W$. We are saying **replace what was in the memory locations associated with the variable C (or X$) with the result of addition of A to B (or V$ + W$)**. This replacement concept is important in creating workable mathematical equations. However, it also means that the "=" sign has two meanings — replacement, as we have seen above, and equality in logical comparisons. We will see the use of the "=" sign as an equality concept when we discuss branching.

Thus far, we have presented an extremely simple program which performs a simple calculation, but does nothing with it. What about printing it out?

Input and Output

The second important area of programming is inputting data and instructions into the computer and, correspondingly, getting the information out. Input and output instructions are very simple in BASIC. Unfortunately, this simplicity can be a significant problem because sometimes obviously trivial tasks are difficult to do. There are only two commands which must be mastered to do adequate input and output elements in a program — PRINT and INPUT. We can see the use of PRINT in our earlier example:

```
10 A = 2
20 B = 3
25 D = 6
30 C = A + B
35 PRINT A,B,C
40 END
```

In this example LINE 35 will print the numbers "2," "3," and "6" on the same line separated by spaces. Or, correspondingly, we could have printed out the string, "CITY IS NEW YORK," using line 35:

```
10 V$ = "CITY IS "
20 W$ = "NEW YORK"
30 X$ = V$ + W$
35 PRINT X$
```

There are four particular areas of discussion regarding input and output concerns in BASIC:

1. The output unit (screen, printer, etc.)
2. The location on the screen or page (top left, bottom right, etc.)
3. The format of numeric data (For example, the number 2.343567 might be best written as 2.34. Is this relatively simple task possible?)
4. The types of file structures produced and used in BASIC

The Output Unit

A variety of ways can be used to indicate on what unit you would like to see the output. On an Apple II, for example, the printer is turned on before the program is run. Any print command in the program will automatically be directed to the printer while also showing on the screen. In an IBM PC, alternatively, the type of print command itself will indicate whether or not the output line will appear on the printer or on the screen. Thus, while PRINT will put the output on the screen, LPRINT will put it on the printer. To print both on the screen and on the printer both statements are needed. Hence:

```
10 PRINT "This is a short program"
20 LPRINT "This is a short program"
30 END
```

Both LPRINT and PRINT are needed in this little program to print the phrase on both the printer and on the screen.

Location

Putting the information on the screen in the right place is done in BASIC in a variety of ways. There are both extremely simple ways and relatively sophisticated methods. It must be understood that while BASIC is relatively constant from machine to machine, the screen and page formatting routines vary widely. In the IBM PC there is a LOCATE statement which will move the printing to the desired location on the screen. The screen can be divided into 25 rows and either 40 or 80 columns. The original APPLE II came with only 40 columns, the Commodore VIC-20 uses 32 columns, and some early Radio Shack micros use 64 columns. In general there is currently standardization on the 25 row by 80 column format, and we shall use this screen size in our examples. To locate the phrase "This is a short program" on row 5 and starting in column 40 the program would look like this:

```
5 LOCATE 5,40
10 PRINT "This is a short program."
15 END
```

The output on the screen would look like this:

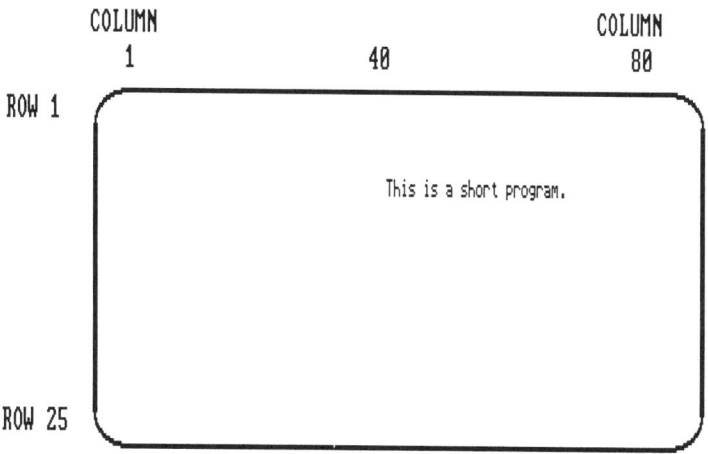

There are various ways to get around the screen depending on the BASIC being used. For example, in APPLE BASIC there are HTAB (horizontal) and VTAB (vertical) statements which permit the placing of characters anywhere on the screen. While the commands will vary depending on the particular BASIC being used, the general concept remains the same.

There is also an important message here which is not immediately obvious — each individual string of characters to be displayed requires separate handling. Structuring a screen full of data to look decent and to present the appropriate information is often no easy task. It is not uncommon to spend a goodly portion of programming time on screen displays. One way to avoid this unfortunate preoccupation with screen display in programming is to use an electronic spreadsheet. This helps explain why spreadsheet programs are so popular.

Numeric Formats

Amazingly, sometimes simple tasks are difficult in BASIC. The ability to format numeric data to make it look presentable is relatively complex. For example, there was no way in early APPLE II BASIC to make "45.6789" into "45.68" for presentation on screen or printer. There is additional software you can buy to do this task, but it was not possible in the BASIC sold with the machine. However, many BASIC's have PRINT USING statements. The process of making a number with a variable number of decimal points into a number with two decimals looks like this:

```
10 PRINT USING "######.##",45.6789
20 END
```

Doing this will produce "45.68" on screen or printer. Also, one can put multiple numbers in the same format on the same line. For example:

```
10 PRINT USING "###.#",34.789,23.111,.789
20 END
```

will produce:

```
34.8    23.1    0.8
```

Unfortunately, this method of formatting numeric output is cumbersome, and not nearly as powerful as other languages like Pascal. Also, as you might expect, one can also use variables with PRINT USING

```
10 A = 22.789
20 B = 789.06321
30 PRINT USING "####.##",A,B
40 END
```

This will produce:

```
22.79    789.06
```

File Characteristics and Manipulation

Thus far we have discussed the PRINT and PRINT USING statements. They represent the simplest of the output instructions to the computer. Both programs and the data used by the programs can be stored on floppy or hard disks, or sent to another computer through telecommunications channels such as telephone wires.

The version of BASIC discussed here is sold by Microsoft, and is available for a wide number of computers. This particular strain of BASIC is an "interpreter" version. This means that each line of program code is converted to the language which the computer understands on a one-by-one basis and then carries out. In the simple three line program below, the BASIC interpreter will read line 10 and carry out the operation of assigning 34 to the variable "ALPHA." Then the interpreter will also do the next two lines one at a time.

```
10 ALPHA = 34
20 BETA = ALPHA * 2
30 PRINT BETA
```

In a compiler version of BASIC, the entire program is converted to machine language before being run. This distinction is made here because an interpreter and compiler store programs in different formats. The BASIC interpreter program must be present in computer memory before the user can attempt to run any program. An interpreter BASIC program is stored in a special file readable only by the interpreter itself, and it contains the file extension, "BAS." Hence, the program "LINEAR" has the name, "LINEAR.BAS."

In interpreter BASIC, programs themselves are stored on disk by using the command SAVE. The programmer saves LINEAR.BAS with the command below, with the interpreter program supplying "BAS."

```
SAVE "LINEAR"
```

However, what if you want to save data you have been working with, a mailing list you have created, or the like? Such information is saved on a "text" file. BASIC permits the saving and retrieving of text files in either a random or sequential fashion. Sequentially accessed files are read in from the beginning of the file on the disk to the end of the file. Randomly accessed files permit any record within the file to be directly read from or written to without reading all the records preceding.

For example, suppose you have written a program to store a mailing list of all your clients and have sorted the names in order so the file is stored alphabetically on the disk. Finding information for a client named Jones, stored somewhere in the middle of a sequentially stored text file, would require reading all records starting at the beginning of the alphabet until the Jones record was found. In a randomly accessed text file, Jones could be immediately retrieved without reading a number of other records first.

In either kind of file, random or sequential, the way the characters are stored is easy to understand. Each character, for example, in the string "CITY IS NEW YORK," takes up one position on the disk. Hence, "CITY IS NEW YORK" takes up 16 positions on the disk. Remember that disks can hold hundreds of thousands of characters, so that there is sufficient room for relatively large files on a floppy disk. Of course, most word processing programs store their files in this text mode also. Within BASIC one can save "text" files by writing the information to the disk. The exact details can be found elsewhere but, in general, accessing a file for either reading or writing requires three steps:

1. Open a file
2. Read from the file or write to the file
3. Close the file

Different instructions exist for different machines but the general routine is the same.

There is only one elementary command for inputting information into a program in BASIC from the keyboard — INPUT. The use of this command is very simple:

```
10 PRINT "What is the name and population of your city?"
20 INPUT CITY$,POPULATION
30 END
```

The screen will prompt with:

?

at which you could respond:

```
?Griggstown,14589
```

The name "Griggstown" will be placed in the memory locations associated with CITY$ and the number "14589" placed in the location keyed to POPULATION. Note that a comma is expected between the two variables. While this instruction is very simple it is powerful enough to handle virtually all keyboard inputs you might desire in a program.

What, however, if you would like to have a substantial set of numeric or alphabetic data used by your program which you would like to avoid inputting each time the program is run? Then one can use DATA and READ statements. For example, one might want to run a simple program to calculate the number of trips generated by a number of households using different assumptions. Assuming there are three classes of households — infrequent travelers, moderately frequent travelers, and very frequent travelers — then we proceed as below:

```
10 DATA 6,8,10
20 READ RATE1,RATE2,RATE3
30 PRINT "How many households with low trip rates?"
40 INPUT HH1
50 PRINT "How many with moderate trip rates?"
60 INPUT HH2
70 PRINT "How many with high trip rates?"
80 INPUT HH3
90 TOTAL = (RATE1*HH1) + (RATE2*HH2)+ (RATE3*HH3)
100 PRINT "The total number of trips is ",TOTAL
110 END
```

Without warning we have just written a program which does something, albeit a simple calculation, which demonstrates a number of concepts as well as documenting the use of DATA and READ statements. The mathematics of line 90 will be discussed shortly in the next section. Also, it is possible to combine PRINT and INPUT statements on one line. For example:

```
70 INPUT "How many with high trip rates",HH3
```

can replace both lines 70 and 80.

The DATA and READ statements are fairly easy to understand. Essentially, we can view the constants in the DATA statement as sequentially ordered with the first one on the left at the top of the "stack." The variables in the READ statement are also ordered. Each variable read will pick up the next constant in the DATA statement.

The whole process is controlled by a stack pointer which "points" to the next constant to be picked up by the next READ statement. The RESTORE statement will reset the stack pointer to the first constant in the DATA statement. Hence:

```
10 DATA 10,20,30,40
20 READ A,B 'This statement puts 10 into A and 20 into B
30 RESTORE 'This instruction sets the pointer at the "top" - 10
40 READ C 'This READ starts at the top putting 10 into C
50 PRINT A,B,C
60 END
```

will produce:

```
10      20      10
```

Interesting? While there are only specific instances where DATA and READ are useful, these two statements along with INPUT constitute a powerful set of data-gathering techniques. Of course, one can read data from text files as well.

Mathematical and Logical Operations

BASIC can do a wide variety of mathematical and logical operations. We have already discussed the first concept important to understanding mathematical operations — the notion of replacement. For example:

```
100 TRIPS = 5 + 9
```

means to add 9 to 5 and place the answer in the memory location associated with the variable TRIPS.

Mathematical expressions follow certain rules:

1. The processing is from left to right
2. The symbols are processed in a hierarchy from first (a) to last (e):
    a. Parentheses ()
    b. Exponentiation ^
    c. Multiplication and floating point division * /
    d. Integer division \ (In the IBM PC BASIC)
    e. Addition and subtraction + -

For example:

```
120 FACTOR = 2*5+3-1*5 means that: FACTOR = 8
```

But:

```
130 FACTOR = 2*(5+3)-1*5 means that: FACTOR = 11
```

Also:

```
150 BLACKJACK = (3*6)+7*9/21 means that: BLACKJACK = 21
```

A set of logical operators is used. These operators have a hierarchy also:

1. NOT
2. Inequalities and equalities
    a. < > (not equal)
    b. = (equal)
    c. < (less than)
    d. > (greater than)
    e. <= (less than or equal to)
    f. >= (greater than or equal to)
3. AND
4. OR

These logical operators will be better understood when we move to the next topic.

Branching

As was suggested earlier, computer languages are LINEAR constructs. A program will deviate from carrying out the next instruction below only when a branch occurs. This ability to branch gives the computer its power: it can make decisions based on explicit rules. There are two types of branches:

1. Unconditional
2. Conditional

Below is an example of an unconditional branch:

```
230 GOTO 1000 '1000 is a line number
```

In fact, unconditional branches are rather uninteresting. The more important case is the conditional branch. The simplest case is the IF..THEN branch. It is really all you need to know to do very nice programming. Examples of the IF..THEN are:

```
20 IF A>5 THEN PRINT "Excess Capacity"
150 IF (NUMHOUSEHOLDS * PERSONSINHOUSEHOLD) > 1000 THEN GOTO 200
400 IF CITY$ = "CAMDEN" THEN INDEX=9
```

Note that the logical operators listed in the previous section are used in these branches. In a conditional branch it is important to remember that **if the condition is not met, the program will fall through and do the next series of instructions below.** Thus, if the condition in the line 150 example is not met — if multiplying NUM-HOUSEHOLDS by PERSONSINHOUSEHOLDS yields a number less than or equal to 1,000 — then the program drops through and does the NEXT successive line number in the program.

In some BASIC's there is an IF..THEN...ELSE command. The IBM PC has this command but Apple II BASIC does not. This branch has the following structure:

```
300 IF A>3 THEN B$="yes" ELSE B$="no"
```

Also note that certain BASIC's allow multiple THEN's and ELSE's in the same statement. Remember that one should move to such complexity only if one feels that the benefits in programming compactness outweigh the loss in legibility.

Loops

Our final concept is the one which allows those repetitive operations for which computers are so famous — loops. The standard loop in BASIC is the FOR...NEXT statement. It is important to understand how the loop works.

```
60 FOR I = 1 TO 50
70 PRINT "Program runs"
80 NEXT I
```

This program will print "Program runs" 50 times on the screen. The variable I is called the counter. The number "1" is the initial value of the counter and "50" is the final one. The program will do all operations between the FOR statement and the NEXT statement which closes the loop. Note that a loop can use the counter value in an operation.

```
100 FOR J = 5 TO 15
110 PRINT J
120 NEXT J
```

will print the numbers 5 to 15 on the screen. Also one can "step" the counter to increment by a value different than one.

```
200 FOR K = 2 TO 10 STEP 2
210 PRINT "Housing"
220 NEXT K
```

will print "Housing" 5 times, stepping from 2 to 10 by 2's.

However, it can become more complex. For example, it is possible to determine the final value of the counter from user input.

```
80 INPUT "How many houses? "; N
90 FOR I = 1 TO N
100 PRINT "One more house"
110 NEXT I
```

Note that the variable N is supplied by the user in response to the INPUT statement asking about the number of times the phrase "One more house" should be printed. One can also "nest" loops, or place one inside another.

```
300 DIM A(30,20)
310 FOR I = 1 TO 30
    320 FOR J = 1 TO 20
        330 A(I,J) = 9
    340 NEXT J
350 NEXT I
```

This program first dimensions (DIM) an array of 30 rows and 20 columns and then puts the number "9" in all 600 cells. Basically, an array is nothing more than a grid of cells with rows and columns. In mathematics we call it a matrix. We generally deal with a two-dimensional array or matrix in most situations. For example, we might decide to depict a gridded map of a piece of land on the screen. Such a two-dimensional representation is best done as an array.

Writing a Program

The essential elements of programming in BASIC have been presented. Obviously, there is more to programming than can be contained in one chapter. There are many planners and managers who will never write a program. However, as soon as you turn on a computer you will be using a program written by someone else. It is also highly conceivable that you may have to instruct a programmer about the kinds of programs you need in your work. Writing a program can prove to be instructional on a number of levels.

Often it is useful to develop the logic of the BASIC program by developing a flowchart. A flowchart is a graphic representation of the logic inherent in the program. Often a flowchart will help the programmer see the structure of the program more easily than he or she would by examining a listing. Flowcharts use a set of symbols to indicate the various program steps. Lamoitier (1982) has suggested that there are three levels of flowchart design:

System flowchart	The interrelationships among programs, files, and equipment
Conceptual flowchart	An overview of the components of a large program
Detailed flowchart	An expansive and complete presentation of the program instructions

The system-level flowchart is not of importance here. As we shall see, the conceptual flowchart will be reconstituted in the next chapter as a "structure chart" when structured programming is discussed. The detailed flowchart highlighting specific instructions in a program uses symbols as shown in Exhibit 6-1.

Only a limited number of symbols can be used to describe program logic in detail. The general processing symbol is used predominantly for calculations. The decision symbol is keyed to the conditional branch instruction. The input-output symbol represents interactions with disk files, keyboard, or printer. The entry or exit point symbol acts as a program beginning or end symbol. The connector permits the transfer of program logic to somewhere else on the page, while the offpage connector sends the program to another page.

In writing a program, you must address the following issues:

1. What is the purpose of the program?
2. By whom will the program be used? For example, a program designed to be used by virtually anyone must be more "user-friendly" than one written only for your use.

3. How often will the program be used? A program used every day should be designed optimally — fast and efficient. One used only once or infrequently need not be so well designed. Remember, better design means more programming time.
4. What kind of input is expected, e.g., keyboard only, a text file, etc.?
5. What kind of output is to be produced — printout, screen displays, graphics, etc.? For example, programs designed to be run in color mean that the user must have a color monitor on his or her system. Graphics output means that the printer is equipped with a graphics capacity.

Exhibit 6-1

Components of a Flowchart

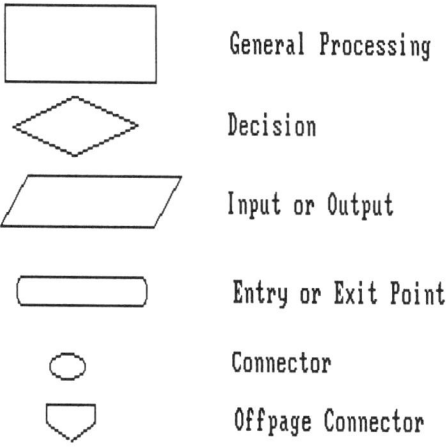

These are only a few of the questions which can be asked of any program that either you write, you use or you evaluate for possible purchase. Given this set of questions, a beginning knowledge of BASIC, and a flowcharting capacity, you can begin to program.

Programming: Minimal BASIC 157

A Set of BASIC Commands

The following set of BASIC commands, though minimal, will allow a wide range of programming tasks to be accomplished. Obviously, there are many more powerful commands which many current BASIC versions have. Also, there are continual developments of a standard BASIC which may eventually allow the user to move among computer systems without having to adjust radically. In this chapter, the following initialization command was used before starting a new program:

NEW — Clears memory to write a new program

The following are file manipulation commands:

SAVE — Saves a program in memory onto disk or other storage media
LOAD — Loads a program from disk or elsewhere into memory

The following is a set of "minimal BASIC" commmands:

Input/Output Commands

PRINT — Prints on the screen

```
120 PRINT "This writes on the screen"
```

LPRINT — Prints on the printer

```
340 LPRINT "This puts out to the printer"
```

PRINT USING — Prints formatted numeric data on the screen

```
790 PRINT USING "##.##";PERSONSHOUSEHOLD
```

INPUT — Queries the user on the screen with a question requiring an answer which is stored as a variable.

```
560 INPUT "How many cities"; CITY
```

READ — Puts the information in DATA statements into variables

```
200 READ INCOME, EDUCATION, AGE
210 DATA 14100,15.2,56
```

Branching and Conditional Operations

GOTO   Unconditional branch to another line number

```
600 GOTO 2000 'Branch to line 2000
```

IF..THEN   Conditional branch or operation

```
880 IF POP>1000 THEN GOTO 5000 'Conditional branch
300 IF TOWN="Warren" THEN A = B+5 'Does an addition
```

Loops

FOR..NEXT   Does repetitive operations

```
100 FOR I = 1 TO 100
110     PRINT "This is a lot of JUNK"
120 NEXT I
```

Matrices

DIM   Dimensions matrices (arrays)

```
DIM POPULATION(20), TRIPRATE(20,5)
```

A Program to Compute an Average

This set of minimal BASIC commands can be used to do a wide range of programming. Obviously, there are other powerful BASIC commands which are extremely useful. Also, the move to other programming languages like Pascal or C will introduce you to a wide variety of other commands and general programming approaches. The simple fact is that you will have to be continually ready to learn new techniques and to explore. Our first program is a simple calculation of an average of any group of numbers. The program listing is shown in Exhibit 6-2, and a flowchart is shown in Exhibit 6-3. The program uses the following commands:

Exhibit 6-2

A Program to Compute an Average

```
100 '*******************************
110 '* AVERAGE CALCULATION PROGRAM *
120 '*******************************
130 '
140 CLS '*Clears the screen-varies among BASIC's*
150 '
160 INPUT "How many numbers ";N
170 '
180   FOR I = 1 TO N
190     PRINT "What is value of number "; I
200     INPUT NUMBER
210     SUM = SUM + NUMBER '* An example of the replacement
220   NEXT I
230 '
240 AVERAGE = SUM / N
250 '
260 PRINT "The average is "; AVERAGE
270 '
280 END
```

Exhibit 6-3

Flowchart of the Average Program

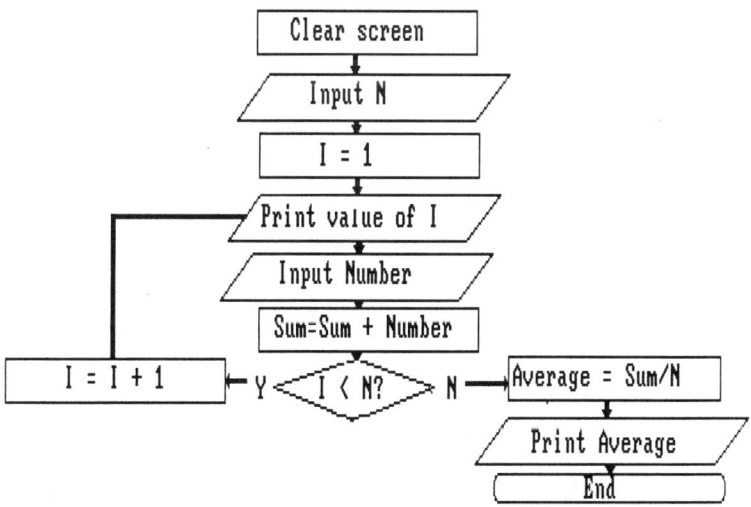

CLS	Clears the screen
INPUT	Queries for an input from the keyboard
FOR..NEXT	A loop
PRINT	Prints to the computer screen
'	The single quote designates a comment in IBM BASIC

The program uses line numbers to order the commands. The structure of the program is straightforward:

Lines	Operations
140	Clears the screen
160	Asks for how many numbers to be used in the average and places the user response in variable N
180-220	A loop, starting with Line 180 and ending with Line 220, which asks the value of each number to be entered into the average calculation. The loop starts at 1 and runs to N, the number of values to be entered. I is the incrementing variable and changes with each loop. Hence, in Line 190 I will increment by one each time the line is printed on the screen. See the example of the output below.
210	An example of the replacement concept. The value of SUM is replaced by the value of SUM + NUMBER. This operation allows you to add each value of NUMBER to the total SUM.
240	This expression calculates the average of the number entered.
260	This command prints on the screen. Remember that in IBM BASIC the LPRINT command prints on the printer. Other BASICS send output to the printer differently.

280   Ends the program.

An example of the output to the screen is shown in Exhibit 6-4. This program run on the IBM PC puts out an "OK" when the program is finished: this is because the program is operating within the BASIC language system of the IBM. Other microcomputers will have different indicators that the program is finished running.

Exhibit 6-4

An Example of Output from the Average Program

```
How many numbers ? 5
What is the value of number 1
? 2
What is the value of number 2
? 6
What is the value of number 3
? 9
What is the value of number 4
? 4
What is the value of number 5
? 6
The average is 5.4
Ok
```

The comments above on lines 180-220 about the incrementing variable I are important. Notice how I changes with each printing of Line 190 because it is inside the loop which ends with line 220, where it says "NEXT I."

The variable AVERAGE is not formatted when printed out in line 260. This means that the number of decimal places in the screen or printer output depends solely on the numbers used. Note that in Exhibit 6-4 the answer, 5.4, had one decimal place. The answer could have just as easily had 5 decimal places. Recall that there is a PRINT USING command in some BASIC's which permits formatting. For use in this program, line 260 becomes:

```
260 PRINT USING "The average is ";"######.##";AVERAGE
```

Conclusion

In this chapter we have presented an overview of BASIC programming. The planner or public manager generally will not be in a position to do extensive programming. However, the increasing power of the microcomputer is not matched by the availability of software. While extensive and increasingly user-friendly packages will be developed in future years, the smaller professions and the specialized tasks these professions undertake will require custom software. Not all needs will be met by the general applications packages, and there will be little incentive for programmers to do custom programming for specialized situations without appropriate compensation. It seems obvious that urban planners and managers will need to either write simple specialized pieces in a straightforward language or commission work to be done either in the organization or by a local consulting firm. This chapter teaches the rudiments, while the next chapter discusses more complex programming techniques and presents a number of examples.

Suggested Further Readings

Graham, Neil. 1982. *Programming the IBM Personal Computer: BASIC*. New York: Holt, Rinehart and Winston.

Lamoitier, Jean-Pierre. 1982. *BASIC Exercises for the IBM Personal Computer*. Berkeley, California: Sybex.

Lien, David A. 1984. *Learning IBM BASIC for the Personal Computer*. Revised Edition. San Diego: Compusoft.

7

Structured Programming

Introduction

In the last chapter the elements of BASIC were outlined. In this chapter the BASIC programming language will be extended by introducing the concept of a structured language and by presenting more complex programming examples. The concept of structured programming is particularly important because a BASIC program can often degenerate into what programmers call "spaghetti code," in which the program is so interrelated that it is difficult to follow and impossible to fix.

After our knowledge of BASIC is firmed up, Pascal will be introduced. Among the structured programming languages available currently, Pascal has the reputation of being an excellent teaching language. It has particular problems, however, which have hindered its use in large-scale system development work. A recent alternative which has emerged is Modula-2, which was designed by Niklaus Wirth, the same person who designed Pascal. The programmer's choice, C, is also a structured language with access to extensive programming libraries and with the ability to interact directly with the microprocessor instruction set and registers. C, however, permits the programmer such a great degree of flexibility that one can get into real trouble without sufficient knowledge of program design.

The Development of Structured BASIC

The BASIC programming language presented here contains inherent dangers to the novice programmer. There are few formal requirements for structuring a BASIC program. The language allows the programmer to write long and complex programs which can be difficult to understand. Observers have suggested that BASIC encourages sloppy programming habits because the user can simply sit down and go at it without much forethought.

Examine the program which is shown in Exhibit 7-1. The program is a simple example which finds the largest number from a set which is entered from the keyboard. It is written in perfectly acceptable BASIC. Note that only the INPUT, IF-THEN, FOR-NEXT and END commands are used in the program. The program works.

Exhibit 7-1

Largest Number Program, Unstructured

```
10 ' This program finds the largest of a set of numbers
20 BIGGEST=0
30 INPUT "how many numbers?",NUM
40 FOR I=1 TO NUM
50 INPUT VALUE
60 IF VALUE < BIGGEST GOTO 80
70 BIGGEST = VALUE
80 NEXT I
90 PRINT "The biggest number is";BIGGEST
100 END
```

This particular program is not particularly difficult to understand, but picture a more extensive program which is written in this same fashion. Programs which are written in this unstructured format are simply not as easy to understand as a more structured version. Contrast this program in Exhibit 7-1 with one which does exactly the same thing but in a structured fashion as shown in Exhibit 7-2. There are two clear differences in these two programs. The structured program is easier both to read and to understand; however, it also requires more effort on the part of the programmer to organize the content and design. The particular pieces of the structured programming approach shown in Exhibit 7-2 will be discussed below following a few general comments.

Structured programming as presented here is an imposition on an essentially unstructured version of BASIC by Microsoft which is supplied with virtually all microcomputers. Also emerging are a number of structured versions of BASIC which will be discussed subsequently.

Exhibit 7-2

Largest Number Program, Structured

```
10 'This program finds the largest of a set of numbers
20 '
25 '    BIGGEST         The variable holding the largest number
26 '    NUM             The number of numeric values to be entered
27 '    VALUE           THe numeric value of the current entry
28 '
30      GOSUB 100 ' Initialization subroutine
40      GOSUB 200 ' Compare subroutine
50      GOSUB 300 ' Print Subroutine
60 '
70 END
80 '
100 ' *****************************
110 ' * INITIALIZATION SUBROUTINE *
120 ' *****************************
121 '
130     BIGGEST=0 ' Initialize BIGGEST
140     INPUT "How many numbers?",NUM
145 '
150 RETURN
160 '
200 ' **********************
210 ' * COMPARE SUBROUTINE *
220 ' **********************
230 '
240 FOR I=1 TO NUM
250     INPUT VALUE
260     IF VALUE < BIGGEST GOTO 280
270     BIGGEST = VALUE
280 NEXT I
290 '
295 RETURN
296 '
300 ' ********************
310 ' * PRINT SUBROUTINE *
320 ' ********************
330 '
340 CLS ' Clear the screen
350 '
360 PRINT "The biggest number is";BIGGEST
370 '
380 RETURN
```

The Characteristics of Structured BASIC

Introduction

The structured BASIC to be discussed here is based on the tenets of structured programming as found in Pascal. (It should be understood that there are others who have their own views of structuring BASIC which can act as a complement to our discussion.) Arthur Luehrmann (1984a, 1984b, 1984c) has developed a useful system for making BASIC structured. The system presented here uses some of the language of the Luehrmann approach. There are several elements important to making BASIC programs more intelligible and straightforward. The proposed system has three components:

1. The use of a "top-down" programming method using a main program with modules
2. Pre-declaration of all variables with definitions in Remarks statements
3. Program legibility, through the extensive use of remarks, empty lines, and indentation of programming statements

Top-Down Programming with Modules

The first important element of a system to make BASIC programs more legible is called the "top-down" approach. The program design should proceed from general to specific. An important concept of top-down programming is the use of program modules or blocks. These modules are subroutines which are run from the main program. In BASIC, these subroutines are usually called by GOSUB statements.

There are a number of steps to doing top-down programming using modules. First, the general structure of the program should be outlined, perhaps graphically, in terms of blocks or modules. Second, the main program should be written in BASIC. Third, the individual modules should be written in BASIC. Even at this stage particularly detailed sections can be sketched in to work on later. Fourth, the program should be completed by writing all remaining routines. At every stage, the program is tested to the extent possible for logic and syntax errors.

Exhibit 7-2 contains the structured version of the program to find the largest number of a set. In Exhibit 7-3 there is a graphic representation of the program using a version of a tree diagram popularized by Bowles (1977: 261-291). In this upside-down tree, or "structure chart", the root (**Find Largest Number**) is connected by branches to the three modules, **Initialize, Compare,** and **Print**. In BASIC these are subroutines, each of which contains leaves, or commands, within them. In this tree structure, rectangles are operations and the rounded rectangles are loops. It is also possible to use traditional flowcharting techniques such as discussed by Lamoitier (1982) and presented in Chapter 6, in which the programming logic is diagrammed in linear sequence from top to bottom.

Exhibit 7-3

Structure Chart, Largest Number Program

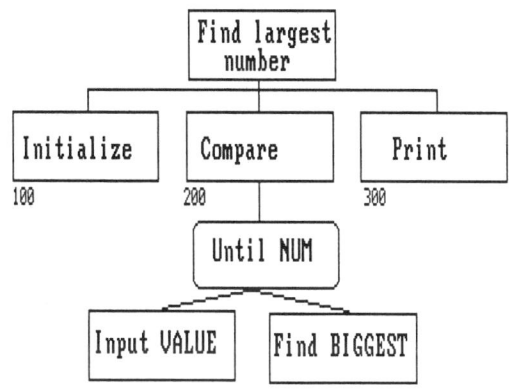

The tree diagram can be related to the program listing in Exhibit 7-2. The main program consists of lines 10 through 70. Lines 30 through 50 are the three GOSUB's which branch to the three subroutines. For example, when the program hits line 30, the GOSUB 100 command sends the program to line 100. The program will process the instructions starting in line 100 until a RETURN (line 150) is encountered. When the RETURN is processed the program returns to line 40, the line after line 30 from which the subroutine was accessed. The three individual modules used by the main program are listed starting with line 100. The Initialization subroutine runs from line 100 to the RETURN in line 150. The Compare subroutine starts in line 200 and returns to the main program in line 295. The Print subroutine starts in line 300 and returns in line 380.

The rounded rectangle in Exhibit 7-3 containing "Until NUM" represents a loop. It is best interpreted as stating that the two rectangles below the loop, "Input VALUE" and "Find BIGGEST," will be done until the incrementing variable I (lines 240-280) reaches the value NUM.

Top-down programming would begin with the tree diagram or flow chart, develop the main program consisting predominantly of GOSUB's although other relatively short routines could be included, and end with the detailed programming of the subroutines.

Pre-Declaration of Variables

As shown in Exhibit 7-2, lines 25 through 27 contain a series of variable names and a brief description of the use of the variable in the program. In a formal structured programming language like Pascal, all variables must be declared by type — integer, real, etc. — before being used in the program. This pre-declaration forces the programmer to think through carefully what variables are really necessary for the tasks assigned. Also, this pre-declaration has an added benefit: if the programmer should misspell a variable name in the program, the error would be caught by the Pascal compiler.

There is no such need for pre-declaration in BASIC. Lines 25 through 27 are simply REMARKS, or comments about the program which are not processed. Remember that the single quote (') in front will mark a line as a comment.

What we have done is to alter the concept of pre-declaration to include a description of the variable. This description makes it easier to follow the program. There is no need in BASIC to follow Pascal and to declare each variable by type — real, string, etc. The variable name itself contains information about the kind of variable it is. String variables will have a "$" after them, such as CITY$, while variables stored in the computer as integers will be noted by a "%" following.

Program Legibility

The final component of structured programming is clarity of presentation. Note the amount of space around the program statements and the use of comments in Exhibit 7-2. Any line beginning with a single quote (') or the word REM is a comment. One can even put comments after a statement as shown in line 30, where "Initialization subroutine" is a comment. Also note the use of indentation, such as lines 250 through 270, which places a set of operations within a FOR-NEXT loop. All of these devices are designed to improve legibility. While this concern may seem trivial in small programs, these simple rules are extremely useful in more extensive programming efforts.

The Linear Model Revisited

There are a number of relatively simple mathematical models which are useful in a wide variety of applications. One of these is the linear model widely used to project the future values of demographic and other planning and management variables. The structure of the linear model was discussed in Chapter 4 in the initial presentation of the electronic spreadsheet. For purposes here, the linear model can be thought of as extrapolating the average growth of past time periods into the future. Following the tenets of structured programming, the linear model program can be broken into four modules:

1. Setting up or initializing the model
2. Putting in the data
3. Calculating the linear model equation
4. Printing out the answers

These four modules are graphically presented in a structure chart in Exhibit 7-4.

Exhibit 7-4

Structure Chart, Linear Model

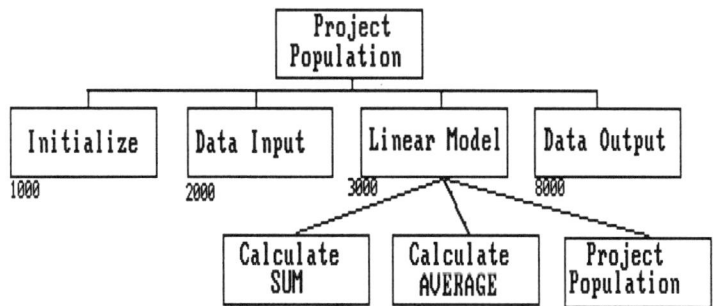

The listing of the linear model program in structured BASIC is found in Exhibit 7-5. These two program instructions discussed earlier are repeated for emphasis since they are in the program:

GOSUB   The command to branch to a programming module. Upon reaching a RETURN command, the program will return to the **next** instruction after the GOSUB from which the branch came.

DIM(A) Dimensions, or sets aside in random access memory, an area with the number of variable locations equal to A. The HISTDATA(20) array in line 1030 has 20 variable locations — HISTDATA(1), HISTDATA(2), etc.

The following is a lengthier description of the different components of the program.

Lines   **Operations**

100-180   Pre-declaration of the different variables in the program. This is always a good idea, and in fact, a formal declaration of all variables is required in the programming language Pascal.

200-230   The four GOSUB's which branch to the four different modules. The GOSUB in Line 200 sends the program to Line 1000, where all commands down to the first RETURN encountered (Line 1120) are done. The program then returns to Line 210, where it branches to Line 2000, and so on.

1000-1130   The Initialization Subroutine which queries the user about the number of historical data points, N, and the number of time periods into the future for which projections are desired, P.

2000-2100   The Data Input Subroutine is done as a loop. Note that the historical data array — HISTDATA(I) — is dimensioned for 20 values. This program contains **no** mechanism to prevent the user from entering a number greater than 20 in line 1070, where the number of historical periods is asked. Should the user enter a

Structured Programming 171

number of historical periods greater than 20, the values for the 21st and successive periods would have no place to go. The program would "crash." The program could be easily modified to solve this problem as we shall see.

3000-3270   The Linear Model Subroutine.

3060   The number of intervals between data points is one less than the number of periods.

3080   While not necessary in most BASIC's, the variable SUM is set to zero before being used in Line 3120.

3120   An example of replacement of SUM with the result of the addition of SUM and CHANGE.

3210-3240   The linear equation in a loop. The most recent data value is HISTDATA(N), which is added to the AVERAGE historical change multiplied by the number of periods I into the future.

8000-8110   The Print Subroutine uses TAB commands to space the labels and answers on the screen. Multiple PRINT and PRINT USING statements will print on the same line if the last entry on any line in the group is a semicolon.

This simple linear model is a straightforward example of a structured programming approach in BASIC. Variables are declared as comments and are briefly defined, sufficient comments are used to make the program instructions clear, and subroutines, or modules, are used to do carry out the tasks. To reinforce this approach, let us extend this model to do exponential and modified exponential modeling as well as linear.

A Three Model Projection Program

In Chapter 4 the exponential and modified exponential models were presented. The linear model program can be edited easily to

Exhibit 7-5

Listing, Linear Model Program

```
10  '****************************
20  '****************************
30  '**   SIMPLE LINEAR MODEL   **
40  '****************************
50  '****************************
60  '
70  '
80  '          VARIABLE DEFINITION
90  '
100 '  AVERAGE          The average change across all historical periods
110 '  CHANGE           The difference in values between time periods
120 '  FUTUREDATA)I)    Array of future data
130 '  HISTDATA(I)      Array of historical data
140 '  I                The incrementing variable used in loops
150 '  INTERVALS        No. of historical periods - 1
160 '  N                Number of historical time periods
170 '  P                Number of future time periods
180 '  SUM              The total of all changes across all periods
190 '
200     GOSUB 1000  ' Initialization Subroutine
210     GOSUB 2000  ' Data Input Subroutine
220     GOSUB 3000  ' Linear Model Calculations
230     GOSUB 8000  ' Data Output Routine
240 '
250 END '*End the program*
980 '
990 '
1000 '*****************************
1010 '* INITIALIZATION SUBROUTINE *
1020 '*****************************
1030 DIM HISTDATA(20),FUTUREDATA(20)
1040 '
1050 CLS '*Clear the screen*
1060 '
1070    INPUT "How many historical periods"; N
1080    PRINT
1090    PRINT "How many time periods into the future"
1100    INPUT "  do you want to project ";P
1110 '
1120 RETURN
1130 '
2000 '*************************
2010 '* DATA INPUT SUBROUTINE *
2020 '*************************
2030 '
2040    FOR I = 1 TO N
2050       PRINT "What is the value in Period "; I
2060       INPUT HISTDATA(I)
2070    NEXT I
```

Exhibit 7-5, continued

```
2080 '
2090 RETURN
2100 '
3000 '*****************
3010 '* LINEAR MODEL *
3020 '*****************
3030 '
3040 ' *Calculate total change in data over past historical periods*
3050 '
3060   INTERVALS = N - 1 '*Intervals are no.of periods minus 1*
3070 '
3080   SUM = 0 '*Initialize SUM to 0*
3090 '
3100     FOR I = 1 TO INTERVALS
3110       CHANGE = HISTDATA(I+1) - HISTDATA(I)
3120       SUM = SUM + CHANGE
3130     NEXT I
3140 '
3150 ' *Calculate average change*
3160 '
3170   AVERAGE = SUM / INTERVALS
3180 '
3190 ' * Project the data for P periods into the future
3200 '
3210     FOR I = 1 TO P
3220       FUTUREDATA(I) = HISTDATA(N) + (AVERAGE * I)
3230             ' * N is the most recent period of historical data*
3240     NEXT I
3250 '
3260 RETURN
3270 '
8000 '***************************
8010 '* DATA OUTPUT SUBROUTINE *
8020 '***************************
8030 '
8040     PRINT
8050     PRINT "Time Period"; TAB(21); "Value"
8060     FOR I = 1 TO P
8070       PRINT TAB(5);
8080       PRINT USING "#"; N+I;
8090       PRINT TAB(17);
8100       PRINT USING "#";FUTUREDATA(I)
8110     NEXT I
8120 '
8130 RETURN
```

include these two models as options. The expanded model is shown in Exhibit 7-6. There are only three changes in the linear model program to accommodate these other two models as options. First, the variable definitions have been expanded in lines 181 to 183 to include necessary ones for the exponential and modified exponential models — RATE, U, and K. Second, a model selection subroutine has been added starting at line 3000. Also note the check on acceptable answers in line 3120. This error check forces the user to respond with a 1, 2, or 3. This is the first example of "bulletproofing" in which the program protects itself from incorrect entries. Third, the exponential and modified exponential models are newly added subroutines.

The exponential model starting in line 5000 uses the same structure as the linear model starting in line 4000, but contains different equations at the appropriate points. The CHANGE equation in line 5090 is different from that in the linear model, as is line 5150 where RATE is calculated. Finally, line 5200 contains the exponential equation using the most recently available data point, HISTDATA(N), and multiplying it by the compound interest formula:

$$\text{FUTUREDATA(I)} = \text{HISTDATA(N)} * (1 + \text{RATE})^I$$

where "^I" is the way of writing I as an exponent. Note that I, the incrementing variable, is used as the power of the exponential equation.

The modified exponential model again uses the same structure as the linear model. However, an additional input is needed from the user — the carrying capacity, K. Line 6100 asks the user for a capacity and checks to make certain in line 6130 that it is not less than the most recent data point, HISTDATA(N). The CHANGE equation in line 6220 is derived from the modified exponential equation calculating U, the unused capacity ratio, and the average of the sums calculated in line 6280. The final equation in line 6330 is directly comparable to the equation in Chapter 4.

Structured programming is a way of increasing program legibility. It also requires additional time and effort. The benefits of a structured programming approach are most apparent in two situations — the development of complex programs and the continuing use of a particular program which will require periodic updating. It is easy to see that a complex program is best written as a set of modules which can be isolated from other parts of the program. It is possible to develop and test modules independently by setting up appropriate

Exhibit 7-6

Listing, Three Model Program

```
10  '*******************************
20  '*******************************
30  '**    THREE PROJECTION MODELS **
40  '*******************************
50  '*******************************
60  '
70  '
80  '           VARIABLE DEFINITION
90  '
100 '   AVERAGE         The average change across all historical periods
110 '   CHANGE          The difference in values between time periods
120 '   FUTUREDATA)I)   Array of future data
130 '   HISTDATA(I)     Array of historical data
140 '   I               The incrementing variable used in loops
150 '   INTERVALS       No. of historical periods - 1
160 '   N               Number of historical time periods
170 '   P               Number of future time periods
180 '   SUM             The total of all changes across all periods
181 '   RATE            Exponential model rate of change
182 '   U               Unused capacity ratio in modified exponential model
183 '   K               Carrying capacity in modified exponential model
190 '
200      GOSUB 1000  ' Initialization Subroutine
210      GOSUB 2000  ' Data Input Subroutine
215 ' ****************************************************
220      GOSUB 3000  ' Model Selection and Calculation
225 ' ****************************************************
230      GOSUB 8000  ' Data Output Routine
240 '
250 END '*End the program*
980 '
990 '
1000 '*******************************
1010 '* INITIALIZATION SUBROUTINE *
1020 '*******************************
1030 DIM HISTDATA(20),FUTUREDATA(20)
1040 '
1050 CLS '*Clear the screen*
1060 '
1070    INPUT "How many historical periods"; N
1080    PRINT
1090    PRINT "How many time periods into the future"
1100    INPUT "  do you want to project ";P
1110 '
1120 RETURN
1130 '
```

Exhibit 7-6, continued

```
2000 '*************************
2010 '* DATA INPUT SUBROUTINE *
2020 '*************************
2030 '
2040    FOR I = 1 TO N
2050       PRINT "What is the value in Period "; I
2060       INPUT HISTDATA(I)
2070    NEXT I
2080 '
2090 RETURN
2100 '
3000 '********************
3010 '* MODEL SELECTION *
3020 '********************
3030 '
3040 PRINT "You have a selection of three models"
3050 PRINT
3060 PRINT "    1. The Linear Model"
3070 PRINT "    2. The Exponential Model"
3080 PRINT "    3. The Modified Exponential Model"
3090 PRINT
3100 INPUT "Which model do you want to use - enter the number";MODELNUMBER
3105 PRINT
3110 '
3120    IF MODELNUMBER <1 OR MODELNUMBER >3 THEN GOTO 3040 '*Error check*
3130 '
3140    IF MODELNUMBER = 1 THEN GOSUB 4000 '*Do Linear Model*
3150    IF MODELNUMBER = 2 THEN GOSUB 5000 '*Do Exponential Model*
3160    IF MODELNUMBER = 3 THEN GOSUB 6000 '*Do Modified Exponential Model*
3170 '
3180 RETURN
3190 '
4000 '*****************
4010 '* LINEAR MODEL *
4020 '*****************
4030 '
4040 ' *Calculate total change in data over past historical periods*
4050 '
4060    INTERVALS = N - 1 '*Intervals are no.of periods minus 1*
4070 '
4080    SUM = 0 '*Initialize SUM to 0*
4090 '
4100    FOR I = 1 TO INTERVALS
4110       CHANGE = HISTDATA(I+1) - HISTDATA(I)
4120       SUM = SUM + CHANGE
4130    NEXT I
4140 '
```

Exhibit 7-6, continued

```
4150 ' *Calculate average change*
4160 '
4170   AVERAGE = SUM / INTERVALS
4180 '
4190 ' * Project the data for P periods into the future*
4200 '
4210   FOR I = 1 TO P
4220     FUTUREDATA(I) = HISTDATA(N) + (AVERAGE * I)
4230         ' * N is the most recent period of historical data*
4240   NEXT I
4250 '
4260 RETURN
4270 '
5000 ' ********************
5010 ' * EXPONENTIAL MODEL*
5020 ' ********************
5030 '
5040   INTERVALS = N - 1 '*Intervals are no.of periods minus 1*
5050 '
5060   SUM = 0 '*Initialize SUM to 0*
5070 '
5080     FOR I = 1 TO INTERVALS
5090       CHANGE = (HISTDATA(I+1) - HISTDATA(I))/ HISTDATA(I)
5100       SUM = SUM + CHANGE
5110     NEXT I
5120 '
5130 ' *Calculate average rate of change*
5140 '
5150   RATE = SUM / INTERVALS
5160 '
5170 ' * Project the data for P periods into the future*
5180 '
5190   FOR I = 1 TO P
5200     FUTUREDATA(I) = HISTDATA(N) * ( 1 + RATE)^I
5210         ' * N is the most recent period of historical data*
5220   NEXT I
5230 '
5240 RETURN
5250 '
6000 '******************************
6010 '* MODIFIED EXPONENTIAL MODEL *
6020 '******************************
6030 '
6040 PRINT
6050 PRINT "You have selected the modified exponential model."
6060 PRINT " This model requires that you select a capacity limit."
6070 PRINT " which is larger than the value of the most recent"
6080 PRINT " historical value"
```

Exhibit 7-6, continued

```
6090 PRINT
6100 INPUT "What limit do you select"; K
6110 PRINT
6120 '
6130    IF HISTDATA(N) < K THEN GOTO 6170 '*Capacity value OK*
6140 PRINT "Warning: Capacity value LESS than most recent historical value"
6150    GOTO 6090
6160 '
6170   INTERVALS = N - 1 '*Intervals are no.of periods minus 1*
6180 '
6190   SUM = 0 '*Initialize SUM to 0*
6200 '
6210     FOR I = 1 TO INTERVALS
6220       CHANGE = (K - HISTDATA(I+1)) / (K - HISTDATA(I))
6230       SUM = SUM + CHANGE
6240     NEXT I
6250 '
6260 ' *Calculate the capacity ratio - U*
6270 '
6280   U = SUM / INTERVALS
6290 '
6300 ' * Project the data for P periods into the future
6310 '
6320     FOR I = 1 TO P
6330       FUTUREDATA(I) = K - ((K - HISTDATA(N)) * U^I)
6340           ' * N is the most recent period of historical data*
6350     NEXT I
6360 '
6370 RETURN
6380 '
8000 '***************************
8010 '* DATA OUTPUT SUBROUTINE *
8020 '***************************
8030 '
8040     PRINT
8050     PRINT "Time Period"; TAB(21); "Value"
8060     FOR I = 1 TO P
8070       PRINT TAB(5);
8080       PRINT USING "#"; N+I;
8090       PRINT TAB(17);
8100       PRINT USING "#";FUTUREDATA(I)
8110     NEXT I
8120 '
8130 RETURN
```

dummy inputs. For example, the modified exponential module could be tested independently by putting dummy values in the HISTDATA array and K, and then printing out the FUTUREDATA array. This test could then be replicated on a calculator or matched against known results from a textbook or other source.

The second reason to do structured programming is to make the program easier to maintain. Any program, large or small, used continually should be written in a structured format for easier maintenance. If there is a need to rewrite a part of the program, the work will be easier to do. In general, the program will be easier to fix, or debug, should there be a problem.

Programming the Population Allocation Model

A spreadsheet version of the Hansen population allocation model was presented in Chapter 5. The model begins with 1980 data and allocates a regional population projection value for 1990 to zones within the region. Factors are identified as predictors of the capacity of each zone to attractive development. These factors can be weighed in terms of relative importance.

Exhibit 7-7

Structure Chart, Population Allocation Model

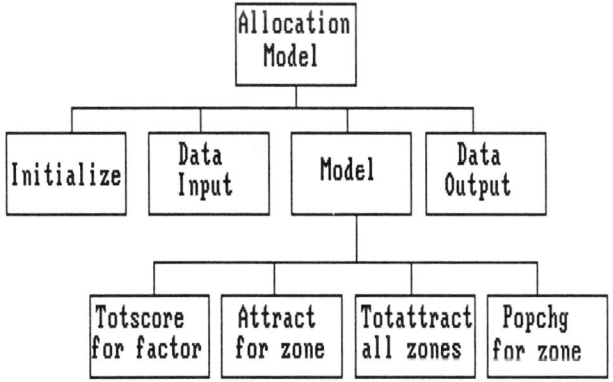

The BASIC version of this model will follow the structured programming concepts outlined earlier. The model is particularly interesting in its manipulation of one- and two-dimensional matrices. The structure chart is shown in Exhibit 7-7. The program listing is in Exhibit 7-8. The program structure is broken into four modules in this example — initialization, data input, model calculation, and data output. This is similar to the linear model in Exhibit 7-4.

Examining the listing in Exhibit 7-8 will help in understanding how the program is constructed.

Lines	Operations
100-210	The main program with four subroutines
1000-1150	The initialization subroutine dimensioning the arrays used and making variables beginning with letters A to H and L to Z double precision. Only variables beginning with I, J, or K are single precision: these three letters are reserved for loop incrementors and upper bounds which require single precision. In the IBM BASIC for the microcomputer, single precision variables are accurate to six digits, even though seven will print out. When dealing in large numbers, such as in millions of dollars or in model construction, double precision is a must. In general, **always** use double precision if there is any doubt about accuracy. Double precision variables are significant to 17 digits.
2000-2420	The data input subroutine queries the user for the number of zones and the 1980 population in those zones. Also, the number, names and weights of the factors are asked.
2130-2160	A check is made to see if 1990 projected regional population is greater than 1980 population by using a conditional branch.
2340-2390	A nested loop is used to read the factor scores in a two dimensional array, SCORE, with the rows the zones and the columns the different factors. The K loop is nested inside the I loop. This means that the array will

Structured Programming

be filled by going across the factors for a particular zone. Hence, for zone 1 the scores will be filled in for the first, second, third, etc., factors.

3000-3240   The model calculation subroutine generates zonal attractiveness values as a base to zonal population change from 1980 to 1990.

3020-3060   These nested loops sum the scores for each factor K into the TOTSCORE array. Note the reversal of the nested loops. The zonal loop I is nested within the factor loop K. This is done because we are moving **down** a column of the SCORE array to sum scores for a factor. In lines 2340-2390 we are moving across rows of the SCORE array.

3080-3120   Another nested loop in which we move across the SCORE array, adding values into an attractiveness score (ATTRACT) for each zone I. This loop follows the structure of the attractiveness equation in Chapter 5.

3140-3160   Sums the zonal attractiveness values.

3180-3210   A loop which calculates the attractiveness proportion (ATTRACTPROP) and the change in population (POPCHG) for each zone.

4000-4220   The screen print routine displays the results of the model run. The same output could be put into a printer using LPRINT commands.

This population allocation model extends our knowledge of how to build a model in BASIC by including matrix manipulations as an element in the program structure. Obviously, models can be quite a bit more complex than this one, as we shall see in the fiscal impact model discussed next.

Exhibit 7-8

Listing, Population Allocation Model

```
100  ' *******************************
110  ' * POPULATION ALLOCATION MODEL *
120  ' *******************************
130  '
140  '
150       GOSUB 1000 ' INITIALIZATION SUBROUTINE
160       GOSUB 2000 ' DATA INPUT SUBROUTINE
170       GOSUB 3000 ' MODEL CALCULATION SUBROUTINE
180       GOSUB 4000 ' DATA OUTPUT SUBROUTINE
190  '
200 END
210  '
1000 ' ***** INITIALIZATION SUBROUTINE *****
1010 '
1020 DIM POP80(15) ' 1980 POPULATION BY ZONE
1030 DIM SCORE(15,5) 'THE ZONE I BY SCORE K MATRIX
1040 DIM FACTORNAME$(5) ' THE NAMES OF FACTORS
1050 DIM WEIGHT(15) ' FACTOR WEIGHTS
1060 DIM POPCHG(15) ' POPULATION CHANGE 1980-90
1070 DIM ATTRACT(15) 'ZONAL ATTRACTIVENESS SCORE
1080 DIM ATTRACTPROP(15) ' ZONAL ATTRACTIVENESS PROPORTION
1090 DIM TOTSCORE(5) ' TOTAL OF ALL FACTOR SCORES
1100 '
1110      DEFDBL A-H ' VARIABLES A TO H - DOUBLE PRECISION
1120      DEFDBL L-Z ' VARIABLES L TO Z - DOUBLE PRECISION
1130 '
1140 RETURN
1150 '
2000 ' ***** DATA INPUT SUBROUTINE *****
2010 '
2020 CLS
2030 INPUT "NUMBER OF ZONES TO BE ALLOCATED ";INUMZONE
2040 PRINT
2050 '
2060 FOR I = 1 TO INUMZONE
2070    PRINT "POPULATION OF ZONE ";I;" IS";
2080    INPUT POP80(I)
2090    TOTPOP80 = TOTPOP80 + POP80(I)
2100 NEXT I
2110 '
2120 PRINT
2130 INPUT "PROJECTED 1990 POPULATION ";TOTPOP90
2140      IF TOTPOP90 > TOTPOP80 THEN GOTO 2180
2150 PRINT "Projected population in 1990 is NOT GREATER than 1980"
2160 GOTO 2120
2170 '
2180      TOTPOPCHG = TOTPOP90 - TOTPOP80
```

Exhibit 7-8, continued

```
2190 '
2200 PRINT
2210 INPUT "NUMBER OF FACTORS TO BE USED IN ANALYSIS ";IFACTOR
2220 PRINT
2230 '
2240 FOR K = 1 TO IFACTOR
2250   PRINT "WHAT IS NAME OF FACTOR ";K
2260   INPUT FACTORNAME$(K)
2270 NEXT K
2280 '
2290 FOR K = 1 TO IFACTOR
2300   PRINT "WEIGHT OF FACTOR ";FACTORNAME$(K)
2310   INPUT WEIGHT(K)
2320 NEXT K
2330 '
2340 FOR I = 1 TO INUMZONE
2350   FOR K = 1 TO IFACTOR
2360     PRINT "INPUT SCORE FOR ZONE ";I;" - FACTOR ";FACTORNAME$(K)
2370     INPUT SCORE(I,K)
2380   NEXT K
2390 NEXT I
2400 '
2410 RETURN
2420 '
3000 ' ***** MODEL CALCULATION SUBROUTINE *****
3010 '
3020 FOR K = 1 TO IFACTOR
3030   FOR I = 1 TO INUMZONE
3040     TOTSCORE(K) = TOTSCORE(K) + SCORE(I,K)
3050   NEXT I
3060 NEXT K
3070 '
3080 FOR I = 1 TO INUMZONE
3090   FOR K = 1 TO IFACTOR
3100     ATTRACT(I) = ATTRACT(I) + (WEIGHT(K)*(SCORE(I,K)/TOTSCORE(K)))
3110   NEXT K
3120 NEXT I
3130 '
3140 FOR I = 1 TO INUMZONE
3150   TOTATTRACT = TOTATTRACT + ATTRACT(I)
3160 NEXT I
3170 '
3180 FOR I = 1 TO INUMZONE
3190   ATTRACTPROP(I) = ATTRACT(I)/TOTATTRACT
3200   POPCHG(I) = TOTPOPCHG * ATTRACTPROP(I)
3210 NEXT I
3220 '
3230 RETURN
3240 '
```

Exhibit 7-8, continued

```
4000 ' ***** DATA OUTPUT ROUTINE *****
4010 '
4020 CLS
4030 PRINT "POPULATION ALLOCATION MODEL"
4040 PRINT "PROJECTED TOTAL 1990 POPULATION   ";TOTPOP90
4050 '
4060 FOR K = 1 TO IFACTOR
4070   PRINT "FACTOR ";K;" - ";FACTORNAME$(K);"  WEIGHT = ";WEIGHT(K)
4080 NEXT K
4090 '
4100 PRINT "ZONE";TAB(13);"1980 POP";TAB(25);"PROP ATTRACT";TAB(45);
     POP CHG 1980-90";TAB(68);"1990 POP"
4105 '
4110 FOR I = 1 TO INUMZONE
4120   PRINT TAB(2);I;
4130   PRINT TAB(10);
4140   PRINT USING "#";POP80(I);
4150   PRINT TAB(28);
4160   PRINT USING ".#";ATTRACTPROP(I);
4170   PRINT TAB(45)
4180   PRINT USING "#";POPCHG(I);
4190   PRINT TAB(65);
4200   PRINT USING "#";POP80(I)+POPCHG(I)
4210 NEXT I
4215 '
4220 RETURN
```

The Fiscal Impact Model

The Concept

The most extensive program in this chapter is a complex fiscal impact model. It contains a wide variety of commands and addresses a variety of issues, including numeric precision, iterative modeling, and an extensive variable list. It is presented not to dazzle or overwhelm, but rather to show the kinds of issues an urban planner or manager would face in writing or supervising a complex program with extensive keyboard queries and a time series output.

One of the recurring elements of local planning is the calculation of fiscal impacts of development. The fiscal impact process is particularly amenable to computer analysis. In fact, mainframe fiscal impact models have existed for a number of years. Burchell and Listokin (1978:345-359) described twelve different models, all of which were designed in the late 1960's or 1970's. This section will present a relatively straightforward fiscal impact model in BASIC which is based on a model developed at the Center for Urban Policy Research of Rutgers University. It is particularly appropriate as a programming example because it is an iterative model which can produce a time series output. This means that the program which will be discussed contains a series of loops. Also, the model is complex enough to demonstrate the advantages of structured programming. Parenthetically, the model could also be done in a spreadsheet environment, and the reader may want to examine how such a model would look done as a spreadsheet.

A fiscal model calculates the potential costs and revenues from a proposed development. For example, a developer may propose the construction of a new residential subdivision or a shopping center. These new residences will send children to local schools and will require provision for police and fire protection. The shopping center will generate traffic on adjacent roads and will also require police and fire protection. Correspondingly, this residential or shopping center development will generate revenues from property taxes and other sources, such as user fees.

Ideally, all relevant impacts of development should be considered in model design. These impacts would include both transportation and environmental elements as well as the fiscal implications of development. Realistically, the inclusion of all of these factors is more than can be done here. However, designing programs in modules will permit the easier introduction of new elements. The structured programming approach advocated, which includes the widespread use of these modules, ensures flexibility of model design to a much greater degree than non-structured approaches.

The fiscal impact model which we are proposing calculates a municipal tax rate based on the following equation:

$$MTAXRT_I = (MEXP_I - MREV.NONPROP_I) / VALTOT_I$$

where:

MTAXRT	Municipal tax rate for period I
MEXP	Municipal expenditures during period I
MREV.NONPROP	Municipal revenues generated from non-property tax sources (e.g. — transfers, user fees) during I

VALTOT Total assessed value of all property, including both proposed development and existing development

The tax rate is the percentage of all property valuation needed to generate the revenues needed from the property tax to cover the municipal expenses (MEXP) for period I. In general, the time period I is a year. Note that non-property revenues (MREV.NONPROP) are subtracted from municipal expenditures. Expanding the revenue equation we have the following:

$$MREV_I = MREV.DEV_I + MREV.SS_I$$

which says that total municipal revenue (MREV) equals property tax revenue from new development (MREV.DEV) plus all revenues from existing development (MREV.SS), labeled "steady state." In turn:

$$MREV.DEV_I = MREV.PROPDEV_I + MREV.NONPROPDEV_I$$

where:

MREV.DEV The total revenue generated from new development during period I

MREV.PROPDEV The revenue generated from taxes on the proposed new development in I

MREV.NONPROPDEV The revenue generated from the new development from non-property tax sources, such as a developer contribution

The model solves for the tax rate which would be generated if the proposed project would be added to the tax rolls of the municipality. An analyst can compare the tax rate with the proposed project against the one which exists without it. Depending on the expenses generated by the new development, the total municipal expenses may increase as a result of the proposed development to a degree that causes the tax rate to rise rather than to fall. Proponents of development hope that the revenues generated from the new project will exceed the additional municipal costs incurred and that the tax rate will fall. The key is the calculation of the additional municipal costs.

The "steady state" variables refer to the current and projected costs and revenues in the municipality and school district **without** construction of the proposed development being analyzed in the model. These steady state revenues from intergovernmental transfers, from other income sources, and from property taxes based on valuation of property can be inflated or deflated in percentage terms across time periods. Municipal expenses can be inflated or deflated as well.

$$MEXP_I = MEXP.DEVRES_I + MEXP.DEVNON_I + MEXP.SS_I$$

MEXP	Total municipal expenses in period I
MEXP.DEVRES	The new expenses incurred from residential development
MEXP.DEVNON	The expenses incurred from new non-residential development, such as offices, shopping centers, and the like
MEXP.SS	Already-existing "steady state" municipal costs for period I

The calculation of cost from new developments can be done by a variety of methods, including the per capita multiplier method, case studies, service standard method, comparable city analysis, a proportional valuation method, or an employment anticipation approach (Burchell and Listokin, 1978). The different methods all have advantages and drawbacks, and no attempt can be made here to discuss the various options in detail. Instead, the reader should consult Burchell and Listokin (1978) for an extended discussion of the various alternatives.

In our model, residential developments will be handled by a per capita method. There may be a number of different types of housing built, such as apartments with different numbers of bedrooms, single-family homes, or townhouses. Each will, on the average, have different numbers of people living in the units and different numbers of school children. The model must handle both the time periods, I, and the different kinds of residential development, J.

$$MEXP.DRES_I = \sum_J [PERSUNIT_J * MCOSTPERS_I * NUMRESUNITS_{I,J}]$$

where:

MEXP.DRES	Expenses caused directly by all proposed residential development for residential types J in period I
PERSUNIT	Average number of persons per dwelling unit for residential type J
MCOSTPERS	The estimated cost per person to the municipality in time period I
NUMRESUNITS	Number of units of residential type J built during period I

This per capita approach assumes that costs to the municipality will vary closely with the number of new residents added to the community through the new development.

School district costs can also be estimated using the per capita method. The cost equation is stated in terms of the number of pupils.

$$\text{SEXP.DEVRES}_I = \sum_J [\text{PUPUNIT}_J * \text{SCOSTPUP}_I * \text{NUMRESUNITS}_{I,J}]$$

where:

SEXP.DEVRES	The expenses to the school district from the total number of students generated by all dwelling units of type J in the proposed development in time period I
PUPUNIT	Average number of pupils per dwelling unit of type J
SCOSTPUP	The average cost to educate a pupil in time period I

A wide range of non-residential land uses may also be constructed as part of the development package. One way to estimate the municipal costs of non-residential projects was done by Burchell and Listokin (1983) for Weehawken, New Jersey. The equation for expenses generated by non-residential development is:

$$\text{MEXP.DEVNON}_I = \sum_J (\text{MCOSTWKR}_I * \text{WORKERS}_J)$$

and:

$$\text{WORKERS}_J = (\text{TOTFTNON}_{I,J}/1000) * \text{WKRFT}_J$$

where:

MEXP.DEVNON	Municipal expenses attributed to non-residential development across all types J for period I
MCOSTWKR	The average cost to the municipality of providing services to a worker in time period I
WORKERS	The number of workers for land use category J for period I
TOTFTNON	The total square feet of proposed development in land use category J during period I
WKRFT	Number of workers per 1,000 square feet for land use category J

Note that the model uses a set of definitions which suggest a series of periods in which different types of construction can occur. In fact, the model is set up to handle a twenty-year stream of staged development of a wide variety of land use categories. Even more, provisions are included in the model to alter the "steady state" set of expenses and revenues to reflect anticipated changes in future years. As an example, it might be suggested that the community will have a gradual increase in property tax revenues in real dollars because of other developments which are also expected to occur in the next few years.

The Computer Program

The outline of model structure above provides a useful framework for understanding the computer program which will be presented. The total tax burden on local residents consists of municipal costs and the municipal portion of school district and county costs. The revenues generated by a municipality consists of property tax revenues, intergovernmental transfers, such as state tax dollars transferred to the municipality as a grant or allocation, and other sources such as municipal user or license fees. The program will calculate municipal, school district and county tax rates as they change over time. The model is essentially one big loop, in which the cost, revenue and tax rate calculations are done by year for as many years as are specified in the user input to the program.

The program is lengthy but not difficult to understand. The structure chart is in Exhibit 7-9. There are 10 modules in the program which can be categorized into three general phases.

1. The data input and initialization phase
2. The calculation phase
   a. Cost model
   b. Valuation model
   c. Non-property revenue model
   d. Tax rate model
   e. General revenue model
3. The output phase

Exhibit 7-9

Structure Chart, Fiscal Impact Model

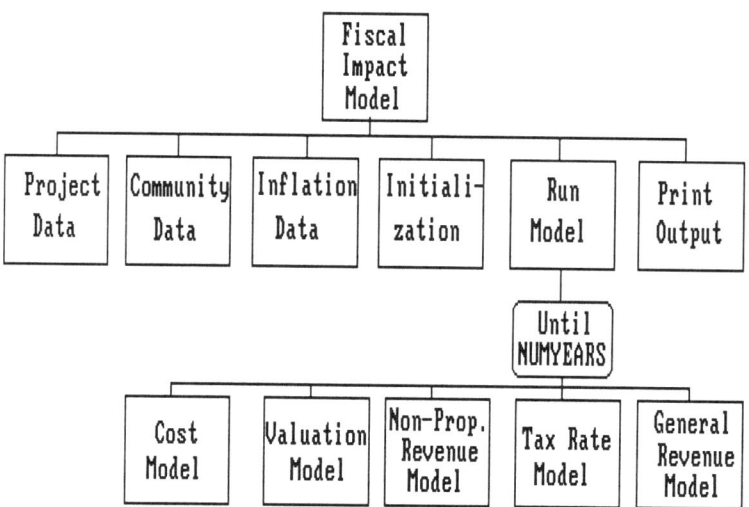

There is one inescapable conclusion from even a cursory glance at the program listing in Exhibit 7-10. The input routines needed to fill in the data necessary to run the model represent the greatest num-

Structured Programming 191

ber of lines in the program. The actual model is relatively straightforward, although one needs to be clear about how to make the model run through time correctly and how to set up the equations. The program contains the folowing major elements:

Lines	Operations
60	Defines the variables which begin with M, S, or V as double precision with 17 significant digits.
100-345	An extensive list of arrays with relatively long names, such as SREV.NONPROPDEV, meaning school revenues generated from newly developed non-residential property. The reader may think these names silly, but they are reasonably clear. Other labeling strategies may be more appropriate. Note that most of the arrays contain either 20 or 6 cells. The length 20 arrays contain room for up to 20 years of development, while the length 6 arrays mean that up to 6 different residential or non-residential development types may be entered. There are also three two-dimensional arrays of 20 by 6 — the number of residential units and the total square footage of either residential or non-residential units. The 20 by 6 arrays are two-dimensional, and it is entirely possible to have arrays with three dimensions or more.
800-900	The subroutines in a structured format.
1000-2140	The project data entry subroutine. Both I and J are used in the loops. Note how the nested loops in lines 1190-1270 work to fill a 20 by 6 array of the number of residential units (NUMRESUNITS) to be developed. In line 1250 the subscript is written (J,I), filling J years within I residential type. Remember, a 20 by 6 array is visualized as having 20 rows (the years) and 6 columns (the residential types). The use of I and J as incrementing variables is arbitrary. K and L could have been used, or any other variable names thought appropriate.

1060	The number of years for which the program is to run (NUMYEARS) is entered here in response to an INPUT statement. Since the dimension of the arrays is 20, no more than a 20 can be entered.
1065	A check on data entry — a number less than 1 or greater than 20 sends the program back to line 1060.
1100	Skip the section on inputting data on residential development and go to the nonresidential section
1120	The FOR..NEXT loop has an upper bound (NUMRESTYPES) determined by user input in line 1090.
3000-3992	The community expense and revenue input section.
3130-3140	It is possible in many BASIC's to refer to cell 0 in an array, and this fact is used in this model. The base year (year 0) contains the "steady state" revenues and expenses at the beginning of the analysis. Hence, the total operating expenses of the community at the beginning of the calculations is stored in MEXP.SS(0), the cell 0 of the array.
3340-3380	A check on whether the beginning municipal revenues equal municipal expenses. If equal, the program goes forward to 3420.
4000-4580	The inflation factor model. It is possible to enter an inflation factor for each of the steady state variables on both the revenue and the expense sides. Note the use of the GRAB$ variable and the VAL statement. This use is an example of bulletproofing. The answers to the INPUT statement are entered into a string variable, GRAB$. The string is then converted to a numeric value in the VAL command. This is done because an answer containing a letter or special character ("a12", for example) to any INPUT to a numeric variable will produce a "REDO FROM START" comment from the BASIC interpreter. This is **not** desirable. Such an approach should be used on all input com-

mands in this program. Bulletproofing was not done simply because of the additional lines of code generated.

5000-5220 The initialization subroutine. Sets up the year 0 data in preparation for the run. Determines the average cost to the municipality of each person residing in year 0 (MCOSTPERS(0)), and each worker (MCOST-WKR(0)). Determines the average cost to the school district per pupil (SCOSTPUP(0)). These will vary as a function of the PCTMEXP and PCTSEXP inflation values queried in line 4140-4190 in the inflation factor model.

6000-6270 The cost model. New development is added to the current stock and total municipal and school expenses calculated. Both steady state expenses and new developments will be inflated by the appropriate inflation factors.

6060-6090 A FOR..NEXT loop which sums municipal expense increases due to new residential development. Note that the cost associated with each residential type (MEXP.DEVRES(I)) is summed into itself in line 6070 — an example of replacement.

6170-6190 The calculation of an inflation factor for the steady state development.

7000-7320 The valuation model. Total valuation is the sum of steady state development and all new development.

7220-7250 The current steady state valuation (VALSS(I)) is the sum of last time period's steady state valuation inflated plus the value of last period's new development.

8000-8310 The non-property revenue model. This model inflates (or deflates) the base year revenues from intergovernmental transfers and other non-property based revenues to the current year. Note that there are a set of program lines referring to non-property based revenues from new development (MREV.NONPROPDEV)

Exhibit 7-10

Listing, Fiscal Impact Model

```
10  ' ***********************************
20  ' * FISCAL IMPACT SIMULATION MODEL *
30  ' ***********************************
40  '
50  KEY OFF '*Turn off key at bottom of screen*
60  DEFDBL M,S,V '*Define variables beginning with M,S,V as double precision*
70  '
80  '*Dimension all arrays*
90  '
100 DIM NUMRESUNITS(20,6) '*Up to 6 housing types in each of 20 years*
105 DIM PERSUNIT(6) '*Average number of persons per unit*
110 DIM PUPUNIT(6) '*Average number of pupils per unit*
115 DIM LABELRES$(6) '*Residential development labels*
120 DIM LABELNONRES$(6) '*Nonresidential development labels*
121 DIM MCOSTPERS(20) '*Municipal cost per person*
122 DIM MCOSTWKR(20) '*Municipal cost per worker*
123 DIM SCOSTPUP(20) '*School cost per pupil*
125 DIM MEXP(20)   '*Total municipal expenditures*
130 DIM MEXP.DEVNON(20) '*Nonresidential development expenditures*
135 DIM MEXP.DEVRES(20) '*Residential development expenditures*
140 DIM MEXP.SS(20) '*Steady state municipal revenues*
145 DIM MREV(20) '*Total municipal revenues*
150 DIM MREV.DEV(20) '*Municipal revenues from new development*
155 DIM MREV.INTGOVDEV(20) '*Intergovernmental development revenues*
160 DIM MREV.INTGOVSS(20) '*Intergovernmental steady state revenues*
165 DIM MREV.NONPROP(20) '*Total nonresidential property revenues*
170 DIM MREV.NONPROPDEV(20) '*Nonresidential development property revenues*
175 DIM MREV.NONPROPSS(20) '*Nonresidential steady state property revenues*
180 DIM MREV.OTHDEV(20) '*Other development revenues*
185 DIM MREV.OTHSS(20) '*Other steady state revenues*
190 DIM MREV.PROPDEV(20) '*Total development property revenues*
195 DIM MREV.PROPSS(20) '*Steady state property revenues*
200 DIM MREV.SS(20) '*Steady state revenues*
205 DIM SEXP(20)   '*Total school expenditures*
210 DIM SEXP.DEVRES(20) '*Residential development expenditures*
215 DIM SEXP.SS(20) '*Steady state school revenues*
220 DIM SREV(20) '*Total school revenues*
225 DIM SREV.DEV(20) '*School revenues from new development*
230 DIM SREV.INTGOVDEV(20) '*Intergovernmental development revenues*
235 DIM SREV.INTGOVSS(20) '*Intergovernmental steady state revenues*
240 DIM SREV.NONPROP(20) '*Total nonresidential property revenues*
245 DIM SREV.NONPROPDEV(20) '*Nonresidential development property revenues*
250 DIM SREV.NONPROPSS(20) '*Nonresidential steady state property revenues*
255 DIM SREV.OTHDEV(20) '*Other development revenues*
260 DIM SREV.OTHSS(20) '*Other steady state revenues*
265 DIM SREV.PROPDEV(20) '*Total development property revenues*
270 DIM SREV.PROPSS(20) '*Steady state property revenues*
275 DIM SREV.SS(20) '*Steady state revenues*
```

Exhibit 7-10, continued

```
280 DIM MTAXRT(20)  '*Municipal tax rate*
285 DIM STAXRT(20)  '*School tax rate*
290 DIM TOTFTNON(20,6) '*Nonresidential total square footage*
295 DIM TOTFTRES(20,6) '*Residential total square footage*
300 DIM UNITSQFTRES(6) '*Residential unit square footage*
305 DIM VALDEV(20)  '*Total value of new development*
310 DIM VALDEVNON(20) '*Total value of nonresidential development*
315 DIM VALDEVRES(20) '*Total value of residential development*
320 DIM VALSQFTNON(6) '*Square foot value of nonresidential types*
325 DIM VALSQFTRES(6) '*Square foot value of residential types*
330 DIM VALSS(20)  '*Value of steady state development*
335 DIM VALTOT(20) '* Total value of ALL*
340 DIM WKRFT(6) '*The average square feet consumed per worker*
345 DIM WORKERS(6) '* Total workers by nonresidential type*
400 ' ********** Main Program **********
800            GOSUB 1000   '*PROJECT DATA SUBROUTINE*
810            GOSUB 3000   '*COMMUNITY EXPENSES AND REVENUES*
815            GOSUB 4000   '*INFLATION FACTOR MODEL*
820            GOSUB 5000   '*INITIALIZATION ROUTINE*
830     FOR I = 1 TO NUMYEARS
840            GOSUB 6000   '* COST MODEL*
850            GOSUB 7000   '* VALUATION MODEL*
860            GOSUB 8000   '* NON-PROPERTY REVENUE MODEL*
870            GOSUB 9000   '* TAX RATE MODEL*
880            GOSUB 10000  '* GENERAL REVENUE MODEL*
890     NEXT I
900            GOSUB 20000  '*PRINT ROUTINE*
910 '
920 END '************ End of Program ****************
930 '
990 ' *************************************
1000 ' *        DATA SUBROUTINE            *
1005 ' *************************************
1010 CLS
1020 PRINT "The fiscal impact simulation model can handle up to 20 years"
1030 PRINT "  of development data and can estimate costs and revenues"
1040 PRINT "  over a twenty year period as well"
1050 PRINT
1060 INPUT "How many years of development analysis ";NUMYEARS
1065    IF NUMYEARS<1 OR NUMYEARS>20 THEN GOTO 1060  ' TEST BOUNDARIES
1070 CLS
1080 PRINT "RESIDENTIAL DEVELOPMENT"
1090 INPUT "Enter the number of development types(up to 6)";NUMRESTYPES
1095    IF NUMRESTYPES<0 OR NUMRESTYPES>6 THEN GOTO 1080 ' TEST BOUNDARIES
1100    IF NUMRESTYPES = 0 THEN GOTO 1700  '*Skip residential data queries*
1110 PRINT
1120    FOR I = 1 TO NUMRESTYPES
1130       PRINT "Name of housing type "I
1140       INPUT LABELRES$(I)
1150    NEXT I
1160 '
```

Exhibit 7-10, continued

```
1170 PRINT
1180 '
1190   FOR I = 1 TO NUMRESTYPES
1200     CLS
1210     PRINT "     RESIDENTIAL UNIT DATA MATRIX - ";LABELRES$(I)
1220     PRINT " Year";TAB(14);"Number of Units"
1230       FOR J = 1 TO NUMYEARS
1240         PRINT TAB(5);J;TAB(20);
1250         INPUT NUMRESUNITS(J,I)
1260       NEXT J
1270   NEXT I
1280 '
1290 ' *Input Persons per Unit*
1300 CLS
1310 PRINT "PERSONS PER UNIT INPUT"
1320 PRINT
1330 PRINT "Enter the average number of persons per dwelling unit type"
1340 PRINT
1350 '
1360   FOR I = 1 TO NUMRESTYPES
1370     PRINT LABELRES$(I);TAB(20);
1380     INPUT PERSUNIT(I)
1390   NEXT I
1400 PRINT
1410 ' *Input the number of school children per dwelling unit"
1420 '
1430 PRINT "NUMBER OF SCHOOL CHILDREN PER UNIT"
1440 PRINT
1450 PRINT "Enter the average number of school children per unit type"
1460 PRINT
1470   FOR I = 1 TO NUMRESTYPES
1480     PRINT LABELRES$(I); TAB(20);
1490     INPUT PUPUNIT(I)
1500   NEXT I
1510 '
1520 PRINT
1530 PRINT "VALUE AND SCALE OF RESIDENTIAL DEVELOPMENT"
1540 PRINT
1550 PRINT "Enter the value per square foot of each residential type"
1560 PRINT
1570   FOR I = 1 TO NUMRESTYPES
1580     PRINT LABELRES$(I);TAB(20);
1590     INPUT VALSQFTRES(I)
1600   NEXT I
1610 PRINT
1620 PRINT "Enter the average square foot size of the residential unit"
1630 PRINT
1640   FOR I = 1 TO NUMRESTYPES
1650     PRINT LABELRES$(I);TAB(20);
1660     INPUT UNITSQFTRES(I)
1670   NEXT I
```

Exhibit 7-10, continued

```
1680 '
1700 CLS
1710 PRINT "OFFICE, INDUSTRIAL AND COMMERCIAL DEVELOPMENT"
1720 PRINT
1730 PRINT "How many different types of non-residential development  - "
1740 PRINT "   shopping centers, offices, manufacturing facilities  - "
1750 INPUT "   will be constructed (up to 6)"; NUMNONRESTYPES
1760 PRINT
1765    IF NUMNONRESTYPES<0 OR NUMNONRESTYPES>6 THEN GOTO 1730
1770    IF NUMNONRESTYPES = 0 THEN GOTO 2130
1780    FOR I = 1 TO NUMNONRESTYPES
1790       PRINT "Name of nonresidential type ";I
1800       INPUT LABELNONRES$(I)
1810    NEXT I
1820 '
1830    FOR I = 1 TO NUMNONRESTYPES
1840       CLS
1850       PRINT "     NONRESIDENTIAL DATA MATRIX   -   ";LABELNONRES$(I)
1860       PRINT " Year";TAB(14);"Amount of Square Feet"
1870          FOR J = 1 TO NUMYEARS
1880             PRINT TAB(5);J;TAB(20);
1890             INPUT TOTFTNON(J,I)
1900          NEXT J
1910    NEXT I
1920 '
1930 PRINT
1940 PRINT "VALUE AND SCALE OF NON-RESIDENTIAL DEVELOPMENT"
1950 PRINT
1960 PRINT "Enter the value per square foot of each type"
1970 PRINT
1980    FOR I = 1 TO NUMNONRESTYPES
1990       PRINT LABELNONRES$(I);TAB(20);
2000       INPUT VALSQFTNON(I)
2010    NEXT I
2020 '
2030 PRINT
2040 PRINT "NUMBER OF WORKERS PER 1,000 SQUARE FEET FOR NONRESIDENTIAL SPACE"
2050 PRINT
2060 PRINT "Enter the number of workers per 1,000 square feet"
2070 PRINT
2080    FOR I = 1 TO NUMNONRESTYPES
2090       PRINT LABELNONRES$(I);TAB(20);
2100       INPUT WKRFT(I)
2110    NEXT I
2120 '
2130 RETURN
2140 '
3000 ' ******************************************************
3010 ' * COMMUNITY AND SCHOOL DISTRICT EXPENSES AND REVENUES *
3020 ' ******************************************************
3030 '
```

Exhibit 7-10, continued

```
3040 CLS
3050 PRINT "MUNICIPAL DATA"
3060 PRINT
3070 PRINT "Following data drawn from municipal and school district"
3080 PRINT "   records on operating expenditures and revenues."
3090 PRINT "Total operating expenditures must equal total revenues"
3100 PRINT "   in the base year (Year 0) for the model to calculate "
3110 PRINT "   the initial municipal and school tax rates."
3120 PRINT
3130 PRINT "Total Operating Expenditures";
3140 INPUT MEXP.SS(0)
3150 PRINT
3160 PRINT "Total Revenues"
3170 PRINT "   From Property Taxes";TAB(20);
3180 INPUT MREV.PROPSS(0)
3190 PRINT "   From Intergovernmental Transfers";TAB(20);
3200 INPUT MREV.INTGOVSS(0)
3210 PRINT "   From Other Sources";TAB(20);
3220 INPUT MREV.OTHSS(0)
3230 PRINT
3240 '
3250 ' * Add up the revenue sources *
3260    MREV.NONPROPSS(0)=MREV.INTGOVSS(0)+MREV.OTHSS(0)
3270    MREV.SS(0) = MREV.PROPSS(0) + MREV.NONPROPSS(0)
3280 '
3290 ' * For initial data (Round 0) total expenses and revenues equal
3300 '    steady state expenses and revenues
3310    MREV(0) = MREV.SS(0)
3320    MEXP(0) = MEXP.SS(0)
3330 '
3340     IF MREV(0) = MEXP(0) THEN GOTO 3420 ' *Continue queries*
3350 '
3360 PRINT "WARNING — Total revenues do not equal total expenses in"
3370 PRINT "   initial data (Round 0). "
3380 INPUT "Press return to enter data again";JUNK$
3390 '
3400     GOTO 3040
3410 '
3420 PRINT
3430 PRINT "Municipal Population";TAB(20);
3440 INPUT MPOPULATION
3450 PRINT
3460 PRINT "Total number of employees in municipality"
3470 INPUT MEMPLOYMENT
3480 PRINT
3490 PRINT "This model uses a per capita method of calculating "
3500 PRINT "   municipal and school costs. The residential and "
3510 PRINT "   non-residential valuation of real estate is required"
3520 PRINT "   in order to estimate resident and employee costs."
3530 PRINT
3540 PRINT "Residential assessed property total";TAB(20);
```

Exhibit 7-10, continued

```
3550 INPUT VALUATION.RES
3560 PRINT
3570 PRINT "Non-residential assessed property total";TAB(20);
3580 INPUT VALUATION.NONRES
3590 PRINT
3600 PRINT
3610 '
3620 '
3630 ' * SCHOOL DISTRICT DATA*
3640 CLS
3650 PRINT "SCHOOL DISTRICT DATA"
3660 PRINT
3670 PRINT "Total Operating Expenditures";
3680 INPUT SEXP.SS(0)
3690 PRINT
3700 PRINT "Total Revenues"
3710 PRINT "   From Property Taxes";TAB(20);
3720 INPUT SREV.PROPSS(0)
3730 PRINT "   From Intergovernmental Transfers";TAB(20);
3740 INPUT SREV.INTGOVSS(0)
3750 PRINT "   From Other Sources";TAB(20);
3760 INPUT SREV.OTHSS(0)
3770 PRINT
3780 '
3790 '* Add up revenue sources*
3800  SREV.NONPROPSS(0)=SREV.INTGOVSS(0)+SREV.OTHSS(0)
3810  SREV.SS(0) = SREV.PROPSS(0) + SREV.NONPROPSS(0)
3820 '
3830 ' * For initial data (Round 0) total expenses and revenues equal
3840 '   steady state expenses and revenues
3850   SREV(0) = SREV.SS(0)
3860   SEXP(0) = SEXP.SS(0)
3870 '
3880    IF SREV(0) = SEXP(0) THEN GOTO 3970 '*OK, continue*
3890 '
3900 PRINT "WARNING - Total revenues do not equal total expenses in"
3910 PRINT "   initial data (Round 0). "
3920 '
3930 INPUT "Press return to enter data again";JUNK$
3940 '
3950       GOTO 3640
3960 '
3970 PRINT "Total Number of Pupils";TAB(20);
3980 INPUT SPUPILS
3990 PRINT
3991 '
3992 RETURN
4000 '
4010 ' ****************************************************************
4020 ' * STEADY STATE PERCENT CHANGES IN REVENUE, EXPENSES, VALUATION *
```

Exhibit 7-10, continued

```
4030 ' *****************************************************************
4040 CLS
4050 PRINT "The following percent changes in steady state conditions"
4060 PRINT "  are used by the model to account for such factors as"
4070 PRINT "  inflation, changes in government policy, etc."
4080 PRINT "Values entered are annual percentage changes(plus or minus),"
4090 PRINT "  and should be entered as percents - 4.8 percent is entered"
4100 PRINT "  as 4.8. Enter 0 if no percent change is to be used."
4110 '
4120 PRINT
4130 PRINT "Enter the percent changes for expenses"
4140 PRINT "  Municipal expenses";TAB(40);
4150 INPUT GRAB$
4160   PCTMEXP = (VAL(GRAB$)/100)
4170 PRINT "  School expenses";TAB(40);
4180 INPUT GRAB$
4190   PCTSEXP = (VAL(GRAB$)/100)
4200 PRINT
4210 PRINT "Enter the percent change for revenues"
4220 PRINT "  Municipal revenues"
4230 PRINT "     Steady state intergovernmental";TAB(40);
4240 INPUT GRAB$
4250   PCTMREV.INTGOVSS = (VAL(GRAB$)/100)
4260 PRINT "     Steady state other ";TAB(40);
4270 INPUT GRAB$
4280   PCTMREV.OTHSS = (VAL(GRAB$)/100)
4350 PRINT
4360 PRINT "  School revenues"
4370 PRINT "     Steady state intergovernmental";TAB(40);
4380 INPUT GRAB$
4390   PCTSREV.INTGOVSS = (VAL(GRAB$)/100)
4400 PRINT "     Steady state other";TAB(40);
4410 INPUT GRAB$
4420   PCTSREV.OTHSS = (VAL(GRAB$)/100)
4490 '
4500 ' * Determine steady state increase in valuation other than
4510 '    targeted development *
4520 PRINT
4530 PRINT "Percent increase in steady state valuation"
4540 INPUT GRAB$
4550   PCTVALSS = (VAL(GRAB$)/100)
4560 '
4570 RETURN
4580 '
5000 '*************************
5010 '* INITIALIZATION MODULE *
5020 '*************************
5030 '
5040 ' *Calculate the municipal cost per resident and employee*
5050 '
5060   VALSS(0) = VALUATION.RES + VALUATION.NONRES
```

Exhibit 7-10, continued

```
5070    PCTRESVAL = VALUATION.RES / VALSS(0)
5080    PCTNONRESVAL = 1 - PCTRESVAL
5090    MCOSTPERS(0) = (MEXP.SS(0) * PCTRESVAL) / MPOPULATION
5100    MCOSTWKR(0) = (MEXP.SS(0) * PCTNONRESVAL) / MEMPLOYMENT
5110  '
5120    SCOSTPUP(0) = SEXP.SS(0)/SPUPILS
5130    VALTOT(0) = VALSS(0)
5140  '
5190    MTAXRT(0) = (MEXP(0) - MREV.NONPROPSS(0))/ VALTOT(0)
5200    STAXRT(0) = (SEXP(0) - SREV.NONPROPSS(0))/ VALTOT(0)
5210  '
5220 RETURN
6000  ' *************************
6010  ' * GENERAL COST MODEL    *
6020  ' *************************
6030  '
6031    MCOSTPERS(I) = MCOSTPERS(I-1) * (1 + PCTMEXP)
6032    MCOSTWKR(I) = MCOSTWKR(I-1) * (1 + PCTMEXP)
6033    SCOSTPUP(I) = SCOSTPUP(I-1) * (1 + PCTSEXP)
6034  '
6040  ' *Development residential costs*
6050  '
6060    FOR J = 1 TO NUMRESTYPES
6070 MEXP.DEVRES(I) = MEXP.DEVRES(I) +(PERSUNIT(J) * MCOSTPERS(I) *
     NUMRESUNITS(I,J))
6080 SEXP.DEVRES(I) = SEXP.DEVRES(I) + (PUPUNIT(J)*SCOSTPUP(I) *
     NUMRESUNITS(I,J))
6090    NEXT J
6100  '
6110  ' *Development non-residential costs*
6120    FOR J = 1 TO NUMNONRESTYPES
6130      WORKERS(J) = INT((TOTFTNON(I,J)/1000) * WKRFT(J))
6140      MEXP.DEVNON(I) = MEXP.DEVNON(I) +(MCOSTWKR(I)*WORKERS(J))
6150    NEXT J
6160  '
6170  ' *Steady state residential and nonresidential costs*
6180    MEXP.SS(I) =  (MEXP(I-1) * (1 + PCTMEXP))
6190    SEXP.SS(I) =  (SEXP(I-1) * (1 + PCTSEXP))
6200  '
6210  ' *Total the cost elements*
6220    MEXP(I) = MEXP.DEVRES(I) + MEXP.DEVNON(I) + MEXP.SS(I)
6230    SEXP(I) = SEXP.DEVRES(I) + SEXP.SS(I)
6240  '
6260 RETURN
6270  '
7000  ' ********************
7010  ' * Valuation module *
7020  ' ********************
7030  '
```

Exhibit 7-10, continued

```
7040 '*Total the residential square footage*
7050    FOR J = 1 TO NUMRESTYPES
7060       TOTFTRES(I,J) = (NUMRESUNITS(I,J)*UNITSQFTRES(J))
7070    NEXT J
7080 '
7090 ' * Determine value of current residential development*
7100    FOR J = 1 TO NUMRESTYPES
7110       VALDEVRES(I) = VALDEVRES(I) + (VALSQFTRES(J)* TOTFTRES(I,J))
7120    NEXT J
7130 '
7140 ' * Determine the value of the current non-residential development*
7150    FOR J = 1 TO NUMNONRESTYPES
7160       VALDEVNON(I)=VALDEVNON(I)+(VALSQFTNON(J)* TOTFTNON(I,J))
7170    NEXT J
7180 '
7190 ' * Current development value = sum of residential plus non-residential*
7200    VALDEV(I) = VALDEVRES(I) + VALDEVNON(I)
7210 '
7220 ' * The current steady state valuation is the sum of
7230 '     adjusted steady state valuation from last time period PLUS
7240 '     value of development from last time period*
7250    VALSS(I) = (VALSS(I-1)*(1 + PCTVALSS)) + VALDEV(I-1)
7260 '
7270 ' * Current total value is sum of steady state plus
7280    VALTOT(I) = VALDEV(I) + VALSS(I)
7300 '
7310 RETURN
7320 '
8000 ' *******************************
8010 ' * NON-PROPERTY REVENUE MODULE *
8020 ' *******************************
8030 '
8040 ' *Calculate the steady state residential/non-residential revenues*
8050 '     NOTE:No property revenues included
8060 '
8070 ' *Bring steady state other and intergovernmental revenues forward
8080 '   to current time period adjusting for inflation*
8090    MREV.OTHSS(I) = MREV.OTHSS(I-1) * (1 + PCTMREV.OTHSS)
8100    MREV.INTGOVSS(I) = MREV.INTGOVSS(I-1) * (1 + PCTMREV.INTGOVSS)
8110    SREV.OTHSS(I) = SREV.OTHSS(I-1) * (1 + PCTSREV.OTHSS)
8120    SREV.INTGOVSS(I) = SREV.INTGOVSS(I-1) * (1 + PCTSREV.INTGOVSS)
8130 '
8140 '
8150 ' * Calculate current non-property steady state revenues*
8160    MREV.NONPROPSS(I) = MREV.OTHSS(I) + MREV.INTGOVSS(I)
8170    SREV.NONPROPSS(I) = SREV.OTHSS(I) + SREV.INTGOVSS(I)
8180 '
8190 '
8200 ' * Calculate non-property revenues from development*
8210    MREV.NONPROPDEV(I) = MREV.OTHDEV(I) + MREV.INTGOVDEV(I)
8220    SREV.NONPROPDEV(I) = SREV.OTHDEV(I) + SREV.INTGOVDEV(I)
```

Exhibit 7-10, continued

```
8230 '
8240 '
8250 ' *Calculate total nonproperty revenues*
8260    MREV.NONPROP(I) = MREV.NONPROPDEV(I) + MREV.NONPROPSS(I)
8270    SREV.NONPROP(I) = SREV.NONPROPDEV(I) + SREV.NONPROPSS(I)
8280 '
8300 RETURN
8310 '
9000 ' *******************
9010 ' * Tax rate model *
9020 ' *******************
9030 '
9040    MTAXRT(I) = (MEXP(I) - MREV.NONPROP(I))/ VALTOT(I)
9050    STAXRT(I) = (SEXP(I) - SREV.NONPROP(I))/ VALTOT(I)
9060 '
9070 RETURN
9080 '
10000 ' **************************
10010 ' * GENERAL REVENUE MODEL *
10020 ' **************************
10030 '
10040 ' *Calculate property revenues from development*
10050    MREV.PROPDEV(I) = VALDEV(I) * MTAXRT(I)
10060    SREV.PROPDEV(I) = VALDEV(I) * STAXRT(I)
10070 '
10080 ' *Calculate steady state property revenues*
10090    MREV.PROPSS(I) = VALSS(I) * MTAXRT(I)
10100    SREV.PROPSS(I) = VALSS(I) * STAXRT(I)
10110 '
10120 ' * Calculate total development revenues*
10130    MREV.DEV(I) = MREV.PROPDEV(I) + MREV.NONPROPDEV(I)
10140    SREV.DEV(I) = SREV.PROPDEV(I) + SREV.NONPROPDEV(I)
10150 '
10160 ' * Calculate total steady state revenues*
10170    MREV.SS(I) = MREV.PROPSS(I) + MREV.NONPROPSS(I)
10180    SREV.SS(I) = SREV.PROPSS(I) + SREV.NONPROPSS(I)
10190 '
10200 ' *Calculate total revenues*
10210    MREV(I) = MREV.DEV(I) + MREV.SS(I)
10220    SREV(I) = SREV.DEV(I) + SREV.SS(I)
10230 RETURN
20000 ' *****************
20010 ' * PRINT ROUTINE *
20020 ' *****************
20030 '
20040 CLS
20050 PRINT TAB(7); "Municipal"; TAB(22); "Municipal"; TAB(37); "School";
      TAB(52); "School"; TAB(67); "Value of"
20060 PRINT "Years"; TAB(7); "Expenditures"; TAB(22); "Tax Rate"; TAB(37);
      Expenditures"; TAB(52); "Tax Rate"; TAB(67); "New Project"
20070 PRINT
```

Exhibit 7-10, continued

```
20080      FOR I = 0 TO NUMYEARS
20090         PRINT I;
20100         PRINT TAB(7);
20110         PRINT USING ",";MEXP(I);
20120         PRINT TAB(22);
20130         PRINT USING ".#";MTAXRT(I);
20140         PRINT TAB(37);
20150         PRINT USING ",";SEXP(I);
20160         PRINT TAB(52);
20170         PRINT USING ".#";STAXRT(I);
20180         PRINT TAB(67);
20190         PRINT USING ",";VALDEV(I)
20200      NEXT I
20210 '
20220 RETURN
```

in lines 8210 to 8270. These are revenues from fees extracted from developers and the like. This program as written makes **no** current provision for entering any data into this section, but it could be easily added to the project data input subroutine.

9000-9080   The tax rate calculation model.

10000-10230   The revenue calculation model. Note that the non-property revenues (lines 8000-8310) must be calculated before the tax rate model (lines 9000-9080). An examination of the tax rate equation (lines 9040 and 9050) tells why.

20000-20230   A very straightforward printing routine which could be greatly expanded. Recall that a ";" at the end of the line means that the next PRINT line following will be printed on the same line of the output as the previous one.

The program is extensive but easy to grasp in terms of the straightforward calculations which are carried out. Many modeling efforts will have more complex mathematical bases. However, the modeling of a time-series process such as is done here will face many of the same issues — the use of arrays, the concern with carrying data between time periods, and the use of copious INPUT statements. The reader should take time to understand the structure of the program and consider ways of improving it. For example, can a way be found to enter expected developer contributions into the non-property revenue calculations?

The Interface between BASIC and Electronic Spreadsheets

The lengthy input process found in the fiscal impact model raises the issue of alternative ways of entering data into a BASIC model. One clear method is to use the electronic spreadsheet for inputting data and then transferring it to the BASIC program. In the case of the fiscal impact model, one might well do the entire model as a spreadsheet. However, other models in areas such as land use or transportation, such as the one by Lowry, would need to be transferred to a BASIC program.

It is possible to transfer data between BASIC and an electronic spreadsheet. Ideally, a translation program would not be needed. However, while BASIC can directly read "comma delimited" form, Lotus 1-2-3 does not produce it. A comma delimited form means that each datum in a record is separated by a comma. Lotus 1-2-3 instead produces a print file with blanks as separators.

There is an easy solution — Data Interchange Format (DIF). Originally developed by the original sellers of VisiCalc and promulgated by Software Arts, Inc., DIF is a rather strange file format which is both produced and read by Lotus 1-2-3 and other spreadsheets. An extensive discussion of the DIF format is found in Kalish and Mayer (1981). A simple BASIC program converts a worksheet written in DIF into a matrix in BASIC as shown in Exhibit 7-11 below.

Given the matrix of towns and populations entered into a spreadsheet shown in Exhibit 7-12, the data can be extracted from the spreadsheet without the labels and a DIF file created. The extracted data area is highlighted in black. Lotus 1-2-3 requires that the matrix be saved in the usual way, and the reader is forewarned that the process, albeit simple, must be followed correctly.

Given this input, the actual DIF file created by the spreadsheet program would look like Exhibit 7-13 if examined using an editor or word processor. The header section indicates the number of rows and columns in the matrix. The data section contains the tuples, marked "BOT." Careful comparison between the spreadsheet matrix in Exhibit 7-12 and the DIF file listing shows how the data are transferred into the DIF format.

The BASIC program listing in Exhibit 7-11 will turn the DIF

Exhibit 7-11

Listing, a DIF File Read Program in BASIC

```
10000 '******* Program to read a dif file created by a spreadsheet
10010 '
10015 DIM MATRX$(20,20) ' Set MATRX$ to the appropriate size
10020   CLS
10030   PRINT "This program reads a DIF file from a spreadsheet into"
10040   PRINT "  a string matrix (MATRX$) in BASIC. The spreadsheet file"
10050   PRINT "  MUST be saved by the spreadsheet as a DIF
10060 '
10070       INPUT "Name of file ";INDIF$
10080       OPEN INDIF$ FOR INPUT AS #1
10090 ' Read header of DIF file
10100       INPUT #1, TITLE$
10110       INPUT #1,TYPE,NUMBER
10120       INPUT #1,STRNG$
10130 '
10140       IF TITLE$="VECTORS" THEN VECTORS=NUMBER
10150       IF TITLE$="TUPLES" THEN TUPLES=NUMBER
10160       IF TITLE$="DATA" THEN GOTO 10250  'Header done - Data next
10170       GOTO 10100
10180 '
10250 FOR ROW = 1 TO TUPLES 'Tuples = Rows in MATRX$
10260       INPUT #1,TYPE,NUMBER 'Read BOT (Beginning of tuple)
10270       INPUT #1,STRNG$
10280             FOR COL = 1 TO VECTORS 'Vectors = Columns in MATRX$
10290                 INPUT #1, TYPE,NUMBER
10300                 INPUT #1,STRNG$
10310                     IF TYPE = 0 THEN MATRX$(ROW,COL) = STR$(NUMBER)
10320                     IF TYPE = 1 THEN MATRX$(ROW,COL) = STRNG$
10330             NEXT COL
10340 NEXT ROW
10350 '
10360       CLOSE #1 ' The translation is over
```

Exhibit 7-12
Spreadsheet Data for DIF Transfer

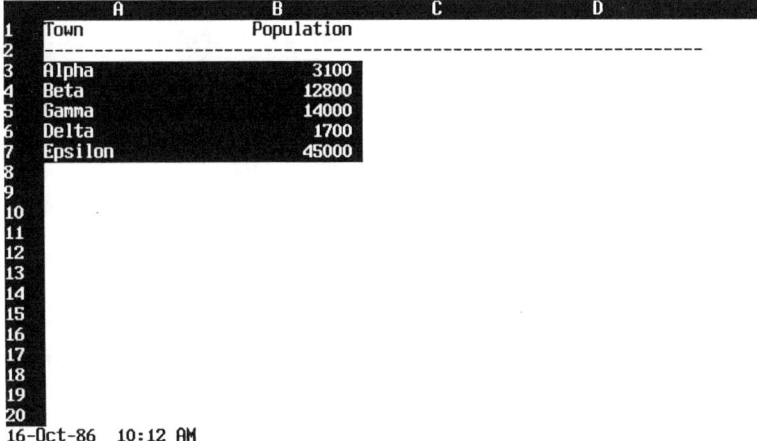

Exhibit 7-13
The DIF File Listing

TABLE	0,12800
0,1	V
""	-1,0
VECTORS	BOT
0,2	1,0
""	"Gamma"
TUPLES	0,1400
0,5	V
""	-1,0
DATA	BOT
0,0	1,0
""	"Delta"
-1,0	0,1700
BOT	V
1,0	-1,0
"Alpha"	BOT
0,3100	1,0
V	"Epsilon
-1,0	0,45000
BOT	V
1,0	-1,0
"Beta "	EOD

file in Exhibit 7-13 into a string array called MATRX$ which can be used in a BASIC program. The program line numbers begin at 10000 so that the program can be inserted as a subroutine with any necessary changes into a larger program. The output matrix is a string array so that either string or numeric data can be entered. You will recall that a string can be converted to a real number by using the VAL function. This means that the MATRX$ array is simply a holding pen from which the programmer will extract the needed data to be placed into the appropriate place in the program. This also means that the DIF subroutine could be used many times in the same program as long as MATRX$ is dimensioned for the largest matrix which will be entered.

Pascal: A Programming Alternative

The second most popular programming language among microcomputer users is Pascal. Developed by Niklaus Wirth, Pascal achieved popularity in the 1970's among microcomputer users because it was the main programming of the UCSD p-System developed at the University of California at San Diego. As outlined in Chapter 3, Pascal was a two-level compiler. The Pascal "source" code, the language one wrote in, was compiled into "pseudo-code," which approximated generic machine-level instruction code. This meant that a run-time compiler which converted this pseudo-code into a machine-specific instruction set was needed. This approach was done for transportability. All that was needed for any particular microprocessor was the run-time compiler. This meant that a p-System Pascal program written for an Apple II micro could be moved to an IBM PC if a run-time compiler were available, although these two computers possessed highly dissimilar microprocessor instruction sets. At one time in the early 1980's, the U.S. Department of Transportation required microcomputer projects which were funded to be written in UCSD Pascal specifically because of the implied portability.

The popularity of Pascal was furthered with the development of Turbo Pascal by Borland International, an inexpensive Pascal editor and compiler available for the IBM Personal Computer and compatibles. The price, the ease of use, and the speed of Turbo-Pascal have made it a favorite. Pascal is an ideal teaching language, stressing the concepts of structured programming.

One easy way to see the advantages and the rigors of Pascal is to examine the linear model program presented in BASIC (Exhibit 7-5) now re-programmed in Pascal. The Pascal version is in Exhibit 7-14. There are a number of general observations about the structure of the linear model Pascal program. First, the program is preceded by a declaration of all variables as either real, integer or arrays. No variable can be used without this declaration. Real, integer, and arrays are program-declared data types and were found in BASIC. However, one of the powers of Pascal is the ability to declare user-defined data types. Thus "Day" declared as a type might take on only the values Monday, Tuesday, up to Saturday. Beyond the scope of the discussion here, this concept of user-defined types bears study if one learns Pascal.

Second, Pascal allows great flexibility in program appearance and emphasizes clarity of presentation. There are no line numbers in Pascal. One usually cannot "GOTO" another part of the program. Modular programming attempts to avoid extended branching back and forth in a program, sometimes labeled "spaghetti code." Eliminating the GOTO does a great deal for clarity. Also, the program lines can be spaced so that they can be easily read.

Third, the linear model program in Pascal is structured in an inverted fashion relative to the BASIC version. In the BASIC version (Exhibit 7-5), the GOSUB's branch to subroutines **below** the main program found in lines 200 to 250. Pascal is exactly the opposite. The subroutines, called "procedures," are listed first, and are **above** the main program found at the bottom of Exhibit 7-14.

Fourth, the distinction in the meaning of the equal sign between equality and replacement is made explicitly in Pascal. Note that in Procedure DataInput the "=" is replaced with a ":=" in the loop beginning:

$$\text{For } I := 1 \text{ to N do}$$

where the ":=" means replacement, or assignment, rather than equality.

Finally, note the use of Begin and End. Pascal is best thought of as a series of single or compound statements bounded by a Begin and an End. Each statement in a procedure ends with a semicolon as seen in Procedure Initialization. However, even compound statements within a loop are bounded by a Begin and an End, as can be seen in Procedure DataInput. The main program itself at the bottom of the listing is also bounded by a Begin and an End.

Once the user is aware of these differences, he or she should

Exhibit 7-14

Listing, Linear Model in Pascal

```pascal
Program Linear;
{Comments are found in curly brackets like these}
VAR
    Average, Change, Sum: Real;
    I, N, P, Intervals: Integer;
    Histdata, Futuredata: Array [1..20] of Real;

Procedure Initialization;
Begin
    Write ('How many historical periods? ');
    Readln (N);
    Writeln ('How many time periods into the future');
    Writeln ('  do you want to project? ');
    Readln (P);
End;

Procedure DataInput;
Begin
    For I := 1 to N do
        Begin
            Writeln ('What is the value in Period ', I);
            Readln (Histdata[I]);
        End;
End;

Procedure Linear;
Begin
{Calculate total change in data over past historical periods}
    Intervals := N-1;
    Sum := 0;
    For I := 1 to Intervals do
        Begin
            Change := Histdata[I+1] - Histdata[I];
            Sum := Sum + Change;
        End;

{Calculate average change}
    Average := Sum / Intervals;

{Project the data for P periods into the future}
    For I := 1 to P do
        Futuredata[I] := Histdata[N] + (Average * I);
End;

Procedure DataOutput;
Begin
    Writeln;
    Writeln ('Time Period     Value');
    For I := 1 to P do
```

Exhibit 7-14, continued

```
        Writeln (N+I:8,Futuredata[I]:14:0);
End;

{*********** Main Program *************}
Begin
    Initialization;
    DataInput;
    Linear;
    DataOutput;
End.
```

find the Pascal program itself very understandable. It follows exactly the modular structure of the BASIC version, using the same logic and the same variable names. However, much more thought must go into the program before writing it, including a specification of all variables and a good sense of the structure. In reading the program, note that Pascal uses "Writeln" for PRINT, and "Readln" for INPUT.

Conclusion

This chapter only briefly touches on Pascal while focusing on structured BASIC because of its ubiquity. It has been shown, however, that a program in structured BASIC can be translated into Pascal. There are extensive options available which build on BASIC as a development environment. Microsoft has introduced QuickBASIC, while Summit Software has BetterBASIC. John Kemeny and Thomas Kurtz, the inventors of the original version, have introduced TrueBASIC. All three are structured versions of the BASIC presented earlier here, with compiled code for speed, optional line numbers, modular design, and the various elements of a structured language like Pascal. If the decision has been to stay with BASIC, then these packages will make programming simpler and produce a faster, more legible product.

The budding programmer can select an alternative stream using Pascal as a base. Wirth, the inventor of Pascal, has introduced Modula-2, a more powerful structured programming language. Modula-2 permits very complex programs to be constructed using "modules" which are a revised version of procedures in Pascal (Wirth, 1985; Christian, 1986; Gleaves, 1984). One involved in a serious programming effort may look to Modula-2 as an option because of the potential of fitting together many modules through the appropriate importing and exporting of information. Modula-2 may become as popular as Pascal if reasonably cheap and easy-to-use compilers become available. One current version by Logitech costs less than $100 for a basic system.

Finally, there is C, a compact, powerful and highly portable language which is widely used in the development of application programs. It is the current choice of many programmers and is available for a wide range of microcomputers. However, there are few restrictions on programmers in terms of what can be done. The basic syntax of C is terse compared with Pascal. Kernighan and Ritchie (1978) wrote the classic text, while others have provided various introductions (Hancock and Krieger, 1982; Kochan, 1983; Plum, 1983). Recently, C++ has been introduced as a superset of C, and contains a set of new language constructs and support for "object-oriented programming."

These are three main streams which a planner or manager can take in programming. The choice is a function of the extent of the intended use, the organizational environment, and the programs which one will be using or will contract out to a consultant. If the tasks are simple, then BASIC is perfectly appropriate. If one is contemplating a complex regional simulation model which will be maintained over a number of years, then the verbosity and legibility of Pascal and Modula-2 become important considerations. These two languages are easy to read and to maintain.

C becomes an option in an environment of other C programmers and programs. Much of the current graphics and mapping software is written in C. However, the compactness which is C's virtue means that updating and maintaining the programs over time may be hard because the program is difficult to understand. C can be written in a verbose manner, but the question is whether or not the programmer will take the time to write understandable code. Programmers, like urban planners and managers, are not immortal and do change jobs. The worst case is to be left with a complex program which no one understands.

In the final analysis, many planners and managers may never write a program. However, everyone will use them and some will develop specifications for the writing of a program by a consultant. In any case, we will all be touched by computer programs in the profession.

Suggested Further Reading

Ottensmann, John R. 1985. *BASIC Microcomputer Programs for Urban Analysis and Planning*. New York: Chapman and Hall.

8

File and Database Management

Introduction

The planner or manager can accomplish a great deal with electronic spreadsheets or original programs. However, there are often situations where she or he would like to electronically store, recall, and update information. This process of information storage and retrieval can be classified under the general terms, file management and database management. File management is the simpler concept. A file management system (FMS) permits a user to store, manipulate, and retrieve a single set of data. Sometimes, a microcomputer-based file management system can permit multiple files of data to be merged into a new file. However, in general, an FMS is involved at a basic level with manipulating a single file.

For example, a planner or manager might wish to keep track of local publicly funded capital projects. For example, there is a federal requirement that states and localities maintain a five-year transportation improvement program updated on a yearly basis. This listing of projects must be classified by federal aid category and funding level by year so that overall expenditures for the state or region can be monitored. Such a federal requirement can be easily satisfied with a file management program available on a microcomputer.

Alternatively, a federal or state agency might have overall responsibility for allocating funds for a wide range of projects within its region. For example, a state parks department might have jurisdiction over all construction and maintenance projects funded with state dollars. Each project might have its own completion date, might require periodic progress reports, and could be geographically dispersed. If the monitoring process is kept simple, a file management system could be designed to update and monitor these projects easily. A simple, widely available, and inexpensive file management system, PC-FILE III, will be presented in this chapter.

A database management system (DBMS) is more complex and more powerful than a file management system. Essentially, a DBMS is a software system which can encompass a set of different files within a common framework, permitting complex operations to be done across these multiple data sets. In the transportation improvement program example above, a single file of highway projects could be entered and maintained on a file management system. However, what if we wished to integrate this file, called TIP, with others in a county system? The county might have a file of coded highway links, labeled NETWORK, for use in transportation planning activities. A general transportation planning model was discussed in an earlier chapter on electronic spreadsheets. Could not the TIP file be related to the NETWORK file, so that the construction and upgrading of highway projects could be located geographically and so that any change in highway characteristics — for example, the number of lanes — could be put into the NETWORK file? This linking of two files becomes best handled by a properly structured database management system.

Unfortunately, there are definitional ambiguities in the file management and database management areas. There are two basic components of a file — fields and records. The most elementary unit is called a **data element** or **field**. These are the individual pieces such as the name, description, or cost of a particular project. In some database literature, a field is known as an **attribute**, a characteristic of some object. In turn, fields, or data elements, are parts of a **record**. A record is a set of fields which describes some entity. Sometimes, records are called segments or tuples. We will generally use field and record in this presentation.

In our state park agency example, any construction or maintenance project is a record. These project records contain fields describing the projects. Records are grouped into a **file**. Hence, all the projects under the jurisdiction of the state parks agency might make up the construction and maintenance file. Different files will generally be of different **record types**, meaning that the set of fields contained would vary. In the transportation improvement program example, two files which would be included are TIP, the listing of all transportation improvement projects in the county, and NETWORK, a listing of all highway links. Each would be a different type of record. In general, a database would be structured as shown in Exhibit 8-1. Note that the files would contain different record types. A well-designed DBMS would be able to permit extensive interaction among files while limiting the amount of redundant information stored.

Exhibit 8-1

A General Representation of a Database

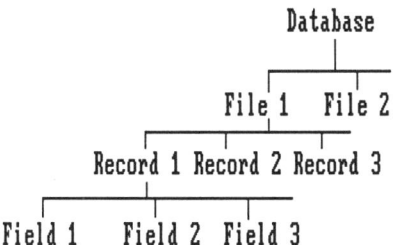

The state park example will be explored in more detail as we examine how a file manager is constructed. A more extensive database system will be developed with the transportation improvement project example.

The Functions of a File or Database Manager

There are five main tasks which the user can carry out with a file management system. These five activities are common to both file management and to DBMS. However, the additional robustness and complexity of a DBMS will be discussed after the topic is introduced later. The five primary tasks are:

1. Creating a file or database
2. Maintaining the file or database with periodic updating
3. Querying the file or database to answer some question
4. Mathematically manipulating the file
5. Printing a summary report

The first task is to **create the file or set of files**. All file managers and database systems have data entry provisions. Typically, data can be directly entered into files from the keyboard, imported from other programs such as an electronic spreadsheet, or "downloaded" from larger computer systems into microcomputer files readable by the database program.

The second task, **maintaining the file**, means either that the file can have additional records placed in it or that any record can be changed given new information. While file and database management software vary in procedure, each will allow a record to be called up and changed. Also, records can be appended to the end of the file.

It is also possible to **ask questions of the file or database** about the information contained. For example, we might be interested in finding out how many projects cost more than $100,000 or have due dates within two months of the current date. Simple file managers and complex database systems, as well as spreadsheets with database functions, such as Lotus 1-2-3, can do this. In DBMS programs a "query language" is often used which allows these questions to be framed in structured phrases. There is continual research into developing query languages which will approximate natural speech and make the use of DBMS easier.

There is the capacity to **do mathematical operations** on files also. In a database program which we will examine, dBASE III PLUS, a procedure can be written which will do mathematical operations. This procedure is a program written in special dBASE language and is stored as a command file which can be run like a BASIC program. Also, one can easily use most file managers and DBMS to do simple calculations such as a summation of project costs. Of course, it is easy to do mathematics in a spreadsheet which is used as a file manager.

Finally, one can **generate reports**. File managers, database managers, and enhanced spreadsheets such as Lotus 1-2-3 have various levels of report-generating capacity. One important element of file organization is "sorting" data in order by alphabetic or numeric fields. For example, we might want to sort the projects in the state park example by dollar amount within counties. DBMS programs and file managers usually offer two options when doing sorting on a field of data — indexing or actual sorts. Indexing is usually preferred because it is more efficient. When indexing, only the selected field is sorted and stored in a special file along with the number of the record. The records themselves remain where they were in the file on disk. This is faster than actual sorting in which the records are physically rearranged on the disk. Both indexed and sorted files can produce reports ordered by the field or fields selected.

There are wide variations in how different microcomputer file and database management programs handle these assorted tasks. Most simple file managers are reasonably easy to understand. Since many file management needs are relatively straightforward in public sector planning and programming activities, it is appropriate to discuss them first.

A Simple File Manager

The General Concept

There are three general ways in which simple file management can be done on a microcomputer at this time. First, there are a number of file management programs which have been developed. These are straightforward software packages which permit easy access to a single file of data. Second, some electronic spreadsheet packages, such as Lotus 1-2-3, contain a simple file management capacity. Third, there are the continually refining sets of integrated packages, such as Framework, Ability, or Enable which combine spreadsheet, file management, word processing, and other functions within a single software package. We will focus on the first two of these file management options — a simple file manager, PC-FILE III, and a spreadsheet with database functions, Lotus 1-2-3.

The file manager, PC-FILE III, is an example of an interesting phenomenon called "shareware." The program offers the package to the general public initially either free or for a modest cost, usually permitting the program to be copied and disseminated to others for evaluation. If the user is happy with the package, then he or she is asked to send a modest contribution to the program developer.

PC-FILE III is an example of a menu-driven program. The opening menu of the program is shown in Exhibit 8-2. The options shown on the screen include some of the traditional elements of a database management system. They are the ability to:

1. Enter data into the fields of a record (ADD)
2. Retrieve a particular record for examination (DISplay or FINd), or modify it (MODify)
3. List a particular set of records on the computer screen, on the printer, or to disk (LISt)

218   *File and Database Management*

4. Sort records alphabetically or numerically (SORt)

This program is particularly easy to use without the need for much instruction. The "F" indicators, such as F1 or F2, are function key indicators on an IBM configuration personal computer keyboard. The "Alt" reference refers to the Alt key on the keyboard.

Exhibit 8-2

The Opening Menu of PC-FILE III

C:PARKS 0 records, disk can hold approx. 32767 more.

```
F1 ADD - Add       a record    | [Alt]F1 BIN - Set binary search on/off
F2 MOD - Modify    a record    | [Alt]F2 GLO - Global update or delete
F3 DEL - Delete    a record    | [Alt]F3 KEY - Set up the smart keys
F4 DIS - Display   a record    | [Alt]F4 NAM - Alter field name or mask
F5 FIN - Find      a record    |
F6 LIS - List or clone         |
F7 SOR - Sort the index        |
F8 UTI - Utilities             |
F9 MEN - Show smart key menu   | [Alt]F9 END - Quit or change database
```

Please press the appropriate function key,
or supply one of the 3-character commands ▶FIN◀

The State Park Example

The state park example can be put into PC-FILE III. The construction and maintenance file might look like Exhibit 8-3. In this file of projects there are four records. Each record consist of seven fields or data elements. The fields represent various kinds of information about the particular record. There is a project number, an indication of whether the project is a construction (Const) or maintenance (Maint) activity, and its name along with various attributes.

The state park construction and maintenance file can be represented in rows and columns as a matrix. Each row is a particular record and each column is a field within the records. This particular structure of rows and columns is sometimes called a "flat file," since it is a two-dimensional matrix. Flat files can be easily represented in a spreadsheet format, as will be shown. Flat files are also useful in understanding **relational** database structures. Exhibit 8-3 contains an example of how one would conceptualize the state park example as a flat file.

Exhibit 8-3

The State Park File Database

Project Number	Type	Name	County	Completion Date	Cost
101	Const	Berry Creek	Salem	Oct. 1987	$100,000
105	Maint	Smithville Park	Atlantic	Jan. 1988	$230,000
109	Const	Elvira Pond	Salem	July 1989	$120,000
103	Const	Cast Iron Bog	Ocean	Dec. 1988	$23,000

To start the database creation process in PC-FILE III, the individual fields must be named and a length — the longest number of characters thought possible — must be determined. Depending on the particular database program used, the field name may have to be short. Even if the program does not require a short name, it is always best to be as brief as possible. You will often have to type in the field name for the different operations possible in a database. Typing in a long name, such as PROJECTNUMBER, is tedious, while PROJNUM is short and conveys the meaning of the field.

The length of the field is required by the program so that appropriate room can be set aside when the record is stored on disk or in memory. Essentially, we are dealing with fixed length records in which a field with 20 possible characters, for example, is stored with 20 available places. In our state park example, the fields in Exhibit 8-4 can be set up in PC-FILE III by using the ADD command.

Exhibit 8-4
The Field Definitions in the State Park File

Field Name	Length	Description
PROJNUM	8	Project number
TYPE	5	Project type
NAME	25	Project name
COUNTY	15	County location of project
MONTH	5	The year of expected completion
YEAR	4	The month of expected completion
COST#	9	The total expected cost

This record consists of 7 fields, totaling 71 characters in length. The number sign after COST indicates that this is a numeric field. The others are stored as characters, or what were called "strings" in BASIC. A variety of tasks can be done on this state park file. Exhibit 8-5 shows the screen in PC-FILE III for adding a record to the state park file. The user simply inserts the appropriate entry into the spaces next to the field label.

Exhibit 8-5
Adding a Record in PC-FILE III

```
ADDing at # 4                                                    ADD
PROJNUM    [103      ]
TYPE       [Const]
NAME       [Cast Iron Bog         ]
COUNTY     [Ocean         ]
MONTH      [12   ]
YEAR       [1988]
COST#      ▶23000    ◀




















To cancel, press (F10) if no data was entered, or (Esc) if data was entered
Enter data. Press (F10) when complete.
```

File and Database Management 221

The state park file can be both sorted and listed. In Exhibit 8-6 the file is listed as it would appear on the printed page. The file was sorted on two fields — YEAR and MONTH — before listing. The primary sort field was YEAR, ordering the records in ascending sequence from lower to higher number by year from 1987 to 1989. The secondary sort field then ordered the records by month from "01" to "12" within the year.

Exhibit 8-6

A List in PC-FILE III

```
                              State Park File
10-25-86 AT 2:50 p.m.                                              Page 1

PROJNUM   TYPE    NAME                    COUNTY          MONTH  YEAR   COST
-------   -----   ----------------------  ---------------  -----  ----  ---------

101       Const   Berry Creek             Salem              10   1987   100000

105       Maint   Smithville Park         Atlantic           01   1988   230000

103       Const   Cast Iron Bog           Ocean              12   1988    23000

109       Const   Elvira Pond             Salem              07   1989   120000

TOTALS
---------------------------
COST               473,000.00    118,250.000  AVG.
Printed 4 of the 4 records.
```

The Role of a File Management Program

A simple file manager is useful for relatively straightforward tasks involving a single dataset. It would be able to keep track of a capital improvement program or zoning and building permit data. Permits for development could be entered and updated in a file manager, with reports issued on a periodic basis. Some file management programs permit custom screen display so that the screen can be made to look like a paper form, making it easier for the inexperienced to use the system.

A file management program will usually contain the capacity to interchange data with other programs. PC-FILE III has the ability to read files from Lotus 1-2-3, other spreadsheets, and word processing programs. It also reads the DIF file format discussed in Chapter 7.

PC-FILE III can also write out files which other programs can use. This capacity is useful in the current microcomputing environment in which no single data storage format exists.

Using Spreadsheets as File Managers

It is also possible to use an electronic spreadsheet as a file manager. However, the spreadsheet must contain some simple file management tools, such as sorting and querying the flat file contained in the spreadsheet. Lotus 1-2-3, as well as other spreadsheet programs like Supercalc 4, contains sort and querying capacity. In the flat file concept, records are the rows and fields are the columns. Entering and changing data in a spreadsheet is straightforward. All that needs to be done is to move to the cell and change it. Records can simply be added anywhere in the file by inserting an empty row and filling it with the appropriate data.

The development of structured spreadsheet design was discussed in Chapter 5. Macros and the concept of a spreadsheet map were introduced at that time to show how one could conceptualize and navigate a large spreadsheet. Macros are very powerful and can be used quite readily in a file management context. The Smiley County Information System is a spreadsheet which uses macros to navigate, to enter data into an on-screen form, and to move the data from the form to the flat file. The flat file itself is a listing of the projects put into the spreadsheet through the data input form. Screen displays of the Information System file are shown in Exhibit 8-7. The two screens define an area from row 195 to row 214 and columns A to J. The file could extend downward as far as necessary to accommodate additional projects. Each capital improvement project record is a row in the file. The fields for each record include the project number, name, and a set of budget allocations by year. This file can be sorted by row using specified fields. It is possible to ask questions of the file using a query command in Lotus 1-2-3, although the process is more awkward than in a file manager such as PC-FILE III.

The opening menu of the Smiley County Information System spreadsheet is shown in Exhibit 8-8. The Alt-S macro (evoked by pressing the Alt and S keys) takes the user to the flat file in Exhibit 8-7. Other macros take the user to the variety of areas in the spreadsheet, including the listing of the macros used.

The spreadsheet map is shown in Exhibit 8-9. The example is

File and Database Management 223

Exhibit 8-7

The Screen Display of the Smiley County File

A196: [W12] READY

	A	B	C	D
195	CAPITAL IMPROVEMENT PROJECT DATABASE			
196				
197				
198	Project No.	Dept.	Project Name	1986
199	---	---	---	---
200	G657	Parks	Green Foote Hollow	0
201	R875	Roads	Million Dollar Highway	600,000
202	W129	Water	Smithville Bags	50,000
203	P341	Parks	Happy Turtle Bog	100,000
204	R124	Roads	Tory Bend Bridge	30,000
205	P453	Parks	Bliss Towers	10,000
206	S786	Sewers	Green Smitten	100,000
207				
208				
209				
210				
211				
212				
213				
214				

02-Feb-87   02:05 PM

E195: [W12] READY

	E	F	G	H	I	J
195						
196						
197						Inflated
198	1987	1988	1989	1990	Total	Total
199	---	---	---	---	---	---
200	0	4,000,000	0	0	4,000,000	5,038,848
201	300,000	0	0	0	900,000	997,920
202	0	0	200,000	80	250,080	326,215
203	200,000	0	0	0	300,000	341,280
204	230,000	0	0	0	260,000	300,672
205	120,000	13,000	0	0	143,000	167,144
206	20,000	40,000	30,000	50,000	240,000	295,998
207						
208						
209						
210						
211						
212						
213						
214						

02-Feb-87   02:05 PM

Exhibit 8-8

The Opening Menu of the Smiley County Spreadsheet

```
A1: [W12] '                                                    READY
```

```
             A         B              C                      D
      1
      2              SMILEY TOWNSHIP INFORMATION SYSTEM
      3
      4              CAPITAL IMPROVEMENT PROGRAM
      5
      6                        MENU
      7              -------------------------------------
      8
      9
     10              ALT-I    Enter project into form
     11
     12              ALT-M    Return to menu
     13
     14              ALT-S    Shows database
     15
     16              ALT-P    Change inflation factor
     17
     18  Map macros: ALT-N    Macro instructions
     19              ALT-D    Description of spreadsheet
     20              ALT-R    Description of range names
     26-Oct-86  08:27 PM
```

Exhibit 8-9

The Smiley County Spreadsheet Map

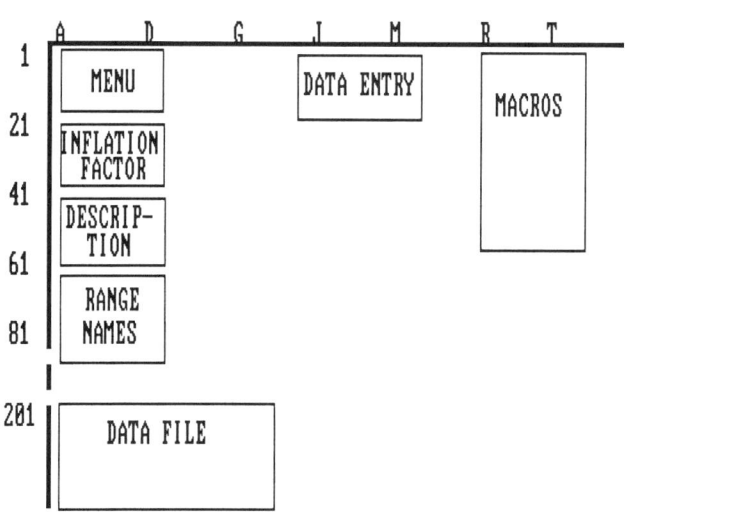

simple but suggests the use of a spreadsheet like Lotus 1-2-3 as a file manager. The spreadsheet is divided into a number of distinct areas. The worksheet when loaded will show the menu in the top left-hand corner. This menu will branch to a variety of tasks depending on user preference. Alt-I will permit the user to enter data into a form which has been created on the screen. Alt-P takes the user to the parameter area; in this case, only an inflation factor to be applied to future expenditures is included. Alt-M always brings up this menu, while Alt-N will bring up the macro area. Alt-R shows the description of range names, while Alt-D shows a simple description of spreadsheet purposes and design.

The interesting twist in this spreadsheet is the use of a data entry form to put information into the flat file. A special menu has been created with macros as part of the data input process. The data input portion of the spreadsheet is shown in Exhibit 8-10. There is a custom menu shown at the top of the data input form which was created through a macro. The "Put" command will transfer the data in the entry form to the "DATA FILE" starting at row 200 (Exhibit 8-9). The unsophisticated user has only to fill in the form which is transferred automatically to the flat file below without having to know a great deal about Lotus 1-2-3.

Exhibit 8-10
Data Input Form, Smiley County Spreadsheet

```
J1: [W12] 'CAPITAL IMPROVEMENT PROJECT -- DATA ENTRY FORM                    MENU
Continue  Put  Erase  Leave  Show
Put record in database
           J           K              L                        M
  1    CAPITAL IMPROVEMENT PROJECT -- DATA ENTRY FORM
  2    **************************************************
  3    Name of CIP Project >>> Green Foote Hollow
  4
  5    Project No. G657         Operating Department >>>>>>  Parks
  6
  7
  8    Projected Expenditures by Year
  9                 Dollars
 10       FY 86 >>           0
 11       FY 87 >>           0
 12       FY 88 >>     1,000,000
 13       FY 89 >>           0
 14       FY 90 >>           0
 15    ----------------------------------------------------------------
 16    Note: ENTER will bring up menu of options
 17          Ctrl-Break will take you out of the macro
 18
 19
 20
28-Oct-86  01:23 PM                          CMD                        CAPS
```

Overall, the example is simple but the idea is powerful. A command-driven program, Lotus 1-2-3, has been made more friendly through a menu-driven overlay. A spreadsheet program has been made into a simple file manager with a custom data entry form. The complete spreadsheet listing is shown in the Appendix. In the spreadsheet listing, the macros used to set up the data entry system are shown to illustrate the flexibility of a spreadsheet program with macro capability.

Database Management Systems

While dealing with a single file is appropriate for many planning and policy analysis situations, some situations will require the manipulation of multiple files in a broader database system. The growing sophistication of users and the rapidly developing technology mean that more complex problems will be tackled. A number of alternative database models have been developed for microcomputer applications. Holsapple (1984) lists five database models — relational, hierarchical, shallow-network, CODASYL-network, and postrelational or extended-network. The one which has achieved the widest recognition at the microcomputer level is the relational database model. Popularized in such versions as the dBASE family of programs, as well as R:base and Oracle, the relational model is intuitively simple while potentially very powerful. The relational model will be presented in detail followed by a brief introduction to dBASE III PLUS, a relational database program.

Before introducing the relational model, it is important to note that a program like dBASE III PLUS can be used as a single file manager. In this context, it is a more powerful (and more expensive) replacement for PC-FILE III. In fact, it is quite common to use dBASE III PLUS, and programs of similar complexity, on single files because of their increased power and flexibility. These more powerful programs offer a programming language of their own, have extensive file handling capacity, and can handle complex queries of the database.

The Relational Model

Introduction

The most widely used database model is the relational design. Introduced by E.F. Codd in 1970, the model is intuitive and easily understood. Most importantly, the relational model is highly flexible in terms of potential use. The model allows the user to ask a wide range of questions of one or more files in a database. These files are viewed as "flat files," in which the records are rows and the fields are columns. It has already been demonstrated that an electronic spreadsheet like Lotus 1-2-3 can be used as a simple file manager by viewing data in the flat file format.

The Transportation Improvement Program Example

The presentation of the conceptual basis of the relational model is best done in terms of a multiple file example. A transportation improvement program (TIP) is a list of all federally sponsored transportation projects. All states and metropolitan areas are required to set up these TIP's to receive federal dollars, and TIP's, in fact, are set up for counties. Let us set up a TIP database for a county with four communities — Alpha, Beta, Gamma and Delta. This database will contain four files — a TIP file (TIP), a highway network file (NETWORK), a file of highway links which will be affected by each TIP project (LINKSET), and a municipality file (MUNI). The structure of the database is shown in Exhibit 8-11.

Exhibit 8-11

The Structure of the TIP Database

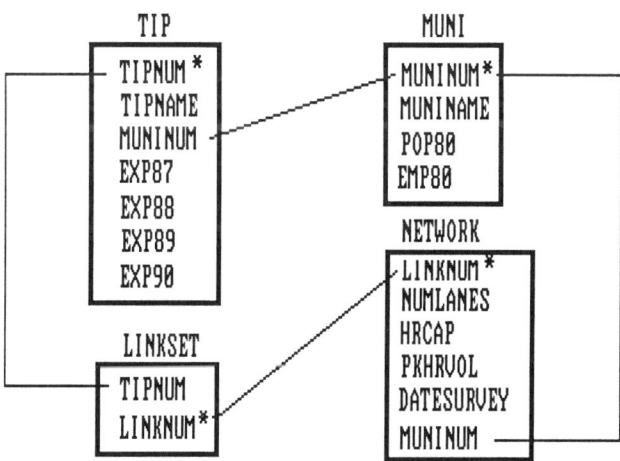

The primary key field is indicated by an "*." This key field is used as a unique identifier of the file and the connection between files.

The TIP file uses TIPNUM, the number of the TIP project, as the primary key field. Also found in the TIP file are fields such TIP-NAME, the name of the project, MUNINUM, the number of the municipality, and data on yearly expenditures (EXP87 to EXP90). The actual data for three projects is found in Exhibit 8-12. In a real situation this data would be greatly expanded to include funding by type of source — federal, state, local, etc. — and a more definitive project description. The first project, the Route 31 widening, will improve a heavily traveled roadway by increasing the lanes from 2 to 4. The second project, the Red Hill Road intersection, will straighten out the road at a dangerous crossing and provide a blinker light. The third, the Mud Creek bridge, will replace a wooden bridge with one of modern design. The expenditures will occur in different years across the 1987-90 period.

Exhibit 8-12

The TIP File Data

TIPNUM	TIPNAME	MUNINUM	EXP87	EXP88	EXP89	EXP90
86-31	Route 31 widening	0901	100000	20000	0	0
86-45	Red Hill Rd. int.	0901	100000	0	0	0
86-68	Mud Creek bridge	0904	0	200000	1200000	100000

The NETWORK file contains data on the different highway links in the county system. The primary field is LINKNUM, a unique identifier which has wide use in planning applications. It can be recalled from the discussion of the urban transportation planning example in Chapter 5 that any link in a highway network can be uniquely numbered. As shown in Exhibit 8-13, a link identifier consists of a beginning node and an ending node. Thus, the LINKNUM 101-102 identifies the link between nodes 101 and 102. There are 25 links in this network located in our four communities of Alpha, Beta, Gamma and Delta. NETWORK also contains data on each link, including hourly design capacity (HRCAP) and actual surveyed counts of peak hour flow (PKHRVOL) along with the date on which the last traffic survey was taken. Other attributes could have been included, such as roadway classification — arterials, expressways, collectors and the like. Usually, such a file contains roads in the county highway system which serve as primary carriers of traffic or feeders to these primary roads: purely local streets are not included in such a file. Also the municipal code (MUNINUM) is included as a field permitting us to develop relations back to the entire MUNI file, as we shall see.

Exhibit 8-13

The NETWORK File Data

LINKNUM	NUMLANES	HRCAP	PKHRVOL	DATESURVEY	MUNINUM
101-102	2	1000	300	19860623	0901
102-103	2	1200	400	19850319	0901
103-104	2	1000	200	19850319	0901
104-116	2	1000	500	19840623	0901
104-105	2	1000	400	19850623	0901
101-117	2	1200	600	19850821	0902
117-118	4	3000	2100	19860820	0902
118-119	2	1400	1000	19860820	0902
105-107	2	1000	300	19860415	0901
106-107	2	1000	300	19860416	0901
106-108	2	1000	300	19860430	0901
108-109	2	1000	200	19850801	0904
109-111	2	1200	400	19860720	0904
109-110	2	600	400	19860721	0904
111-114	2	1200	500	19860712	0901
114-118	2	1200	600	19850620	0902
102-104	2	1000	400	19850516	0901
105-106	2	1000	400	19860518	0901
116-117	2	1000	500	19840331	0902
105-124	2	1000	400	19860521	0901
113-118	4	4000	1600	19860601	0902
113-121	4	4000	1400	19860603	0903
121-122	4	4000	1200	19860606	0903
119-120	3	1200	600	19850715	0903
120-123	3	1200	400	19850712	0903

This NETWORK file is potentially useful in a full-blown computerized transportation planning model in which traffic is assigned to links in the network by means of a mathematical algorithm. Ideally, the simple DBMS proposed here could be expanded to actually assess the effects of a highway investment program on congestion and traffic flows in the county by connecting the TIP file with the NETWORK file.

The MUNI file contains all the municipalities in the county, with an identification code (MUNINUM), name and two demographic variables — population and employment — for each. Exhibit 8-14 shows the data for the four communities. This file could contain a much broader range of descriptors in an actual application.

Exhibit 8-14
The MUNI File Data

MUNINUM	MUNINAME	POP80	EMP80
0901	Alpha	3500	2000
0902	Beta	17800	8000
0903	Delta	33000	15000
0904	Gamma	2200	1000

Finally, the LINKSET file contains the links affected by each TIP project. This file has an interesting structure because of the nature of the problem. A particular transportation improvement project might encompass a number of different transportation links. This can be seen in Exhibit 8-15 which displays the 5 records in the LINKSET file. Note that the TIP project, 86-45, the intersection improvement on Red Hill Road, will affect 3 links — 105-106, 106-108, and 106-107. The file exhibits redundancy — a relational database characteristic — in that the 86-45 project is repeated 3 times. The need for this redundancy in the file structure will be better understood when we later discuss the conceptual basis of the relational model.

Exhibit 8-15
The LINKSET File Data

TIPNUM	LINKNUM
86-31	101-117
86-45	105-106
86-45	106-108
86-45	106-107
86-68	109-110

File and Database Management 231

As will be seen in a subsequent section, the core of the relational database model is the implementation of the connections between the files. These four files are related by key fields which are repeated across files. As has been suggested, the key field is the one by which the file is usually accessed, or identified in the database. The key field in the TIP file is TIPNUM. For NETWORK the key field is LINKNUM, and for MUNI it is MUNINUM. The key field in the LINKSET file is LINKNUM.

Using dBASE III PLUS

Introduction

There are a number of relationships which can be set up using these four data files from the transportation problem. To illustrate we will use dBASE III PLUS, a highly popular database program which is based on the relational model. This program is the most popular microcomputer database program available even though the language and structure are sometimes arcane. This current version of dBASE (there are earlier dBASE II and dBASE III versions) contains a rich variety of ways in which the data can be manipulated. There are four major ways of using dBASE III PLUS.

1. There is a menu-driven structured Assistant with tree-structured commands similar to electronic spreadsheets such as Lotus 1-2-3.
2. There is the capacity to use a well-developed command language, such as LIST or DISPLAY, at period prompts.
3. One can actually program in dBASE III PLUS — it is a programming language which uses modular concepts.
4. Finally, dBASE III PLUS contains an "Applications Generator" in which programs are actually written for the user by answering a series of questions.

These four alternative methods of manipulating a software package represent the landscape of options which many of us will face in the next decade. There have been substantial efforts in reducing complexity in creating and using DBMS software. For example, Symantec has developed Q&A, a natural language DBMS, in which queries are in common language. For example, the phrase "WHICH CUSTOMERS

BOUGHT MORE FURNITURE THAN AVERAGE IN THE LAST 6 MONTHS?" is a valid query in Q&A. While the reader may be struck by the simplicity of such an approach, such simplicity can be at the cost of efficiency. As knowledge is accumulated, the need to reduce keystrokes is more highly valued. The power of Lotus 1-2-3, and similar programs, is that keystrokes are few relative to the power of the commands. Ideally, the successful commercial package in future years will have the capacity to be accessed at a variety of levels proceeding from simple and verbose to complex and terse.

From earlier discussion, it will be recalled that there are five major functions of a file management system — create, maintain, query, manipulate and print. The same holds true for multiple file database systems except that one also must manage the interconnections among the files.

Creating a File

The creation of a file in dBASE III PLUS is a simple task. Recall that there are alternative ways in which the program can be used. At the simplest level dBASE III PLUS, using the Assistant, contains a menu design like Lotus 1-2-3 with a hierarchical command structure, such as is shown in Exhibit 8-16. One simply selects the command CREATE from the menu using cursor keys and proceeds. The CREATE command sets up a screen for setting up the structure of the file in terms of field names, field type (character, numeric, etc.), and field width.

We shall operate at the second level of operation in dBASE III PLUS using commands issued directly by the user — direct command mode — when prompted with a period. Recall that we also had the option of writing an actual program to issue the CREATE command, or using the Applications Generator program available for dBASE III PLUS to have the program written automatically.

The direct command mode is perhaps the simplest way to use a program like dBASE III PLUS, but it does require a knowledge of command language syntax. For example, the NETWORK file would be created as shown in Exhibit 8-17. Since the dBASE family of programs can use a command language format (rather than menus), a way of indicating that the program is ready for input is needed. A period is the "prompt" for dBASE. When a period is at the beginning of the line, the user is expected to input a command.

Exhibit 8-16
A Screen in dBASE III PLUS Assistant

Set Up **Create** Update Position Retrieve Organize Modify Tools   **11:23:06 pm**

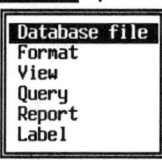

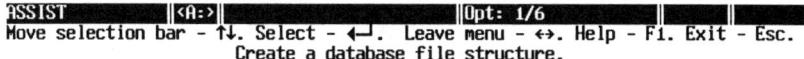

Move selection bar - ↑↓. Select - ↵. Leave menu - ↔. Help - F1. Exit - Esc.
Create a database file structure.

The command CREATE will start the process of putting together a file in dBASE III PLUS. The user types CREATE after the period prompt.

.CREATE

The program will respond by setting up a structure for entering the definition of the NETWORK file. It prompts for a name to the file:

Enter filename:

The user responds "NETWORK." dBASE III PLUS responds with a template for entering the structure of the file. The template is filled in with the fields in the NETWORK file.

Exhibit 8-17
The Creation of the NETWORK File

Field Name	Type	Width	Dec
1. LINKNUM	Character	9	
2. NUMLANES	Numeric	4	0
3. HRCAP	Numeric	9	0
4. PKHRVOL	Numeric	9	0
5. DATESURVEY	Date	8	
6. MUNINUM	Character	5	

The user simply fills in the field names, field type, the width of the field in the record and, if there is a numeric variable, the number of decimal places on a record by record basis. In this example, the user has typed in the six field names from LINKNUM to MUNINUM. There are different types of fields, each of which serves a particular purpose. Character fields are simply a grouping of letters like strings in BASIC or labels in an electronic spreadsheet. LINKNUM and MUNINUM are numeric labels for each of the links in the network and for each municipality, respectively. Numeric fields are those on which calculations will be done. For example, NUMLANES is the number of roadway lanes in the link.

dBASE III PLUS also supports date fields. The program automatically sets the field width at 8 characters. The date January 15, 1987 would be entered "01/15/87" — 8 characters wide with month, day and year separated by slashes. DATESURVEY is the most recent date on which the traffic was surveyed, and PKHRVOL was the actual number of vehicles counted for the peak hour. Dates, exactly because they are so structured into months, days and years, are difficult to handle in a computer program. dBASE III PLUS has developed the date type to make the process easier.

Different database programs will have alternative ways of setting up how a file will be structured, but the overall approach will be the same. In general, competition in the field means that any significant breakthroughs in program design by one vendor will produce a flurry of activity by competing vendors.

Entering the Data

The second task after setting up the file is to input the data into the file structure. Recall that in an electronic spreadsheet each row is considered a record. The columns are the fields. Data is entered directly in the appropriate cell within this row by column framework. In a database program such as dBASE III PLUS, the data are usually entered into either a standard or customized template. The standard template is produced automatically by the program. When filled in with the first record of the NETWORK dataset, the standard template would look like Exhibit 8-18, similar to the PC-FILE III screen for adding a record.

Exhibit 8-18

Adding a Record to the NETWORK File

```
LINKNUM      101-102
NUMLANES        2
HRCAP          1000
PKHRVOL         300
DATESURVEY   06/23/86
MUNINUM      0901
```

The different fields for the NETWORK record are filled in for the various records. The program allocates the number of spaces to each field and sets up an expectation as to what kind of information can be expected. The underlined area is total width of the field. Character fields, such as LINKNUM, are left-adjusted, while numeric fields, such as HRCAP, are right-adjusted. DATESURVEY is a date field, and the program will expect the date to be entered as shown.

It is also possible to develop a customized template inside dBASE III PLUS which could be made to look like a printed form or structured in any fashion one would like. An example of what a customized template would look like for the NETWORK file is shown below.

Exhibit 8-19

A Customized NETWORK Data Entry Screen

```
            Network Listing for Athens County

      Municipality              _____

      Network Link Number       _____

      Number of Lanes           _____

      Peak Hour Capacity        _____

Date Surveyed           _____

Volume                  _____
```

Querying the File

One of the major strengths of a database program is the user's ability to ask questions of the data. Querying a flat file stored in a spreadsheet such as Lotus 1-2-3 (Version 1A or 2) is awkward, since the spreadsheet format must itself be used to do the query. As spreadsheet designs evolve and become better integrated with database management functions, this awkwardness may be reduced in the future. On the other hand, database programs are designed specifically to make the query function straightforward, powerful and easy to use. For example, the NETWORK file can be examined to determine a wide variety of characteristics of the links included in the file. There are a number of commands in dBASE III PLUS which permit one to query the database. For example, the county planner might want to target those four-lane roads which have significant peak hour traffic. Using the NETWORK file containing the links in the network, the DISPLAY command in dBASE III PLUS will list a selected set of records on screen or printer. The following command:

.DISPLAY FOR numlanes=4.AND.pkhrvol>=1600

would generate the following from the NETWORK file:

Exhibit 8-20

Displaying Records in the NETWORK file

Record#	LINKNUM	NUMLANES	HRCAP	PKHRVOL	DATESURVEY	MUNINUM
7	117-118	4	3000	2100	08/20/86	0902
21	113-118	4	4000	1600	06/01/86	0902

The DISPLAY command will select only those links in the network which meet the joint criteria of having 4 lanes and peak hour volumes of 1,600 or greater. The county traffic engineer might wish to find all links which had traffic counts done after June, 1986. The data type DATE can be queried as follows

.DISPLAY FOR YEAR(datesurvey)=1986.AND.MONTH(datesurvey)>06

and will produce the following:

Exhibit 8-21

Displaying Records in NETWORK Surveyed after June, 1986

Record#	LINKNUM	NUMLANES	HRCAP	PKHRVOL	DATESURVEY	MUNINUM
7	117-118	4	3000	2100	08/20/86	0902
8	118-119	2	1400	1000	08/20/86	0902
13	109-110	2	1200	400	07/21/86	0904
14	109-110	2	600	400	07/21/86	0904
15	111-114	2	1200	500	07/12/86	0901

The YEAR(datesurvey) phrase is a function statement which extracts the year from the DATESURVEY field and compares it to 1986. Correspondingly, the MONTH(datesurvey) portion extracts the month and looks to see if it is greater than "06," or the month of June. The output lists all records which meet the survey date criteria of occurring after June, 1986. A database can be queried in a variety of ways using commands such as DISPLAY.

Generating Reports

Database programs can also print out a wide variety of report formats of any or all records in a database. Exhibit 8-22 shows the output from the NETWORK file where particular fields were selected for inclusion and only the links in Alpha (MUNINUM = "0901") were listed. Also, the "Volume/Capacity Ratio" is a calculated field (actual peak hour flow divided by the hourly capacity) set up within the report structure. The command which generated this report uses a predefined report format called NETPRT, sets a condition to pick out only projects in Alpha (MUNINUM = "0901", and sends the output to the printer (TO PRINT). The command looks like the following.

.REPORT FORM NETRPT FOR muninum="0901" TO PRINT

The actual report generated by this command is in Exhibit 8-22.

Exhibit 8-22

Report on the NETWORK File

Page No.   1
10/28/86

Network Listing

Link Number	Municipality	Number of Lanes	Volume/Capacity Ratio
101-102	0901	2	0.30
102-103	0901	2	0.33
103-104	0901	2	0.20
104-116	0901	2	0.50
104-105	0901	2	0.40
105-107	0901	2	0.30
106-107	0901	2	0.30
106-108	0901	2	0.30
111-114	0901	2	0.42
102-104	0901	2	0.40
105-106	0901	2	0.40
105-124	0901	2	0.40

A database manager such as dBASE III PLUS has tremendous capacity to do the relatively straightforward task of querying, sorting and creating reports. However, the power of a relational database program is in its ability to work with multiple files. For example, rather than repeating all the information about the municipality within which the improvement project will be carried out, a reference in the TIP file to MUNI can relate municipality data to the project. MUNINUM, the identification code for the municipality, is found in both the MUNI and the TIP files and is the linkage between the TIP file and the MUNI file. By establishing a relationship between the two files using MUNINUM, all information about a municipality stored in MUNI can be accessed in conjunction with a particular project in the TIP project. The strong preoccupation in relational models with relationships between files is better conceptualized when the relational model is better understood.

Linking Files in a Relational Model

The Conceptual Basis

The relational model contributes both conceptual understanding and implementation tools to help us in the handling of datasets.

The clarity of the basic relational model concepts means that database systems using these concepts are easy to understand.

The more formal presentation of the relational model is in terms of set theory using relational calculus. However, the important aspects of the model can be understood through the use of examples which demonstrate the points to be made. First, the definitional structure of a relational framework needs to be understood. The flat file concept as presented in the section on spreadsheets as file managers must be expanded when dealing with the relational model. Records are represented as rows in the file. These rows are called "tuples" in the relational model. The file itself is called a "relation" or a table. This relation is given a name by which it is known. The columns in the flat file are the fields in our earlier definitions. However, in the relational model the name of the field is called the "attribute," and the potential range of answers for a particular field the "domain."

Using the Athens County transportation planning example, there are four relations, tables or files in the TIP database — TIP, MUNI, NETWORK, and LINKSET. The various fields, or attributes, of the files are each bounded in terms of possible responses; this bounded set is called a domain. For the attribute (or field) TIPNUM the domain is the range of possible identification codes used in the county. The domain of the 1980 population of a municipality (POP80) is all positive numbers no greater than 999,999,999, or the nine-digit width of the field. Obviously, the same domain may apply to more than one field.

Two of the main concerns of the developers of the relational model are the integrity and the usefulness of the database. In the attempt at simplifying the way in which data are organized while maintaining accessibility to the data, the relational model has developed a series of conditions which describe a well-designed database. A particular file, or relation, will take on a variety of "normal forms." These normal forms require that the data be organized in an unambiguous and logical fashion.

The first normal form, sometimes called 1NF, occurs when every value is atomic or non-decomposable. This means that there is only one value at each location in the flat file, and not a set of values (Date, 1981:83-95). In Exhibit 8-23 there is the example of LINKSET files from the transportation improvement program in both non-normalized and normalized forms. In the non-normalized form, the number of the transportation improvement project (TIPNUM) is associated with a set of links (LINKNUM). The shaded area shows that TIP-

NUM 86-45 is associated with three links — 105-106, 106-108 and 106-107. This is sometimes referred to as a 1:N (one to many) relationship. These links would be the ones on which the transportation improvements would be carried out. In the normalized version, there is only one link number in each cell, so that TIPNUM 86-45 is repeated three times for each associated link. Normalized relationships do mean redundancy in a relational model. While the non-normalized form is conceptually viable in some database models, it is not a useful structure in a relational model. The first normal form is shown in the normalized version of the LINKSET file.

Exhibit 8-23

Non-Normalized and Normalized LINKSET Files

The Non-Normalized Version

TIPNUM	LINKNUM
86-31	101-117
86-45	105-106
	106-108
	106-107
86-68	109-110

The Normalized Version

TIPNUM	LINKNUM
86-31	101-117
86-45	105-106
86-45	106-108
86-45	106-107
86-68	109-110

A relation is in second normal form (2NF) when each non-primary key is dependent on the primary key and the file (relation) is in first normal form. For example, the primary key in the TIP file or relation is TIPNUM, the field on which the file will be accessed. Recalling Exhibit 8-11, showing the structure of the four-file database, TIPNAME and the expenditure data, EXP87 through EXP90, are dependent on TIPNUM, since they are uniquely associated with TIP-NUM.

The third normal form (3NF) takes the process a step further by asserting that fields which are not used as keys (nonkey attributes) are independent of each other. For example, Exhibit 8-24 shows the TIP relation at the left (Non-3NF) including the municipality name (MUNINAME) as well as MUNINUM, its identification number. The third normal form would require that we could treat MUNINUM and MUNINAME as independent fields when in fact it cannot be done. Instead the relation is decomposed into TWO relations, or files, as shown at the right of EXHIBIT 8-24 as 3NF. Both these files, TIP and MUNI, are 3NF because all nonkey fields are independent of each other.

Exhibit 8-24

Third Normal Form File Structures

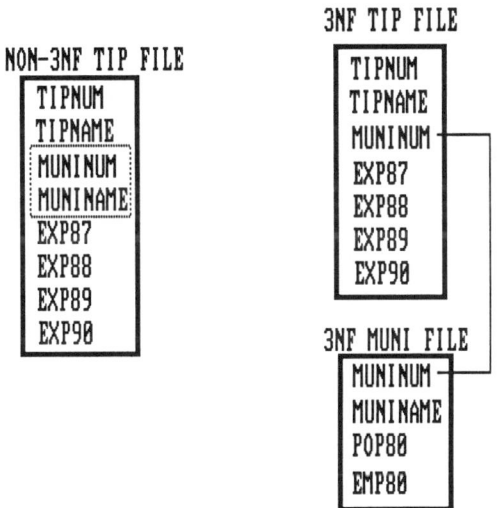

If all of this seems incomprehensible, consider the problem of maintaining a database which violates these assumptions. Assume that the database which we were using contains the non-3NF TIP file in Exhibit 8-24. Consider the problem of moving the project to another community. This would mean that the municipal identification code

(MUNINUM) would have to be changed in the TIP file. Since MUNINUM and MUNINAME are related, we would also have to change the name of the municipality. Should we forget, the database would contain a wrong name for the city. However, the decomposition into two files as shown at the right of Exhibit 8-24 would avoid this problem. The changing of a city identification code in the TIP file would not require any changes in the MUNI file. MUNINUM is the primary key field in the MUNI file, but a non-primary field in the TIP file.

In summary, the normalization process reduces complexity in the database by insisting on well-defined atomic sets. Usually this is done by decomposition of a file or relation with many fields into a series of smaller files or relations with fewer fields. Each file has a primary field identified and all non-primary variables are dependent on these primary fields. However, non-primary fields are not dependent on each other.

Another more powerful normalization criterion has emerged in the field. The "Boyce-Codd Normal Form" (BCNF) was developed to handle the cases where there is more than one primary key in a file (Date, 1981:249-253; Hawryszkiewycz, 1984). To understand BCNF, one must master the concept of functional dependence. A field Y is functionally dependent on field X when a set of values in X uniquely determines a set of values in Y — Y is a function of X. For example, POP80 is functionally dependent on MUNINUM. Knowing the names of cities means that we know the populations of those cities. A file is in BCNF when every field on which other fields are functionally dependent is a primary field. We shall not pursue the BCNF requirements here any further except to say that the Boyce-Codd normal form is a conceptually simpler but more powerful version of the third normal form (3NF). We introduce the concepts of successive stronger relational structures (1NF, 2NF, 3NF and BCNF) because the ideas presented help us in designing databases.

This focus on the criteria by which a relational database will be constructed points out the potential complexity of designing a viable database for planning and public management. However, when reduced to its basics the conceptual underpinnings of the relational model are remarkably simple. We will demonstrate the potential by fleshing out the transportation improvement program example after a brief discussion of how the relational model is being represented in the commercial market.

The Relational Model in the Marketplace

It is important to understand the "hype" around the use of the relational model. In 1985, Codd, the designer of the relational model, criticized mainframe database management systems as claiming to be relational when, in fact, they do not possess all the characteristics of a "true" relational database manager (Codd, 1985a;1985b). Codd sets out 12 rules which define a relational structure. These rules are preceded by a Rule Zero, which states that a relational database system must be able to manage the files contained totally through the relational capacity contained in the system. This means that any database programming system claiming to be relational would not send the user to some nonrelational program to do database functions. For example, a relational database program would not send the user to a BASIC program or to a spreadsheet to insert, correct or delete a record. These tasks would be done inside the DBMS. While this example is obvious, there are situations in large mainframe installations in which users are supposed to use a specialized program in a business language, COBOL, to optimize database system functioning.

While the presentation of each of the 12 rules is beyond concern here, there are two rules which get at the heart of a relational system and reinforce the concepts of normal form presented earlier. Rule 1 states that information is represented by only one thing — values located in flat files. A corollary result of this rule is that even the data definition dictionary, or catalog of field names and files in the DBMS, should itself be a file in the DBMS. In this sense the data in this file is "metadata," describing the data in the rest of the system.

Rule 2 reinforces the simplicity of the relational structure. Each value in the DBMS must be accessible by knowing only the name of the file, the field name, and the value of the "primary" key. Recall that the primary key is the field name which one would most likely look at to find a record. In the transportation improvement program example, the expenditures on a project in 1989 could be accessed by knowing the name of the file, TIP, the field name, EXP89, and the particular value of TIPNUM, the primary field, for which we were searching. While this seems straightforward, this basic concept might not be honored in a large database system.

A controversy has arisen over how well existing mainframe database systems conform to Codd's 12 rules. In general, Codd found no commercial database program which followed all 12 rules, although some did better than others. A number of vendors selling database systems have added relational elements to already-existing hierarchical systems and called their systems relational. The critics of Codd's 12 rules have said that speed of operation and compatibility with existing systems are more important than conceptual purity (Gallant, 1986). This controversy will continue over the next decade. Codd argues that while a relatively fast and powerful relational database program which honors all 12 rules may not have existed in 1985, it does not mean that it will not exist at some future time.

Ironically, a "fourth generation" relational language, IDEAL, was a dismal failure in the development of a state motor vehicle information system in New Jersey (Babcock, 1985). The system was too slow to handle the terminals connected to it, and drivers' licenses and vehicle registrations were not issued in time: the system was 6 months behind at one point. The conceptual simplicity and potential ease of use of a relational database system must be balanced against operational capacity and speed of transaction.

The issue of hype carries over to the microcomputer level. There are several microcomputer-based relational systems available, such as dBASE III PLUS and R:base. These packages are grounded in the relational model, although one could argue that they are not full-fledged relational database systems. While the command language is not straightforward, a typical relational microcomputer system such as dBASE III PLUS can handle multiple files, albeit in a somewhat awkward fashion.

Accessing Multiple Files in dBASE III PLUS

Using the example of the four files in the Athens County transportation system database, one can establish a set of relations across files. In a relational structure, multiple files must first be opened in order to access the information contained. In dBASE III PLUS the user opens the files for use and identifies each alphabetically — A, B, etc. This is done with SELECT and USE commands. Different database programs will use different language constructs.

Recall that there is a general distinction between command and menu-driven programs. Recall that at its most basic level, dBASE III PLUS is a command-driven language. The relationship between two files will be demonstrated using the command language option in dBASE III PLUS. For our example, let us assume that the county planner wishes to determine the various municipal characteristics of the communities in which TIP projects are being done. In this example a relationship will be established between the TIP file, containing the project information, and the file of municipal information, MUNI. A field common to both must be used to establish the relationship. Recalling Exhibit 8-11, the MUNINUM field, containing the municipal identification field, is found in both files. The MUNINUM field is the relational connection which permits information stored in the MUNI file to be available for each TIP project. The relation between these two files, MUNI and TIP, occurs through the MUNINUM variable.

The dBASE III PLUS program requires that one file be designated as "primary" and the other as "secondary" for purposes of establishing a connection. In this example, TIP will be the primary and MUNI the secondary. In order for dBASE III PLUS to make the connection between the two files, the secondary file, MUNI, must be put in order through indexing. In an indexed file, a special separate file is created in which a key field is sorted in order along with the record number which points to where the record is physically located on disk. This special file is small in size relative to the size of the entire file. Indexing is an efficient alternative to actually sorting each record. For a large database sorting takes time and is often unnecessary. It is more efficient to index instead. In indexing only the key field is sorted. This indexing concept is very much like a subject index at the back of a book which is sorted alphabetically and contains the page references on which the subject is discussed.

By indexing on MUNINUM in the MUNI file it will be possible to have dBASE III PLUS set up the relationship between the MUNI and TIP files. This indexing process will create a file of sorted MUNINUM's and the record number associated with the MUNINUM.

In dBASE III PLUS the following set of commands will set up primary and secondary files and establish the connection. The TIP file will be considered as primary and opened in the following way as file A:

```
.SELECT A
.USE TIP
```

The file A designation is simply dBASE III PLUS convention. These two commands open TIP calling it "A."

```
.SELECT B
.USE MUNI
```

These two lines open MUNI as the "B" file.

.INDEX ON MUNINUM to MUNIDEX

This command creates a file called "MUNIDEX" which is the index, and contains only the sorted MUNINUM fields from all the municipal records along with the record number. If one listed the MUNI file indexed on MUNINUM it would be sorted from low to high values.

.SELECT A
.SET RELATION TO MUNINUM INTO MUNI

These two commands select TIP to be worked on and then establish a relationship with the file MUNI through the common variable MUNINUM. The two files are related.

If the process seems awkward or obscure, do not be disheartened. While popular, dBASE III PLUS is cumbersome in its command mode. Menu and icon-driven alternatives may well be viable options. Most important is the conceptual framework behind the example.

Continuing with our example, a listing of variables from both files might look like Exhibit 8-25. The MUNINUM field is taken from the TIP file, while MUNINAME and POP80 come from the MUNI file. The "B->" in front of MUNINAME and POP80 identifies these fields as coming from the "B" file, MUNI.

Exhibit 8-25

Relating the TIP and MUNI Files

Record#	MUNINUM	B->MUNINAME	B->POP80
1	0901	Alpha	3500
2	0901	Alpha	3500
3	0904	Gamma	33000

Other Database Systems

There are a number of other generally recognized database systems. Two kinds will be examined here — **hierarchical** and **network**. Hierarchical data structures can be conceptualized in the shape of tree networks. In the case of the state park file, the general design of one possible hierarchical structure is shown in Exhibit 8-26 along with the four projects in the file. There is an order to the record structure from Type at the top to Project No., Completion Date, and Total Cost at the bottom. All fields, except the top one, are subordinate to the one above. Subordinate elements are sometimes called "children" of the one above. Hence, County is the child of Type. Correspondingly, Type is the parent of County. Each type of project — Construction or Maintenance — is called a segment, which contains both data and pointers to the subordinate elements below. Hence, Construction points to both Salem and Ocean Counties, but not to Atlantic or other counties in the state. The hierarchical structure organizes how the data can be accessed and used. For example, one cannot easily create an alphabetic listing of all projects in the file because of the split between types of projects.

Exhibit 8-26

The State Park File as a Hierarchical Structure

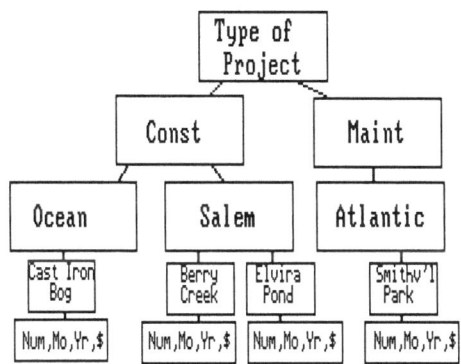

On the other side, hierarchically organized files are excellent for large data sets because they avoid repetition. For example, if the state park agency were dealing with 1,000 projects, 500 of which were construction projects, then there would be 500 separate fields containing the word "Const" in a relational database. However, in a hierarchical database system there would be one segment, "Construction," with pointers to subordinate segments in the tree structure. However, we would all have to agree that the database should be structured in the manner shown in Exhibit 8-26. In a relational system we do not need to make a decision *a priori* about a tree structure. Any field can be related to any other field at any time we choose — ultimate flexibility at some cost in duplication.

Finally, a network database is a more complex but more flexible hierarchical structure. In a network system a database is made up of a collection of sets, and each set is a collection of records. Network systems are based on a proposed national standard developed by a group of the COnference on DAta SYstems Languages (CODASYL). At this time, relational models are the most popular at the microcomputer level. This may change as more complex systems become widely available. For example, Bonczek, Holsapple and Whinston (1984) have proposed that the "extended-network" data model be utilized at the microcomputer level. The extended-network encompasses a set of different data models including network, hierarchical and relational.

Conclusion

It should be clear that simple file management and database problems can be handled easily with a microcomputer. The file manager, PC-FILE III, is a good example of a straightforward but useful implementation. There are many database management systems for the more complex situations. We have briefly examined one, dBASE III PLUS, because of its popularity. However, the development of enhanced spreadsheet programs like Lotus 1-2-3 with database functions — sort, query, maintain, report — provides the user with another option which should be explored.

Suggested Further Readings

Bonczek, Robert H., Clyde W. Holsapple, and Andrew B. Whinston. 1984. *Micro Database Management: Practical Techniques for Application Development.* New York: Academic Press.

Holsapple, C. W. 1984. "A Perspective on Data Models," *PC Tech Journal* 3:7 (July): 113-141.

Martin, James. 1976. *Principles of Data-Base Management.* Englewood Cliffs, New Jersey: Prentice-Hall.

9

Future Directions

Introduction

This chapter examines three aspects of the microcomputer revolution which will especially affect the practice of urban planning and mangement in the next decade. First, there will be an increasing focus on the development and use of expert systems. Langendorf (1985) has suggested that while computer models are designed to handle structured problems, most planning and management issues are either semistructured or unstructured. Expert systems may help to provide a handle on these ill-defined problems by permitting what Britton Harris (1966) once called "transduction" — the two-way movement between theory and practice.

The second area of development is computer mapping and information systems. Up to now, the ability to do extensive mapping and to build urban geographic databases has been limited. Hardware and software have been expensive, and the data entry requirements large. Inexpensive and powerful microtechnology will change this situation, permitting smaller and less affluent organizations to begin to look at mapping applications. We shall briefly explore the areas of computer mapping and urban geographic information systems as background to these potential developments.

Finally, we shall look at the emerging electronic office in urban planning and management. The electronic office will utilize a wide range of technical innovations to assist the management function, including microcomputers and communication networks.

Developing and Using Expert Systems

Introduction

One of the fashionable areas of current research is in the field of expert systems. Such systems are designed to assist decision-makers by applying a set of predefined rules within a logical framework to the solution of a stated problem. The problem may be ill-defined, and a well-designed expert system can assist in better specifying the question. An expert system is a component of the decision support system concept developed in the 1970's. There are three basic elements of a decision support system (Langendorf, 1985). First, the interface between computer and user is isolated from the technicalities of the machine. Second, the system developed is easy to modify. Third, the system includes the capacity to do alternatives analysis, assumption modification, and sensitivity analysis. A simple example of a decision support system is the electronic spreadsheet, which has a reasonable isolation of user, is easy to change, and permits "what-if" analysis. Expert systems are a more robust alternative. They can be designed to use natural language, they are sometimes self-modifying, and they can be highly interactive.

An expert system is a piece of the general area of artificial intelligence (AI), the study of symbolic, nonalgorithmic approaches to problem solving. An expert system comprises two components — a knowledge base and an inference engine. Exhibit 9-1, based on Buchanan and Shortliffe (1984:7), shows the relationships between the user, the system, and the builders of the system.

The system is created through the interaction of the knowledge engineer and the domain expert. In the planning and management area, a set of domain experts might gather to develop the information base and the rules which would govern the interaction of information elements. These experts would gather to focus on a problem amenable to expert system solution within a planning and management context. Such problems generally have the following characteristics:

1. A problem common enough among planners or managers to justify the resource expenditures necessary to build an expert system.
2. A problem which is definable, using available information, with derivable explicit rules that operate on this information.

Exhibit 9-1

The Structure of an Expert System

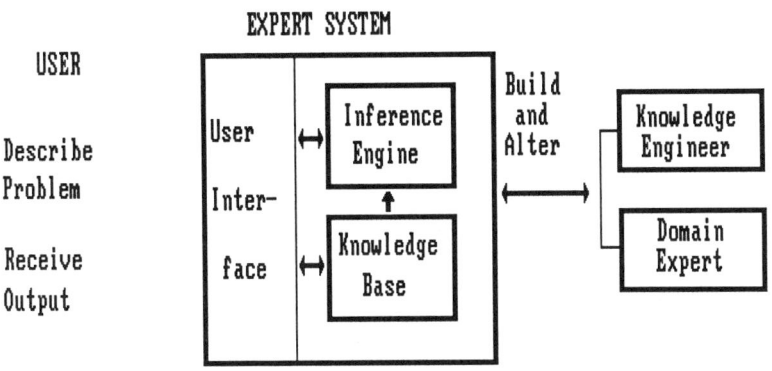

A number of models have been developed in this book; each generates numeric answers. These models were either written as electronic spreadsheets or in BASIC. An expert system changes the questions that are asked of the computer. The presence of explicit logical connections and the rules of inference permit a broader kind of answer. Rather than asking how many people will live in Alpha in 1990, one can ask if the town will grow under certain assumptions, and if so, how much. Rather than knowing the number of vehicles traveling on a roadway near a new shopping center, we can ask if the road will be congested, and if so, how severely. In this sense, the answers reflect the kind of information the decision maker would like to hear.

The traditional quantitative model discussed in the previous chapters would be only one component within a larger expert system envelope. This system framework would permit a larger range of topics to be considered before answering the question — will the town grow, or will there be severe congestion? It might even be possible in a highly developed expert system to analyze the projected growth policies of a community in terms of demographics and land use and transportation impacts. The knowledge base could contain a summary of the experiences of other communities as well as a variety of urban models.

One must distinguish between the expert system itself and the means used to develop and operate it. As suggested earlier, the expert system contains a knowledge base and an inference engine. Recall that a database is a collection of files, each of which contains records made up of fields, or data elements. A knowledge base is more than a database. The knowledge base is an ordered set of data elements along with the established relationships among these data elements. In other words, the knowledge base stores both objects and the relationships among objects. As a contrast, a flat file used in the relational model discussed in Chapter 8 would not itself contain the type of relationship between any two fields.

The knowledge base also contains conditional "if-then" statements. These are central because they permit inferential conclusions to be drawn. One of the pioneer medical expert systems, MYCIN, done at Stanford University, was primarily conceptualized as an extensive set of conditional statements (Buchanan and Shortliffe, 1984). Systems such as MYCIN (written in LISP, an AI language) use backward chaining, or a goal-directed programming structure. In a backward chaining structure, the system starts with a goal and works backwards through the inference rules. In classic formal logic:

If A, then B	(Rule 1)
If B, then C	(Rule 2)
A	(Data)
Therefore C	(Conclusion)

In a backward chaining design (Buchanan and Shortliffe, 1984):

Find out about C	(Goal)
If B, then C	(Rule 1)
If A, then B	(Rule 2)

Therefore If A, then C   (Implicit rule)

Question: Is A true?   (Data)

Using a Programming Language

Earlier we made a distinction between the expert system and the means used to develop and operate it. While all expert systems have an inference engine and a knowledge base, a system can be implemented in a variety of ways. First, one can write an expert system in a procedural programming language, such as BASIC or Pascal. The presence of conditional logic permits the development of expert systems in a standard programming language. For example, Frey (1986) developed an expert system to classify house styles, such as Colonial Revival or Tudor, based on descriptive attributes, such as roof pitch or materials used. Developed primarily to show the use of pattern recognition approaches in expert systems, the program was written in Microsoft BASIC.

Prolog as an Expert System Tool

Second, the system can be written in an AI-based language, such as LISP or Prolog. These languages are declarative rather than procedural, meaning that rather than detailing the procedures required to generate a solution, the user specifies a problem and the computer provides a set of possible solutions. The introduction in 1986 of a number of microcomputer based Prolog interpreters and compilers has made this language an increasingly important option to other procedural languages. The majority of Prolog compilers and interpreters follow the language conventions of Clocksin and Mellish (1984). In Prolog, a program is made up of clauses which are treated as factual information or rules operating on this information. A Prolog database might contain the following clauses:

generates(officelanduse,100)
contains(middlesexcounty,piscataway)

The first clause contains a **predicate**, "generates," and two arguments, "officelanduse" and "100." This clause is a **fact** in Prolog and can be translated into "office land use generates 100 trips per acre per day." The second fact states that "Middlesex County contains Piscataway." Note that the arguments — called atoms in Prolog — in these clauses, such as officelanduse, are written as all lower-case letters. An **atom** in Prolog is a lower-case non-integer constant containing no spaces, such as piscataway or officelanduse.

Rules are the basic clauses which drive the program. Rules are the conditional "if-then" statements which lie at the base of expert systems. In Prolog the following structure is a rule:

congested(route287) :- many(trips)

The ":-" symbol means "if." The rule reads: "Route 287 is congested if trips are many." Understanding Prolog means understanding the process of **instantiation**. Whenever the Prolog program finds an instance among the facts and rules which is supported, then the fact or rule is instantiated. Recalling the earlier discussion about goal seeking and backtracking, Prolog states a goal by using a query command. By using a query, the Prolog interpreter or compiler is directed to instantiate the clause in the query. In Prolog a goal is an uninstantiated query. Prolog will answer "YES" or "NO" to the query, depending on whether or not the goal was instantiated.

Unlike facts, **variables** in Prolog are akin to variables in other languages: they can take on a range of values. Variables start with capital letters, so that Piscataway (a variable) is not equivalent to piscataway (an atom). We shall show the use of variables subsequently in an example expert system. This brief introduction to Prolog would not be complete without a discussion of structures and lists. A structure permits nested facts. For example:

contains(middlesexcounty,piscataway(township, 90000))

This clause can be interpreted as "Piscataway, in Middlesex County, is a township of 90,000 inhabitants." A **list** is an ordered sequence of indeterminate length which contains zero or more elements. Lists are central to AI languages. In fact, the language LISP stands for LISt Processor. Unlike BASIC or Pascal in which an array must be declared with a fixed number of elements, a list in Prolog can be altered at any time.

There are several Prolog compilers and interpreters commercially available and more will come. Only Prolog interpreters were introduced initially. Recall that an interpreter converts the source language into machine code one line at a time. Prolog is a dynamic environment permitting the adding and subtracting of facts and rules at any time, suitable for an interpreter environment. Also, Prolog programs can modify themselves, contradicting the concept of a program completely compiled into machine code which cannot be changed. A number of compilers have emerged regardless (Covington and Vellino, 1986). These Prolog compilers generally will compile the original program but will run the compiled code within an interpreter so that the program can change as it is running. One of these compilers, Turbo Prolog from Borland International, is an inexpensive version from the developers of Turbo Pascal, an excellent and widely used Pascal system for both IBM and Apple Macintosh microcomputers. Turbo Prolog is a structured version of an unstructured language that requires the user to pre-declare all clause types and variables before using it, just as Pascal does. There is great debate over Turbo Prolog, with some suggesting that it is not really Prolog, but a very different creature (Covington and Vellino, 1986; Swaine, 1986). We will use the Prolog V-Plus interpreter from Chalcedony Software, Inc., in the example below. This inexpensive interpreter uses the standard Clocksin and Mellish, also called Edinburgh, syntax.

To show a simple and straightforward example of a Prolog program, we will construct a traffic impact model. The expert system predicts the impact of a proposed development on an adjacent roadway while also accounting for existing traffic. Exhibit 9-2 contains the program listing. The program contains a trips per acre file of land use types and a set of rules which operates using this file. A Prolog program is very flexible in how the various elements are put together. Also, a wide variety of goals can be stated. The traffic impact program is designed to achieve two goals: (1) estimating the expected total hourly volume from existing traffic and from the proposed new development, and (2) adding new trip generation data to the model as the user wishes. Prolog permits easy modification of the database contained. In this sense, a Prolog program can "learn" new information from an exchange with the user.

The traffic impact program in Exhibit 9-2 was created with a separate editor program. The interpreter, Prolog V-Plus, was used to run the traffic impact system. A Prolog program is run by stating a goal which the program will seek to satisfy. We have set up the traffic impact expert system to calculate trip volumes on a roadway. The actual calculation of the trip impacts is done in the *run* rule in the program. We will use "run" as the goal. The user types "run?" at the goal prompt. Prolog seeks to satisfy the condition that "run" is true by carrying out the assigned tasks.

The order of program elements in Prolog is flexible to a degree, and we have placed the facts on the number of trips per acre generated by various land uses first. These facts, of the form

tripacres(sfresidential,100.)

indicate that single-family residential development will generate 100 trips per acre per hour. The *run* rules are next: recall that "run" has been stated as the Prolog goal. The first of these two rules, beginning:

Exhibit 9-2

A Traffic Impact Expert System in Prolog

```
/*A Traffic Impact Expert System*/

/* The trips per acre file */
tripacres(sfresidential,100.).
tripacres(mfresidential,200.).
tripacres(office,400.).

/* The command run? starts Prolog instantiating this rule */
run :-
  getlanduse(Landuse),
  getrestinfo(Acres,Capacity,Volume),
  impact(Landuse,Acres,Capacity,Volume),
  !. % Cut the search at this point if landuse is found.

/* If the landuse is not found in file, Prolog searches this
run :-
  write('The trips cannot be calculated because the landuse'),
  nl,
  write('  category is not included in the dataset.'),
  nl,
  write('Would you like to enter a new category and associated'),
  nl,
  write('  hourly trips per acre? Enter y for yes or n for
  ratom(Answer),
  nl,
  yesisthe(Answer), % Prolog seeks to instantiate this rule
/* Prolog will continue if Yes*/
/* A new landuse will be entered in the trips/acre file */
  write('What is the name of the land use category (in lowercase)?'),
  ratom(Newlanduse),
  nl,
  write('How many trips per hour (with a decimal point)?'),
  ratom(Newtripacres),
  nl,
/* The following clause adds the new tripacres fact to file */
  assertz(tripacres(Newlanduse,Newtripacres)).

getlanduse(Landuse) :-
  write('Enter the following information:'),
  nl,
  write('What is the landuse category (in lowercase)?'),
  ratom(Landuse),
  nl,
  tripacres(Landuse,X).

getrestinfo(Acres,Capacity,Volume) :-
  write('How many acres of development (with a decimal point)?'),
  ratom(Acres),
  nl,
```

Exhibit 9-2, continued

```
write('What is capacity of roadway at the site (decimal)?'),
ratom(Capacity),
nl,
write('What is the highest hourly volume (decimal)?'),
ratom(Volume),
nl.

impact(Landuse,Acres,Capacity,Volume) :-
  tripacres(Landuse,X),
  Trips is Acres * X,
  Totaltrips is (Trips/2) + Volume,
  VC is Totaltrips / Capacity,
  write('The total number of trips at the site are '),
  write (Totaltrips),
  nl,
  write('The volume-capacity ratio is '),
  write(VC),
  nl.

/* Called from the second '' run'' rule */
/*   if found true (or instantiated) will permit */
/*   the user to enter a new land use category */
yesisthe(Answer) :-
  Answer = 'y'.
```

```
run :-
  getlanduse(Landuse),
  getrestinfo(Acres,Capacity,Volume),
  impact(Landuse,Acres,Capacity,Volume,Trips,VC),
  !.      %Cut the search at this point if landuse is found.
```

is the central rule in the program. The ":-" is translated as "if", and the "," means "and." This rule can be translated as: "the *run* rule (the goal) is true **if** the rules *getlanduse* **and** *getrestinfo* **and** *impact* are all true." The "!," a **cut** command, tells Prolog to stop instantiating if the rule is found to be true. The cut is a necessary evil in Prolog to prevent the backtracking process from continuing on when not appropriate.

The reader can begin to see that Prolog is unlike any programming language seen before. The *getlanduse* rule is found in the program listing below the second *run* rule. The *getlanduse* rule first seeks to have the user enter the landuse category through a "write" command. The "ratom" command reads the "atom" typed on the keyboard and binds it to Landuse, a variable containing the name of the type of landuse category. The "nl" commands, required after each "write" command, are simply carriage returns, or "new lines." The final command in the *getlanduse* rule is the most important:

tripacres(Landuse,X).

This clause is instantiated, or found true, only if the Landuse typed in by the user is in the database already. The number of trips, X, will exist only if the landuse exists. Only three landuse categories are included in the Exhibit 9-2 listing — sfresidential (single family), mfresidential (multiple family), and office. This means that if the user types in anything else — say, industrial — then the tripacres clause is not instantiated, or false.

Let us assume that **the tripacres clause is false**, and not instantiated. Backward chaining now occurs. If the tripacres clause is false, this means that the *getlanduse* rule is false, which in turn means that the *run* rule, stated as a goal, is false and not instantiated. This means that Prolog seeks to satisfy "run" as a goal by moving to the **second** *run* rule. The second *run* rule tells the user that the trips cannot be calculated, but that a new landuse category can be added if desired. The *yesisthe(Answer)* rule looks for a "yes" to the question if the user would like to enter a new landuse category trip rate. The variables Newlanduse and Newtripacres contain the newly entered information. The final clause:

assertz(tripacres(Newlanduse,Newtripacres))

puts this new information into the trips per acre file. The Prolog program is actually modified to include this new fact about landuse and trips per acre. The "assertz" command puts the fact last in the set of similar facts, while a similar command "asserta" puts the fact first.

Let us now assume that **the tripacres clause is now true**. This means that the landuse category was found among the trips per acre facts. The *getlanduse* rule is instantiated. Next, Prolog seeks to instantiate the next clause in the **first** *run* rule, the *getrestinfo* rule, which asks the user for the amount of acres in the proposed development (Acres), the capacity of the roadway onto which the traffic will load from the new development (Capacity), and the existing traffic volume on the roadway without the new development (Volume). This rule will always be instantiated as long as the user enters information.

Finally, Prolog will move to the last rule, *impact*. This rule will also always be instantiated since there are no conditions under which any clause could be found to be false. The tripacres(Landuse,X) clause will bind the user input to the Landuse variable entered earlier. Prolog then knows that X represents the number of trips associated. The next three clauses, containing "is," are equations.

Prolog's mathematical capacity is minimal and may be inadequate for the sometimes computationally complex fields like urban planning and management. The basic mathematical operators, such as multiply and divide, are present, but there is little else. The early implementations of Prolog could do only integer arithmetic handling numbers between -32,768 and +32,768. Prolog-V Plus has added floating point arithmetic, an important element for any serious equation-building. Some Prolog implementations permit the inclusion of programs written in other languages to run within Prolog itself. This permits complex mathematical solutions to be done in a more suitable computational language.

The nature of Prolog means that the notation of an equation must be rethought. To say "Y = X" is to test if the statement is true given what Prolog knows. To do assignment, we must say "Y is X." In the *impact* rule, Trips are calculated by the Prolog expression:

$$\text{Trips is Acres} * X$$

Trips refers to the number generated by the new landuse alone during the peak hour. The remaining elements of this model are highly simplistic. One-half of the traffic is added to the existing volume since in the new development traffic will split and go in opposite directions on the roadway: this is the Totaltrips variable. The volume-capacity ratio, VC, is then calculated. Both Totaltrips and VC are written to the screen.

The final command in the *run* rule is the cut, "!". This stops Prolog from going on to the second *run* rule, which assumes that the landuse category entered by the user was not found.

A close examination of Exhibit 9-2 can provide a reasonably good perspective on the use of Prolog as a model building tool in planning and management. Mathematical operations are weak, but the logical structure is powerful. Only a few of the available commands have been discussed, and one would have to invest considerable time to develop a real competency in the language. However, Prolog, or a more powerful successor, may well become very important in the next decade.

Commercial Expert System Packages

There is a third level on which an expert system could be written. A number of commercial expert system packages have become available. These packages have the capacity to handle conditional rules, do backtracking, and query the user in order to reach a conclusion. Amer (1986) has created an expert system to examine alternative transit modes for a developing community on the edge of a metropolitan area. Using EXSYS, a modestly priced expert system development package, Amer used a set of conditional rules to define potential choices in transit modes which would fit the spatial and demographic situation. In EXSYS, probabilities can be assigned to the choices. Below is a sample of a rule:

RULE NUMBER 42

IF:
THE AVERAGE INCOME OF THE POPULATION IS LOW

THEN:
TAXICAB - Probability=3/10
and DIAL-A-BUS - Probability=8/10
and LOCAL BUS, FREQUENT SERVICE=8/10
and LOCAL BUS, INTERMEDIATE SERVICE=8/10
and LOCAL BUS, MININUM SERVICE=8/10

Packages such as EXSYS make the creation of an expert system much easier than writing in Prolog or some other language. However, the potential user must be aware that rule-making can be an extensive and tedious process. There are 71 rules in the Amer modal selection system, and many more could be added to enrich the system.

Conclusion

Expert systems are emerging in planning and management. One benefit of such developments is the codification of knowledge in the field into coherent sets of rules useful in expert systems. Expert systems will not replace intuition, common sense, or experience. They are useful in defined situations which repeat themselves sufficiently to justify the resource commitment required. In general, expert systems can be useful as natural language front ends for complex models written in other languages, as stand-alone packages, and as tools for the development of dynamic databases which can alter themselves.

Mapping the Urban Environment

This brief section will highlight the developments occurring in the computer mapping and geographic information system areas. There are two important thrusts in this area. First, there are the developments in low cost computer thematic mapping packages. Wiggins (1986) has reviewed three — ATLAS AMP, PCMAP, and MULTIMAP. All these packages permit the use of externally generated digitized boundaries, and all allow the user to create map boundaries directly and generate maps on a plotter or printer. A number of vendors sell boundary files of census tracts, municipalities and other geographic units. However, it is also possible to digitize one's own boundaries through these systems.

The digitizing process can be done in a variety of ways. First, the coordinate system must be selected. Widely used coordinate systems include latitude-longitude and State Plane Coordinate. There is also the problem of projecting a curved surface onto a flat piece of paper, so projection techniques are used (Wiggins, 1986). Second, the digitizing must be done. There are three general types of geographic elements which require digitizing. Points, such as the locations of buildings, are simply identified by the coordinates. Lines, highways for example, are identified by beginning and ending points. Polygons can be coded in two ways, either as polygons directly, or as lines coded as chains. This latter technique, sometimes called chain-and-node, is economical in that the lines of a common boundary are digitized only once (Lima, 1985). Polygons are coded by recording each point's coordinates around the shape until the starting point is reached. There is the problem of having two adjacent polygons meet exactly, but careful digitizing and software seem able to prevent problems in the packages reviewed by Wiggins (1986).

The boundary files created provide the outline of the map. A data file, either obtained from outside sources or created by the user, will contain the information to be placed within the map. Often files can be imported from spreadsheet and file management programs. The data entered into the mapping package must be grouped into categories before being displayed. Finally, colors and hatch patterns must be selected for each of these categories.

Microcomputer mapping packages provide a necessary tool for the planner or manager. The second area of development — urban geographic information systems — is both more exciting and more interesting. In its broadest sense, an urban geographic information system (GIS) is a spatially defined database with a query language producing statistical output and maps. Kinzy (1980) has outlined the concept of geoprocessing, while Kevany (1980) has discussed the hardware and software elements of an interactive graphics system. Ideally, there would be an underlying relational database structure which would use the land use parcel as the primary unit of study. Through appropriate aggregation techniques, the parcel data could be encompassed within census tract, planning district, and municipal boundaries.

These information systems are of such a scale that current ones are usually run on mainframe computers. For example, the New York City planning department has developed a system which integrates the U.S. Bureau of Census GBF/DIME (geographic base file/dual independent map encoding) system with a parcel-based digitizing effort (Juhl and Wallick, 1986). Data stored in the central computer can be extracted in a wide variety of ways and used in maps. For example, tax delinquency information from the department of real property can be merged with geographic base data to produce a map.

There are a number of computerized information systems which focus on land use supply. Godschalk and others (1986) examined 24 land use supply systems. Of the 10 started in 1980 or after, half were run solely on a microcomputer. At the microcomputer level the New Haven experience is noteworthy (Kops, Hall, Goetze, and Canto, 1986). The Land Use Information System (LUIS) contains 26,000 parcels with a wide variety of information. Data on parcels include such standard information as address, assessed value, and land use, as well as such variables as fires, code violations and background census data. The parcels do not have X-Y coordinates, but they can be keyed to block faces through a modified DIME file.

The advent of the newer, more powerful micros, such as those driven by the Intel 80386 chip and Motorola equivalents, will make it possible to develop geographic information systems on these machines. New Haven was able to put 26,000 parcels without geographic coordinates on a micro equivalent to the IBM AT with a 40 million byte hard disk, while supporting dumb terminals. New 80386 machines can now have 100 million plus byte disks, and run 4 times faster than an AT. The potential to deliver a comprehensive urban geographic information system on a microcomputer sitting on a nearby desk awaits only the software and the commitment.

Managing the Electronic Office

We conclude with a discussion of the effects of the electronic evolution on the urban planner's or manager's office. We have already touched on some of the tools of the trade — electronic spreadsheets, elementary programming, database management and computer mapping. As time goes on, expert systems will begin to emerge in areas where the potential use will outweigh the resource commitment. Integrated programs which combine many functions, such as Symphony and Framework, may be used in some offices. These integrated programs will make the process of moving between spreadsheet, database and wordprocessing easier. As stated in Chapter 7, DIF file transfers are one current way of moving information among programs, but that method is less attractive than a system which would be transparent to the user. The integration of programs within a common frame will occur by using a graphics interface similar to the icon displays of the Apple Macintosh. The most likely candidate for IBM machines and clones is Windows from Microsoft Corporation. Higher resolution color displays (approximately 1,000 by 1,000 pixels) will be standard in these graphics-based interface systems.

The office itself will change in a number of ways. First, the microcomputers will continue to get more powerful, equaling the power of minicomputers and mainframes. We have discussed this point repeatedly, but the hardware developments have been truly dazzling. Few, if any, in 1977 would have predicted the technology available in 1987. At some point the technological evolution may slow down. The fact remains that the currently available 32-bit processors such as the Intel 80386 may be capable of handling an extensive load in the office. Such machines will handily support local area networks and may be capable of running an urban geographic information system for a smaller community.

Second, there will be tremendous increases in the availability of in-house information through technological advances in magnetic and laser disk storage capacity and access. Local storage of large datasets such as census and other demographic information will be commonplace. The U.S. Bureau of Census is examining the possibility of putting census materials on compact read-only disks (CD-ROM) (Moore and Williams, 1986). A single laser disk can hold the equivalent of about 1,500 floppy disks, or 4 high-density computer tapes. The computer tape version of the 1982 economic census requires five or six tapes, while the same information could be put on one or two compact disks. The user will need a laser disk player and appropriate software to access the census materials. Others have used the larger diameter video disk storage devices to hold pictorial materials. For example, there are communities which have photographed residences and other land use structures and created assessment files on laser disk. The written characteristics of the property can be accompanied by a directly accessible picture.

Third, there will be the increasing use of desktop publishing in producing reports. The development of the laser printer and powerful report production software, which can produce excellent print output without a typesetting machine, will change how planners and managers generate their written work. Desktop publishing permits the author to maintain complete control of the publishing environment and produces camera-ready copy quickly. The initial thrust into desktop publishing came with the Apple Macintosh and the Laserwriter laser printer. Using a page description language called Postscript, it is possible to integrate text in a variety of fonts and styles and graphics into a common document without cutting and pasting. The planner will be able to integrate text and graphics, including maps, into a document and turn out copies quickly and cheaply. The development of high-resolution scanners, which digitize pictures for entry into a computer, means that maps and photographs will be placed within the desktop publishing environment and easily manipulated.

Fourth, networking among micros in the organization will be an expectation. As microcomputer applications become more complex and their uses more ubiquitous, there is a natural evolution toward connecting machines together so that programs and data can be shared. A local area network (LAN) is a system of interconnected microcomputers which can transfer information among machines using one of a set of communications protocols. The actual implementation of a network is quite complex, although as more and more networks are developed, the experiences will provide a basis for simplified installation in the future.

The selection of a network for a planning office involves the following steps:

1. Delineation of the objectives of the networked facility

2. Identification of potential hardware and software options
3. Evaluation of a selected set of hardware/software combinations
4. Selection of a particular system

These four steps smack suspiciously of the planning process which many of us have been taught. Their use here is to emphasize that networking a set of microcomputers requires careful preparation. The flexibility and friendliness of the individual microcomputer system arises precisely because program and data do not have to be shared. A networked facility, established to permit sharing, introduces a degree of complexity which must be addressed. For example, sharing the same database means that the database program must keep track of who is modifying what records, to prevent data corruption.

The lone microcomputer user, happy that he/she does not have to deal with the passwords, protocols and general complexities of a mainframe computer, is rudely awakened when the network is established. Passwords are often required, data and program access may be restricted, and once again, as with the central computer, the user is dependent upon a central "file server" to provide access to information. If the file server is out of service, then the network is unusable. (It is possible to have multiple file servers in some network systems to provide redundancy.) Often, the needs of a public or private sector office are such that a network is essential. Without a network, data, programs and hardware, such as laser printers, can be shared only by exchanging floppy disks or by wheeling equipment from office to office. The reader is cautioned that a network installation does not relieve the user from purchasing the appropriate number of copies of software to cover the machines on which it is being used. Some companies, such as Microrim with its R:BASE System V database package, charge the same price for a single license as for the multiuser version. Many others require a separate copy for each machine, a much more expensive option.

Conclusion

This book has covered a great deal of material, and yet so much more needs to be said. A window on a constantly evolving world of microtechnology has been opened. The reader must somehow place his or her needs and interest within the matrix of options and decide on a direction to go. The key to understanding and using this microtechnology is **flexibility**, both in the software and hardware selected, and in the user's attitude toward these tools.

If one is interested in quick and flexible decision support capacity, then the electronic spreadsheet is the primary tool. However, as spreadsheets get bigger and more complex, the need to utilize structured design principles becomes increasingly important. Many public and private organizations are using the electronic spreadsheet on a daily basis. As these uses become more extensive, increasing concern will have to be shown to documentation and to error checking.

If one is concerned about data management issues and building database management schemes, then the relational model becomes an important conceptual element. It is quite easy to develop a single file management system, but the development of a dynamic multiple file structure is another matter. However, most urban planning and management situations are complex, and deal with multiple files available from a variety of sources. For example, building and construction permits for a new shopping center on a major roadway may be processed by the municipality, but permits to put in a curb cut may be handled by the state. The county may also require a set of approvals before construction. The information needed to handle these requests can reside in a multitude of files.

The advantage of the relational model is that it is both ad hoc and flexible — two central elements of a decision support system useful in planning and management. One could start with a single file designed to do a defined task. If appropriate key fields or "hooks" to other files are included in this first file, then the DBMS could be expanded at any time. Since these are the flat files required by the relational model, they can be queried and manipulated in virtually any way. This flexibility suits the rapidly changing issues and problems which confront urban planning and management.

The development of structured programming using BASIC is another example of a flexible approach. Modular programming — the treatment of a complex problem by breaking it into pieces — means that one can create building blocks which are transferable among problems. The linear model calculation module for projecting population could just as easily be used to project jobs, or any other variable. In a broader sense, many high-level programming languages contain a set of libraries which enrich the language immensely. C has an extensive set of libraries to complement the rather sparse language. Pascal is developing a rich collection of subroutines as well. For example, Borland International's Turbo Pascal has had rather powerful database management and graphics libraries developed. The urban planning and management field may well mature enough to permit the building of specialized libraries to contain the models used and the spatial data analysis routines needed for a projection, an alternatives analysis, or a geographic information system.

Finally, the emerging area of expert systems, particularly in the use of languages such as Prolog, may provide a new definition of flexibility. Operational programs may emerge which in a sense "learn" from the user and add information to an already existing database. Whatever direction future developments may take, the urban planner or manager has a great deal to look forward to and a great deal to do.

Suggested Further Readings

Buchanan, Bruce G and Edward H. Shortliffe, editors. 1984. *Rule-based Expert Systems*. Reading, Massachusetts: Addison-Wesley.

Clocksin, W. F, and C. S. Mellish. 1984. *Programming in Prolog*. Berlin: Springer-Verlag.

Covington, Michael. 1985. "Programming in Logic, Part 1," *PC Tech Journal* 3:12 (December): 82-93.

Covington, Michael. 1986. "Programming in Logic, Part 2," *PC Tech Journal* 4:1 (January): 145-155.

Covington, Michael and Vellino, Andre. 1986. "Prolog Arrives," *PC Tech Journal* 4:11 (November): 52-67.

Sterling, L. and E. Shapiro. 1986. *The Art of Prolog*. Cambridge, Massachusetts: MIT Press.

Appendix

This Appendix contains three cell listings of Lotus 1-2-3 models. The first listing is for the urban transportation planning model in Chapter 5. This is an extensive and complete listing of the model: it consumes about 100K of memory. The model does trip generation, trip distribution and traffic assignment for a five-zone city. A few of the equations are complex — e.g., cells B126 and B311 — but the overall structure is straightforward. Appropriate copying of formulas makes the creation of the template relatively simple. Recall from Chapter 5 that "![B37]" means that the equation in that cell was copied from cell B37.

The second listing is from the comparative cost model in Chapter 5. This listing contains a set of simple macros which move the user around the spreadsheet. To save space some of the descriptions of the spreadsheet are left out of the cell listing, but are shown in Chapter 5.

The third listing is from the Smiley County Information System example in Chapter 8. The macros used are complex, and include an interesting data entry form. This is a model which shows how a spreadsheet format can be used as a file manager.

Exhibit A-1

Cell Listing, Urban Transportation Planning Model

	A	B	C	D	E	F	G
1	'URBAN TRANSPORTATION PLANNING MODEL						
2							
3	'TABLE 1 - RESIDENTIAL TRIP PRODUCTION CHARACTERISTICS						
4							
5			' — % AVG DAILY PT-PURPOSE —				
6	'INCOME	"AVG PT/HH	"HBW	"HBNW	"NHB		
7	'--------	'--------	'--------	'--------	'--------		
8	'0-5	6.4	0.22	0.58	0.2		
9	'5-10	13.4	0.2	0.57	0.23		
10	'10-15	18	0.19	0.56	0.25		
11	'15-20	19.6	0.18	0.56	0.26		
12	'20+	20.5	0.18	0.55	0.27		
13							
14	'TABLE 2 - AUTO OCCUPANCY RATES (NO TRANSIT ASSUMED)						
15							
16	'HBW	1.37		'PASSENGERS PER VEHICLE			
17	'HBNW	1.81					
18	'NHB	1.43					
19							
20	'TABLE 3 - PROPOSED RESIDENTIAL DEVELOPMENT						
21							
22			'-------- NO OF HOUSEHOLDS BY ZONE A				

Exhibit A-1, continued

	A	B	C	D	E	F	G
		ND INCOME					

23	'ZONE	^0-5	^5-10	^10-15	^15-20	^20-25	"TOTAL
24	!--------	!--------	!--------	!--------	!--------	!--------	!--------
25	1	50	20	10	50	60	@SUM(B25..F25)
26	2	20	0	100	0	300	![G25]
27	3	20	0	120	0	120	![G25]
28	4	10	40	150	0	230	![G25]
29	5	10	0	200	0	100	![G25]
30	"TOTAL	@SUM(B25..B29)	![B30]	![B30]	![B30]	![B30]	![B30]
31							
32	'TABLE 4 - PERSON TRIP PRODUCTIONS BY ZONE AND INCOME						
33							
34		'---NO OF PERSONS TRIPS BY ZONE AND INCOME LEVEL---					
35	'ZONE	^0-5	^5-10	^10-15	^15-20	^20-25	"TOTAL
36	!--------	!--------	!--------	!--------	!--------	!--------	!--------
37	1	((B25*$B$8))	+C25*$B$9	+D25*$B$10	+E25*$B$11	+F25*$B$12	![G25]
38	2	![B37]	![C37]	![D37]	![E37]	![F37]	![G25]
39	3	![B37]	![C37]	![D37]	![E37]	![F37]	![G25]
40	4	![B37]	![C37]	![D37]	![E37]	![F37]	![G25]
41	5	![B37]	![C37]	![D37]	![E37]	![F37]	![G25]
42	"TOTAL	![B30]	![B30]	![B30]	![B30]	![B30]	![G25]
43							
44	'TABLE 5 - VEHICLE TRIP PRODUCTIONS, PROPOSED DEVELOPMENT						
45							
46		'— NO OF TRIPS BY PURPOSE, PROPOSED DEVELOPMENT —					

Exhibit A-1, continued

	A	B	C	D	E	F	G
47		"HBW	"HBNW	"NHB	"TOTAL		
48	!--------	!--------	!--------	!--------	!--------		
49	1	(($B37*C$8)+($C37*C$9)+($D37*C$10)+($E37*C$11)+($F37*C$12))/$B$16	![B49]	![B49]	@SUM(B49..D49)		
50	2	![B49]	![B49]	![B49]	![E49]		
51	3	![B49]	![B49]	![B49]	![E49]		
52	4	![B49]	![B49]	![B49]	![E49]		
53	5	![B49]	![B49]	![B49]	![E49]		
54	"TOTAL	![B30]	![B30]	![B30]	![B30]		
55							
56	'TABLE 6 - NONRESIDENTIAL TRIP ATTRACTION CHARACTERISTICS						
57							
58				"DAILY	' — % PURPOSE -		
59	'CODE	'CATEGORY		"TP/ACRE	"HBW	"HBNW	"NHB
60	!--------	!--------	!--------	!--------	!--------	!--------	!--------
61	'*** RETAIL ***						
62	'SHOP CT	'SHOPPING CENTER		66.7*(1/3)*40	0.05	0.6	0.35
63	'COMMERCL	'OTHER COMMERCL		75*(1/3)*40	0.05	0.6	0.35
64	'*** MANUFACTURING ***						
65	'LT IND	'LIGHT INDUSTRIAL		52.4	0.9	0.05	0.05
66	'MANUF	'MANUFACTURING		38.9	0.9	0.05	0.05
67	'IND PK	'INDUSTRIAL PARK		62.8	0.9	0.05	0.05
68	'*** OFFICE ***						
69	'OFFSMALL	'OFFICE<100000SF		137	0.2	0.45	0.35
70	'OFFLARGE	'OFFICE>100000SF		166	0.2	0.45	0.35

Exhibit A-1, continued

	A	B	C	D	E	F	G
71	'*** RESTAURANT ***						
72	'QUALREST	'QUALITY		200	0.05	0.7	0.25
73	'OTHREST	'OTHER		932	0.05	0.54	0.41
74	'FASTFOOD	'FAST FOOD		1825	0.05	0.54	0.41
75	'*** RECREATIONAL ***						
76	'PARK	'LOCAL PARK		6	0	0.9	0.1
77							
78	'TABLE 7 - PROPOSED NONRESIDENTIAL DEVELOPMENT						
79							
80		'-------- PROPOSED NONRESIDENTIAL ACTIVITY IN ACRES -------					
81	'ZONE	"SHOP CT	"COMMERCL	"LT IND	"MANUF	"IND PK	"OFFSMALL
82	'--------	'--------	'--------	'--------	'--------	'--------	'--------
83	1	3	0	0	0	0	1
84	2	0	2	0	3	0	0
85	3	0	0	2	6	10	0
86	4	2	3	0	2	0	4
87	5	0	0	2	0	20	0
88	"TOTAL	![B30]	![B30]	![B30]	![B30]	![B30]	![B30]
89							
90	'ZONE	"OFFLARGE	"QUALREST	"OTHREST	"FASTFOOD	"PARK	"TOTAL
91	'--------	'--------	'--------	'--------	'--------	'--------	'--------
92	1	12	0	0	0	0	@SUM(B83..G83)+@SUM(B92..F92)
93	2	0	0	0	0	10	![G92]
94	3	0	0	0	0	0	![G92]
95	4	0	1	0	0	0	![G92]
96	5	0	0	0	0	0	![G92]
97	"TOTAL	![B30]	![B30]	![B30]	![B30]	![B30]	![B30]
98							
99							
100	'TABLE 8						

Exhibit A-1, continued

	A	B	C	D	E	F	G
	'- VEHICLE TRIP ATTRACTIONS FROM NONRESIDENTIAL						
101							
102		'- VEHICLE TRIP ATTRACTIONS BY LAND USE AND ZONE -					
103	'ZONE	"SHOP CT	"COMMERCL	"LT IND	"MANUF	"IND PK	"OFFSMALL
104	!--------	!--------	!--------	!--------	!--------	!--------	!--------
105	1	+B83*$D$62	+C83*$D$63	+D83*$D$65	+E83*$D$66	+F83*$D$67	+G83*$D$69
106	2	![B105]	![C105]	![D105]	![E105]	![F105]	![G105]
107	3	![B105]	![C105]	![D105]	![E105]	![F105]	![G105]
108	4	![B105]	![C105]	![D105]	![E105]	![F105]	![G105]
109	5	![B105]	![C105]	![D105]	![E105]	![F105]	![G105]
110	^TOTAL	![B30]	![B30]	![B30]	![B30]	![B30]	![B30]
111							
112	'ZONE	"OFFLARGE	"QUALREST	"OTHREST	"FASTFOOD	"PARK	"TOTAL
113	!--------	!--------	!--------	!--------	!--------	!--------	!--------
114	1	+B92*$D$70	+C92*$D$72	+D92*$D$73	+E92*$D$74	+F92*$D$76	@SUM(B105..F114)
115	2	![B114]	![C114]	![D114]	![E114]	![F114]	![G114]
116	3	![B114]	![C114]	![D114]	![E114]	![F114]	![G114]
117	4	![B114]	![C114]	![D114]	![E114]	![F114]	![G114]
118	5	![B114]	![C114]	![D114]	![E114]	![F114]	![G114]
119	^TOTAL	![B30]	![B30]	![B30]	![B30]	![B30]	![B30]
120							
121	'TABLE 9 - NONRESIDENTIAL TRIP ATTRACTIONS BY PURPOSE AND ZONE						
122							
123		'- NO OF NONRESIDENTIAL ATTRACTIONS BY PURPOSE					
124	'ZONE	"HBW	"HBNW	"NHB	"TOTAL		
125	!--------	!--------	!--------	!--------	!--------		

Appendix 275

Exhibit A-1, continued

	A	B	C	D	E	F	G
126	1	(($B105*E$62)+($C105*E$63)+($D105*E$65)+($E105*E$66)+($F105*E$67)+($G105*E$69)+($B114*E$70)+($C114*E$72)+($D114*E$73)+($E114*E$74)+($F114*E$76))	![B126]	![B126]	![E49]		
127	2	![B126]	![B126]	![B126]	![E49]		
128	3	![B126]	![B126]	![B126]	![E49]		
129	4	![B126]	![B126]	![B126]	![E49]		
130	5	![B126]	![B126]	![B126]	![E49]		
131	"TOTAL	![B30]	![B30]	![B30]	![B30]		
132							
133	'TABLE 10 - RESIDENTIAL TRIP ATTRACTIONS BY PURPOSE AND ZONE						
134							
135			'NO. HBNW ATTRACTIONS/HH=			1	
136			'NO. NHB ATTRACTIONS/HH=			0.5	
137							
138	'ZONE	"NO. HH	"HBW	"HBNW	"NHB	"TOTAL	
139	!--------	!--------	!--------	!--------	!--------	!--------	
140	1	+G25	0	+B140*$F$135	+B140*$F$136	![E49]	
141	2	![B140]	0	![D140]	![E140]	![E49]	
142	3	![B140]	0	![D140]	![E140]	![E49]	
143	4	![B140]	0	![D140]	![E140]	![E49]	
144	5	![B140]	0	![D140]	![E140]	![E49]	
145	"TOTAL	![B30]	![B30]	![B30]	![B30]	![B30]	
146							
147	'TABLE 11 - TOTAL TRIP ATTR						

Exhibit A-1, continued

	A	B	C	D	E	F	G
	ACTIONS						
148							
149	'ZONE	"HBW	"HBNW	"NHB	"TOTAL		
150	!--------	!--------	!--------	!--------	!--------		
151	1	+C140+B126	![B151]	![B151]	![E49]		
152	2	![B151]	![B151]	![B151]	![E49]		
153	3	![B151]	![B151]	![B151]	![E49]		
154	4	![B151]	![B151]	![B151]	![E49]		
155	5	![B151]	![B151]	![B151]	![E49]		
156	"TOTAL	![B30]	![B30]	![B30]	![B30]		
157							
158	'TABLE 12 - TOTAL TRIP PRODUCTIONS (FROM TABLE 5)						
159							
160	'ZONE	"HBW	"HBNW	"NHB	"TOTAL		
161	!--------	!--------	!--------	!--------	!--------		
162	1	+B49	![B162]	![B162]	![E49]		
163	2	![B162]	![B162]	![B162]	![E49]		
164	3	![B162]	![B162]	![B162]	![E49]		
165	4	![B162]	![B162]	![B162]	![E49]		
166	5	![B162]	![B162]	![B162]	![E49]		
167	"TOTAL	![B30]	![B30]	![B30]	![B30]		
168							
169	'TABLE 13 - (PRODUCTIONS - ATTRACTIONS)						
170							
171		"HBW	"HBNW	"NHB			
172	!--------	!--------	!--------	!--------			
173		+B167-B156	![B173]	![B173]			
174							
175	'TABLE 14 - PRODUCTION/ATTRACTION ADJUSMENT FACTORS (TP/TA)						
176							
177			'	"HBW	"HBNW	"NHB	
178	!--------	!--------	!--------	!--------	!--------	!--------	
179	'TOTAL PR			+B167	![D179]	![D179]	

Exhibit A-1, continued

	A	B	C	D	E	F	G
180	ODUCTIONS 'TOTAL AT TRACTIONS			+B156	![D180]	![D180]	
181	'FACTOR			@IF((+D180<>0),+D179/D180,0)	![D181]	![D181]	
182							
183	'TABLE 15 - ADJUSTED TRIP PRODUCTIONS AND ATTRACTIONS						
184							
185	'ZONE	1	2	3	4	5	"TOTAL
186	!--------	!--------	!--------	!--------	!--------	!--------	!--------
187	'HBW PRD	+B162	+B163	+B164	+B165	+B166	![G25]
188	'HBW ATT	+B151*$D$181	+B152*$D$181	+B153*$D$181	+B154*$D$181	+B155*$D$181	![G25]
189	'HBNW PRD	+C162	+C163	+C164	![D180]	+C166	![G25]
190	'HBNW ATT	+C151*$E$181	+C152*$E$181	+C153*$E$181	+C154*$E$181	+C155*$E$181	![G25]
191	'NHB PRD	+D162	+D163	+D164	+D165	+D166	![G25]
192	'NHB ATT	+D151*$F$181	+D152*$F$181	+D153*$F$181	+D154*$F$181	+D155*$F$181	![G25]
193							
194	'TABLE 16 - TIME-DISTANCE MATRIX						
195							
196	'ZONE	1	2	3	4	5	
197	!--------	!--------	!--------	!--------	!--------	!--------	
198	1	5	14	7	11	13	
199	2	14	5	21	15	21	
200	3	7	21	5	18	14	
201	4	11	15	18	5	12	
202	5	13	21	14	12	5	
203							
204	'***** HOME-BASED WORK (HBW) TRIP DISTRIBUTIONS *****						
205							
206	'TABLE 17 - HBW F-MATRIX (F						

Exhibit A-1, continued

	A	B	C	D	E	F	G
	RICTION F ACTOR MAT RIX)						
207					'EXPONENT =	0.4	
208							
209	'ZONE	1	2	3	4	5	"TOTAL
210	!--------	!--------	!--------	!--------	!--------	!--------	!--------
211	1	@IF((B198>0),(1/(B198^$F$207)),0)	![B211]	![B211]	![B211]	![B211]	![G25]
212	2	![B211]	![B211]	![B211]	![B211]	![B211]	![G25]
213	3	![B211]	![B211]	![B211]	![B211]	![B211]	![G25]
214	4	![B211]	![B211]	![B211]	![B211]	![B211]	![G25]
215	5	![B211]	![B211]	![B211]	![B211]	![B211]	![G25]
216							
217	'TABLE 18 - HBW TRIP DISTRIBUTIONS (ROUND 1)						
218							
219	'ZONE	1	2	3	4	5	"TOTAL
220	!--------	!--------	!--------	!--------	!--------	!--------	!--------
221	1	(($B$187*(B211*B$188))/(($B211*$B$188)+($C211*$C$188)+($D211*$D$188)+($E211*$E$188)+($F211*$F$188)))	![B221]	![B221]	![B221]	![B221]	![G25]
222	2	(($C$187*(B212*B$188))/(($B212*$B$188)+($C212*$C$188)+($D212*$D$188)+($E212*$E$188)+($F212*$F$188)))	![B222]	![B222]	![B222]	![B222]	![G25]
223	3	(($D$187*	![B223]	![B223]	![B223]	![B223]	![G25]

Exhibit A-1, continued

	A	B	C	D	E	F	G
		(B213*B$188))/(($B213*$B$188)+($C213*$C$188)+($D213*$D$188)+($E213*$E$188)+($F213*$F$188)))					
224	4	((($E$187*(B214*B$188))/(($B214*$B$188)+($C214*$C$188)+($D214*$D$188)+($E214*$E$188)+($F214*$F$188)))	![B224]	![B224]	![B224]	![B224]	![G25]
225	5	((($F$187*(B215*B$188))/(($B215*$B$188)+($C215*$C$188)+($D215*$D$188)+($E215*$E$188)+($F215*$F$188)))	![B225]	![B225]	![B225]	![B225]	![G25]
226	"TOTAL	![B30]	![B30]	![B30]	![B30]	![B30]	![B30]
227							
228	'TABLE 19 - ADJUSTED ATTRACTIONS (A(J,IT)=A(J,IT-1)*(A(J)/(C(J,IT-1))						
229							
230	'ZONE	1	2	3	4	5	
231	!--------	!--------	!--------	!--------	!--------	!--------	
232	'GENERATN						
233	' HBW AT	+B188	![B233]	![B233]	![B233]	![B233]	

Exhibit A-1, continued

	A	B	C	D	E	F	G
234	'DISTRIBT N						
235	' HBW AT	+B226	![B235]	![B235]	![B235]	![B235]	
236	'A(J,IT=1)	@IF(B235<>0,(B233*(B233/B235)),0)	![B236]	![B236]	![B236]	![B236]	
237							
238	'TABLE 20 - HBW TRIP DISTRIBUTION (ROUND 2)						
239							
240	'ZONE	1	2	3	4	5	"TOTAL
241	!--------	!--------	!--------	!--------	!--------	!--------	!--------
242	1	(($B$187*(B211*B$236))/(($B$211*$B$236)+($C$211*$C$236)+($D$211*$D$236)+($E$211*$E$236)+($F$211*$F$236)))	![B242]	![B242]	![B242]	![B242]	![G25]
243	2	(($C$187*(B212*B$236))/(($B$212*$B$236)+($C$212*$C$236)+($D$212*$D$236)+($E$212*$E$236)+($F$212*$F$236)))	![B243]	![B243]	![B243]	![B243]	![G25]
244	3	(($D$187*(B213*B$236))/(($B$213*$B$236)+($C$213*$C$236)+($D$213*$D$236)+	![B244]	![B244]	![B244]	![B244]	![G25]

Exhibit A-1, continued

	A	B	C	D	E	F	G
245	4	($E$213*$E$236)+($F$213*$F$236))) ((($E$187*(B214*B$236))/(($B$214*$B$236)+($C$214*$C$236)+($D$214*$D$236)+($E$214*$E$236)+($F$214*$F$236)))	![B245]	![B245]	![B245]	![B245]	![G25]
246	5	((($F$187*(B215*B$236))/(($B$215*$B$236)+($C$215*$C$236)+($D$215*$D$236)+($E$215*$E$236)+($F$215*$F$236)))	![B246]	![B246]	![B246]	![B246]	![G25]
247	"TOTAL	![B30]	![B30]	![B30]	![B30]	![B30]	![B30]
248							
249	'***** HOME BASED NON-WORK (HBNW) TRIP DISTRIBUTIONS *****						
250							
251	'TABLE 21 - HBNW F-MATRIX (FRICTION FACTOR MATRIX)						
252					'EXPONENT =	0.7	
253							
254	'ZONE	1	2	3	4	5	"TOTAL
255	!--------	!--------	!--------	!--------	!--------	!--------	!--------
256	1	@IF((B198	![B256]	![B256]	![B256]	![B256]	![G25]

Exhibit A-1, continued

	A	B	C	D	E	F	G
		>0),(1/(B198^$F$252)),0)					
257	2	![B256]	![B256]	![B256]	![B256]	![B256]	![G25]
258	3	![B256]	![B256]	![B256]	![B256]	![B256]	![G25]
259	4	![B256]	![B256]	![B256]	![B256]	![B256]	![G25]
260	5	![B256]	![B256]	![B256]	![B256]	![B256]	![G25]
261							
262	'TABLE 22 - HOME BASED NON-WORK (HBNW) TRIP DISTRIBUTIONS (ROUND 1)						
263							
264	'ZONE	1	2	3	4	5	"TOTAL
265	!--------	!--------	!--------	!--------	!--------	!--------	!--------
266	1	(($B$189*(B256*B190))/(($B$256*$B$190)+($C$256*$C$190)+($D$256*$D$190)+($E$256*$E$190)+($F$256*$F$190)))	![B266]	![B266]	![B266]	![B266]	![G25]
267	2	(($C$189*(B257*B190))/(($B$257*$B$190)+($C$257*$C$190)+($D$257*$D$190)+($E$257*$E$190)+($F$257*$F$190)))	![B267]	![B267]	![B267]	![B267]	![G25]
268	3	(($D$189*(B258*B190))/(($B$258*$B$190)+($C$258*$C$190)+($D$258*	![B268]	![B268]	![B268]	![B268]	![G25]

Exhibit A-1, continued

	A	B	C	D	E	F	G
269	4	$D$190)+($E$258*$E$190)+($F$258*$F$190))) (($E$189*(B259*B190))/(($B$259*$B$190)+($C$259*$C$190)+($D$259*$D$190)+($E$259*$E$190)+($F$259*$F$190)))	![B269]	![B269]	![B269]	![B269]	![G25]
270	5	(($F$189*(B260*B190))/(($B$260*$B$190)+($C$260*$C$190)+($D$260*$D$190)+($E$260*$E$190)+($F$260*$F$190)))	![B270]	![B270]	![B270]	![B270]	![G25]
271	"TOTAL	![B30]	![B30]	![B30]	![B30]	![B30]	![B30]
272							
273	'TABLE 23 - ADJUSTED ATTRACTIONS (A(J,IT)=A(J,IT-1)*(A(J)/(C(J,IT-1))						
274							
275	'ZONE	1	2	3	4	5	
276	'--------	'--------	'--------	'--------	'--------	'--------	
277	'GENERATN						
278	' HBNW ATT	+B190	![B278]	![B278]	![B278]	![B278]	
279	'DISTRIBTN						
280	' HBNW ATT	![B235]	![B235]	![B235]	![B235]	![B235]	
281	'A(J,IT=1	![B236]	![B236]	![B236]	![B236]	![B236]	

Exhibit A-1, continued

	A	B	C	D	E	F	G
282	)						
283	'TABLE 24 - HOME BASED NON-WORK (HBNW) TRIP DISTRIBUTIONS (ROUND 2)						
284							
285	'ZONE	1	2	3	4	5	"TOTAL
286	!--------	!--------	!--------	!--------	!--------	!--------	!--------
287	1	(($B$189*(B256*B281))/(($B$256*$B$281)+($C$256*$C$281)+($D$256*$D$281)+($E$256*$E$281)+($F$256*$F$281)))	![B287]	![B287]	![B287]	![B287]	![G25]
288	2	(($C$189*(B257*B281))/(($B$257*$B$281)+($C$257*$C$281)+($D$257*$D$281)+($E$257*$E$281)+($F$257*$F$190-2)))	![B288]	![B288]	![B288]	![B288]	![G25]
289	3	(($D$189*(B258*B281))/(($B$258*$B$281)+($C$258*$C$281)+($D$258*$D$281)+($E$258*$E$281)+($F$258*$F$281)))	![B289]	![B289]	![B289]	![B289]	![G25]
290	4	(($E$189*	![B290]	![B290]	![B290]	![B290]	![G25]

Exhibit A-1, continued

	A	B	C	D	E	F	G
		(B259*B281))/(($B$259*$B$281)+($C$259*$C$281)+($D$259*$D$281)+($E$259*$E$281)+($F$259*$F$281)))					
291	5	((($F$189*(B260*B281))/(($B$260*$B$281)+($C$260*$C$281)+($D$260*$D$281)+($E$260*$E$281)+($F$260*$F$281)))	![B291]	![B291]	![B291]	![B291]	![G25]
292	"TOTAL	![B30]	![B30]	![B30]	![B30]	![B30]	![B30]
293							
294	'***** NON HOME BASED (NHB) TRIP DISTRIBUTIONS *****						
295							
296	'TABLE 25 - NHB F-MATRIX (FRICTION FACTOR MATRIX)						
297					'EXPONENT =	0.7	
298							
299	'ZONE	1	2	3	4	5	"TOTAL
300	!--------	!--------	!--------	!--------	!--------	!--------	!--------
301	1	@IF((B198>0),(1/(B198^$F$297)),0)	![B301]	![B301]	![B301]	![B301]	![G25]
302	2	![B301]	![B301]	![B301]	![B301]	![B301]	![G25]
303	3	![B301]	![B301]	![B301]	![B301]	![B301]	![G25]
304	4	![B301]	![B301]	![B301]	![B301]	![B301]	![G25]

Exhibit A-1, continued

	A	B	C	D	E	F	G
305	5	![B301]	![B301]	![B301]	![B301]	![B301]	![G25]
306							
307	'TABLE 26 - NON HOME BASED (NHB) TRIP DISTRIBUTIONS (ROUND 1)						
308							
309	'ZONE	1	2	3	4	5	"TOTAL
310	!--------	!--------	!--------	!--------	!--------	!--------	!--------
311	1	((($B$191*(B301*B192))/(($B$301*$B$192)+($C$301*$C$192)+($D$301*$D$192)+($E$301*$E$192)+($F$301*$F$192)))	![B311]	![B311]	![B311]	![B311]	![G25]
312	2	((($C$191*(B302*B192))/(($B$302*$B$192)+($C$302*$C$192)+($D$302*$D$192)+($E$302*$E$192)+($F$302*$F$192)))	![B312]	![B312]	![B312]	![B312]	![G25]
313	3	((($D$191*(B303*B192))/(($B$303*$B$192)+($C$303*$C$192)+($D$303*$D$192)+($E$303*$E$192)+($F$303*$F$192)))	![B313]	![B313]	![B313]	![B313]	![G25]
314	4	((($E$191*(B304*B19	![B314]	![B314]	![B314]	![B314]	![G25]

Exhibit A-1, continued

	A	B	C	D	E	F	G
		2))/(($B$304*$B$192)+($C$304*$C$192)+($D$304*$D$192)+($E$304*$E$192)+($F$304*$F$192)))					
315	5	((($F$191*(B305*B192))/(($B$305*$B$192)+($C$305*$C$192)+($D$305*$D$192)+($E$305*$E$192)+($F$305*$F$192)))	![B315]	![B315]	![B315]	![B315]	![G25]
316	'TOTAL	![B30]	![B30]	![B30]	![B30]	![B30]	![B30]
317							
318	'TABLE 27 - ADJUSTED ATTRACTIONS (A(J,IT)=A(J,IT-1)*(A(J)/(C(J,IT-1))						
319							
320	'ZONE	1	2	3	4	5	
321	!--------	!--------	!--------	!--------	!--------	!--------	
322	'GENERATN						
323	' HBNW ATT	+B192	![B323]	![B323]	![B323]	![B323]	
324	'DISTRIBTN						
325	' HBNW ATT	![B235]	![B235]	![B235]	![B235]	![B235]	
326	'A(J,IT=1)	![B236]	![B236]	![B236]	![B236]	![B236]	
327							
328	'TABLE 28 - NON HOME BASED (NHB) TRIP DISTRIB						

Exhibit A-1, continued

	A	B	C	D	E	F	G
329	UTIONS (ROUND 2)						
330	'ZONE	1	2	3	4	5	"TOTAL
331	!--------	!--------	!--------	!--------	!--------	!--------	!--------
332	1	(($B$191*(B301*B326))/(($B$301*$B$326)+($C$301*$C$326)+($D$301*$D$326)+($E$301*$E$326)+($F$301*$F$326)))	![B332]	![B332]	![B332]	![B332]	![G25]
333	2	(($C$191*(B302*B326))/(($B$302*$B$326)+($C$302*$C$326)+($D$302*$D$326)+($E$302*$E$326)+($F$302*$F$326)))	![B333]	![B333]	![B333]	![B333]	![G25]
334	3	(($D$191*(B303*B326))/(($B$303*$B$326)+($C$303*$C$326)+($D$303*$D$326)+($E$303*$E$326)+($F$303*$F$326)))	![B334]	![B334]	![B334]	![B334]	![G25]
335	4	(($E$191*(B304*B326))/(($B$304*$B$326)+($C$304*$C$326)+($D$304*$D$326)+($E$304*$E	![B335]	![B335]	![B335]	![B335]	![G25]

Exhibit A-1, continued

	A	B	C	D	E	F	G
		$326)+($F$304*$F$326)))					
		A	B	C	D	E	F
336	5	(($F$191*(B305*B326))/(($B$305*$B$326)+($C$305*$C$326)+($D$305*$D$326)+($E$305*$E$326)+($F$305*$F$326)))	![B336]	![B336]	![B336]	![B336]	![G25]
337	"TOTAL	![B30]	![B30]	![B30]	![B30]	![B30]	![B30]
338							
339	'TABLE 29 - TOTAL TRIPS FROM DISTRIBUTION MODEL						
340							
341	'ZONE	1	2	3	4	5	"TOTAL
342	!--------	!--------	!--------	!--------	!--------	!--------	!--------
343	1	+B242+B287+B332	![B343]	![B343]	![B343]	![B343]	![G25]
344	2	![B343]	![B343]	![B343]	![B343]	![B343]	![G25]
345	3	![B343]	![B343]	![B343]	![B343]	![B343]	![G25]
346	4	![B343]	![B343]	![B343]	![B343]	![B343]	![G25]
347	5	![B343]	![B343]	![B343]	![B343]	![B343]	![G25]
348	"TOTAL	![B30]	![B30]	![B30]	![B30]	![B30]	![B30]
349							
350							
351	!****** TRIP ASSIGNMENT PHASE ******						
352							
353	'TABLE 30 - LINK TIMES (IN MINUTES)						
354							
355	'LINK	'TIME					
356	!--------	!--------					
357	1	6					
358	2	5					

Exhibit A-1, continued

	A	B	C	D	E	F	G
359	3	5					
360	4	6					
361	5	8					
362	6	6					
363	7	3					
364	8	3					
365	9	5					
366	10	10					
367	11	5					
368	12	6					
369	13	8					
370	14	3					
371	15	4					
372	16	4					
373	17	5					
374	18	6					
375	19	5					
376	20	3					
377	21	3					
378	22	4					
379	23	7					
380	24	3					
381	25	5					
382	26	3					
383	27	5					
384	28	4					
385	29	9					
386	30	3					
387	31	5					
388	32	3					
389	33	4					
390							
391	'TABLE 31 - ASSIGNMENT PHASE (1=ALL, 0<VALUE<1 =PROPORTION)						
392	' EITHER SINGLE OR MULTIPLE PATHS CAN BE ASSIGNED						
393							
394		'ZONAL INTERCHANGES					
395		'--------	'--------	'--------	'--------	'--------	'--------

Exhibit A-1, continued

	A	B	C	D	E	F	G
396	'LINK	"1-1	"1-2	"1-3	"1-4	"1-5	"2-2
397	'--------	'--------	'--------	'--------	'--------	'--------	'--------
398	1	0	1	0	0	0	0.2
399	2	0	1	0	0	0	0.5
400	3	0	0	0	0	0	0.5
401	4	0	0	0	0	0	0.2
402	5	0	0	0	0	0	0.2
403	6	0	0	0	0	0	0.2
404	7	0.5	1	0	1	0	0
405	8	0.5	0	1	0	1	0
406	9	0.2	0	0	0	0	0
407	10	0.2	0	0	0	0	0.2
408	11	0.2	0	0	0	0	0
409	12	0.2	0	0	0	0	0
410	13	0	0	0	0	0	0
411	14	0	0	0.4	0	0	0
412	15	0	0	0	0	0	0
413	16	0	0	0.6	0	0	0
414	17	0	0	0	0	0	0
415	18	0	0	0	0	0.4	0
416	19	0	0	0	0	0.4	0
417	20	0	0	0	0	0.4	0
418	21	0	0	0	0	0.6	0
419	22	0	0	0	0	0	0
420	23	0	0	0	0	0.6	0
421	24	0	0	0	1	0	0
422	25	0	0	0	1	0	0
423	26	0.2	0	0	0	0	0.2
424	27	0	0	0	0	0	0.2
425	28	0	0	0	0	0	0
426	29	0	0	0	0	0	0
427	30	0	0	0	0	0	0
428	31	0	0	0	0	0	0
429	32	0	0	0	0	0	0
430	33	0.2	0	0.4	0	0	0
431	'--------	'--------	'--------	'--------	'--------	'--------	'--------
432							
433	'TABLE 32 − LINK VOLUMES						
434							
435	'ZONES	"1-1	"1-2	"1-3	"1-4	"1-5	"2-2
436	'--------	'--------	'--------	'--------	'--------	'--------	'--------
437	'TOT TRIPS	+B343	+C343+B344	+D343+B345	+E343+B346	+F343+B347	+C344
438	'--------	'--------	'--------	'--------	'--------	'--------	'--------
439	1	+B$437*B398	![B439]	![B439]	![B439]	![B439]	![B439]

Exhibit A-1, continued

	A	B	C	D	E	F	G
440	2	! [B439]	! [B439]	! [B439]	! [B439]	! [B439]	! [B439]
441	3	! [B439]	! [B439]	! [B439]	! [B439]	! [B439]	! [B439]
442	4	! [B439]	! [B439]	! [B439]	! [B439]	! [B439]	! [B439]
443	5	! [B439]	! [B439]	! [B439]	! [B439]	! [B439]	! [B439]
444	6	! [B439]	! [B439]	! [B439]	! [B439]	! [B439]	! [B439]
445	7	! [B439]	! [B439]	! [B439]	! [B439]	! [B439]	! [B439]
446	8	! [B439]	! [B439]	! [B439]	! [B439]	! [B439]	! [B439]
447	9	! [B439]	! [B439]	! [B439]	! [B439]	! [B439]	! [B439]
448	10	! [B439]	! [B439]	! [B439]	! [B439]	! [B439]	! [B439]
449	11	! [B439]	! [B439]	! [B439]	! [B439]	! [B439]	! [B439]
450	12	! [B439]	! [B439]	! [B439]	! [B439]	! [B439]	! [B439]
451	13	! [B439]	! [B439]	! [B439]	! [B439]	! [B439]	! [B439]
452	14	! [B439]	! [B439]	! [B439]	! [B439]	! [B439]	! [B439]
453	15	! [B439]	! [B439]	! [B439]	! [B439]	! [B439]	! [B439]
454	16	! [B439]	! [B439]	! [B439]	! [B439]	! [B439]	! [B439]
455	17	! [B439]	! [B439]	! [B439]	! [B439]	! [B439]	! [B439]
456	18	! [B439]	! [B439]	! [B439]	! [B439]	! [B439]	! [B439]
457	19	! [B439]	! [B439]	! [B439]	! [B439]	! [B439]	! [B439]
458	20	! [B439]	! [B439]	! [B439]	! [B439]	! [B439]	! [B439]
459	21	! [B439]	! [B439]	! [B439]	! [B439]	! [B439]	! [B439]
460	22	! [B439]	! [B439]	! [B439]	! [B439]	! [B439]	! [B439]
461	23	! [B439]	! [B439]	! [B439]	! [B439]	! [B439]	! [B439]
462	24	! [B439]	! [B439]	! [B439]	! [B439]	! [B439]	! [B439]
463	25	! [B439]	! [B439]	! [B439]	! [B439]	! [B439]	! [B439]
464	26	! [B439]	! [B439]	! [B439]	! [B439]	! [B439]	! [B439]
465	27	! [B439]	! [B439]	! [B439]	! [B439]	! [B439]	! [B439]
466	28	! [B439]	! [B439]	! [B439]	! [B439]	! [B439]	! [B439]
467	29	! [B439]	! [B439]	! [B439]	! [B439]	! [B439]	! [B439]
468	30	! [B439]	! [B439]	! [B439]	! [B439]	! [B439]	! [B439]
469	31	! [B439]	! [B439]	! [B439]	! [B439]	! [B439]	! [B439]
470	32	! [B439]	! [B439]	! [B439]	! [B439]	! [B439]	! [B439]
471	33	! [B439]	! [B439]	! [B439]	! [B439]	! [B439]	! [B439]
472	!--------	!--------	!--------	!--------	!--------	!--------	!--------

	H	I	J	K	L	M	N
395	!--------	!--------	!--------	!--------	!--------	!--------	!--------
396	"2-3	"2-4	"2-5	"3-3	"3-4	"3-5	"4-4
397	!--------	!--------	!--------	!--------	!--------	!--------	!--------
398	1	0.4	1	0	0	0	0.2
399	1	1	1	0	0	0	0
400	0	0	0	0	0	0	0
401	0	0	0	0	0	0	0
402	0	0	0	0	0	0	0
403	0	0.6	0	0	0	0	0.2
404	0.5	0	0.4	0	0.5	0	0
405	0.5	0	0.4	0	0.5	0	0
406	0.5	0	0	0	0.5	0	0
407	0	0	0	0	0	0	0
408	0	0	0	0	0	0	0

Exhibit A-1, continued

	H	I	J	K	L	M	N
409	0	0	0	0.2	0	0	0
410	0	0	0	0.2	0	0	0
411	0.5	0	0	0.33	0.5	0	0
412	0	0	0	0.33	0	0	0
413	0.5	0	0	0.33	0.5	1	0
414	0	0	0	0.2	0	0	0
415	0	0	0	0.2	0	0.3	0
416	0	0	0	0	0	0.3	0
417	0	0	0	0	0	0.3	0
418	0	0	1	0	0	0.7	0
419	0	0	0.6	0	0	0	0.2
420	0	0	0.4	0	0	0.7	0
421	0	0.4	0.6	0	1	0	0.2
422	0	0.4	0	0	1	0	0.33
423	0.5	0	0	0	0.5	0	0
424	0	0	0	0	0	0	0
425	0	0.6	0	0	0	0	0.33
426	0	0	0	0	0	0	0.33
427	0	0	0	0	0	0	0
428	0	0	0	0	0	0	0
429	0	0	0	0	0	0	0.2
430	0	0	0	0.2	0	0	0
431	!--------	!--------	!--------	!--------	!--------	!--------	!--------
432							
433							
434							
435	"2-3	"2-4	"2-5	"3-3	"3-4	"3-5	"4-4
436	!--------	!--------	!--------	!--------	!--------	!--------	!--------
437	+D344+C345	+E344+C346	+F344+C347	+D345	+E345+D346	+F345+D347	+E346
438	!--------	!--------	!--------	!--------	!--------	!--------	!--------
439	![B439]	![B439]	![B439]	![B439]	![B439]	![B439]	![B439]
440	![B439]	![B439]	![B439]	![B439]	![B439]	![B439]	![B439]
441	![B439]	![B439]	![B439]	![B439]	![B439]	![B439]	![B439]
442	![B439]	![B439]	![B439]	![B439]	![B439]	![B439]	![B439]
443	![B439]	![B439]	![B439]	![B439]	![B439]	![B439]	![B439]
444	![B439]	![B439]	![B439]	![B439]	![B439]	![B439]	![B439]
445	![B439]	![B439]	![B439]	![B439]	![B439]	![B439]	![B439]
446	![B439]	![B439]	![B439]	![B439]	![B439]	![B439]	![B439]
447	![B439]	![B439]	![B439]	![B439]	![B439]	![B439]	![B439]
448	![B439]	![B439]	![B439]	![B439]	![B439]	![B439]	![B439]
449	![B439]	![B439]	![B439]	![B439]	![B439]	![B439]	![B439]
450	![B439]	![B439]	![B439]	![B439]	![B439]	![B439]	![B439]
451	![B439]	![B439]	![B439]	![B439]	![B439]	![B439]	![B439]
452	![B439]	![B439]	![B439]	![B439]	![B439]	![B439]	![B439]
453	![B439]	![B439]	![B439]	![B439]	![B439]	![B439]	![B439]
454	![B439]	![B439]	![B439]	![B439]	![B439]	![B439]	![B439]
455	![B439]	![B439]	![B439]	![B439]	![B439]	![B439]	![B439]
456	![B439]	![B439]	![B439]	![B439]	![B439]	![B439]	![B439]
457	![B439]	![B439]	![B439]	![B439]	![B439]	![B439]	![B439]

Exhibit A-1, continued

	H	I	J	K	L	M	N
458	![B439]	![B439]	![B439]	![B439]	![B439]	![B439]	![B439]
459	![B439]	![B439]	![B439]	![B439]	![B439]	![B439]	![B439]
460	![B439]	![B439]	![B439]	![B439]	![B439]	![B439]	![B439]
461	![B439]	![B439]	![B439]	![B439]	![B439]	![B439]	![B439]
462	![B439]	![B439]	![B439]	![B439]	![B439]	![B439]	![B439]
463	![B439]	![B439]	![B439]	![B439]	![B439]	![B439]	![B439]
464	![B439]	![B439]	![B439]	![B439]	![B439]	![B439]	![B439]
465	![B439]	![B439]	![B439]	![B439]	![B439]	![B439]	![B439]
466	![B439]	![B439]	![B439]	![B439]	![B439]	![B439]	![B439]
467	![B439]	![B439]	![B439]	![B439]	![B439]	![B439]	![B439]
468	![B439]	![B439]	![B439]	![B439]	![B439]	![B439]	![B439]
469	![B439]	![B439]	![B439]	![B439]	![B439]	![B439]	![B439]
470	![B439]	![B439]	![B439]	![B439]	![B439]	![B439]	![B439]
471	![B439]	![B439]	![B439]	![B439]	![B439]	![B439]	![B439]
472	!--------	!--------	!--------	!--------	!--------	!--------	!--------

	O	P	Q
394	'ZONAL IN		
395	!--------	!--------	
396	"4-5	"5-5	
397	!--------	!--------	
398	0	0	
399	0	0	
400	0	0	
401	0	0	
402	0	0	
403	0	0	
404	0	0	
405	0	0	
406	0	0	
407	0	0	
408	0	0	
409	0	0	
410	0	0	
411	0	0	
412	0	0	
413	0	0	
414	0	0	
415	0	0.2	
416	0	0.2	
417	0	0.5	
418	1	0.5	
419	0.6	0	
420	0	0.2	
421	0	0	
422	0.6	0	
423	0	0	
424	0	0	
425	0	0	

Exhibit A-1, continued

	O	P	Q
426	0.4	0	
427	0	0.2	
428	0	0.2	
429	0.4	0.2	
430	0	0	
431	!--------	!--------	
432			
433			
434			
435	"4-5	"5-5	
436	!--------	!--------	^TOTAL
437	+F346+E347	+F347	^VOLUMES
438	!--------	!--------	!--------
439	![B439]	![B439]	@SUM(B439..P439)
440	![B439]	![B439]	![Q439]
441	![B439]	![B439]	![Q439]
442	![B439]	![B439]	![Q439]
443	![B439]	![B439]	![Q439]
444	![B439]	![B439]	![Q439]
445	![B439]	![B439]	![Q439]
446	![B439]	![B439]	![Q439]
447	![B439]	![B439]	![Q439]
448	![B439]	![B439]	![Q439]
449	![B439]	![B439]	![Q439]
450	![B439]	![B439]	![Q439]
451	![B439]	![B439]	![Q439]
452	![B439]	![B439]	![Q439]
453	![B439]	![B439]	![Q439]
454	![B439]	![B439]	![Q439]
455	![B439]	![B439]	![Q439]
456	![B439]	![B439]	![Q439]
457	![B439]	![B439]	![Q439]
458	![B439]	![B439]	![Q439]
459	![B439]	![B439]	![Q439]
460	![B439]	![B439]	![Q439]
461	![B439]	![B439]	![Q439]
462	![B439]	![B439]	![Q439]
463	![B439]	![B439]	![Q439]
464	![B439]	![B439]	![Q439]
465	![B439]	![B439]	![Q439]
466	![B439]	![B439]	![Q439]
467	![B439]	![B439]	![Q439]
468	![B439]	![B439]	![Q439]
469	![B439]	![B439]	![Q439]
470	![B439]	![B439]	![Q439]
471	![B439]	![B439]	![Q439]

Exhibit A-2

Cell Listing, Comparative Cost Model

	A	B	C	D	E
1	'COST ANALYSIS OF TWO PROJECTS, 10 YEAR PERIOD				
2					
3					
4		'MENU OF ALTERNATIVE MACROS			
5		'------------- ------------- ------------- -------------			
6		'ALT-P	'Change parameters, including wage rates,		
7			' discount rate, etc. and show		
8			' discounted option totals		
9					
10		'ALT-S	'Show the spreadsheet		
11					
12		'ALT-G	'Show graph of discounted values		
13					
14		'ALT-M	'Returns to macro menu		
15					
16		'ALT-N	'Go to macro instructions		
17					
18		'ALT-D	'Go to description of the spreadsheet		
19					
20		'ALT-R	'Go to range names with descriptions		
21					
22					
23					

Exhibit A-2, continued

	A	B	C	D	E
24		'PARAMETERS AND COMPARISON OF OPTIONS			
25					
26					
27	'WAGE RATE - CLASS 1				7.5
28	'WAGE RATE - CLASS 2				15
29					
30	'YEARLY WAGE RATE PERCENT INCREASE				0.06
31	'LENGTH OF WORK WEEK				35
32	'YEARLY MAINTENANCE INFLATION FACTOR				0.05
33					
34	'DISCOUNT RATE				0.1
35					
36		'** PRESENT VALUE OF OPTION 1			+J58
37		'** PRESENT VALUE OF OPTION 2			+J78
38					
39					
40					
41		'OPTION 1			
42		'............	'............	'.........	'.........
43		^CAPITAL		'......... --- LABOR COSTS ----	
44		^& FIXED	^MAINT.	'---- CLASS 1 ----	
45	'YEAR	^COSTS	^COSTS	'EMPLOYEES	^WAGE RT
46	'.........	'............	'............	'.........	'.........
47	1	600000	30000	5	+E27
48	2	600000	+$C$47*(1+$E$32)^A47	5	+$E$27*(1+$E$30)^A47
49	3	15000	![C48]	5	![E48]

Exhibit A-2, continued

	A	B	C	D	E
50	4	15000	![C48]	5	![E48]
51	5	15000	![C48]	5	![E48]
52	6	15000	![C48]	5	![E48]
53	7	15000	![C48]	5	![E48]
54	8	15000	![C48]	5	![E48]
55	9	15000	![C48]	5	![E48]
56	10	15000	![C48]	5	![E48]
57	!--------	!--------	!--------	!--------	!--------
58					
59					
60					
61		'OPTION 2			
62		!--------	!--------	!--------	!--------
63		^CAPITAL		!--------	
				--- LABOR COSTS ----	
64		^& FIXED	^MAINT.	!---- CLASS 1 ----	
65	'YEAR	^COSTS	^COSTS	'EMPLOYEES	^WAGE RT
66	!--------	!--------	!--------	!--------	!--------
67	1	300000	20000	8	![E47]
68	2	300000	+$C$67*(1+$E$32)^A67	8	![E48]
69	3	10000	![C68]	8	![E48]
70	4	10000	![C68]	8	![E48]
71	5	10000	![C68]	8	![E48]
72	6	10000	![C68]	8	![E48]
73	7	10000	![C68]	8	![E48]
74	8	10000	![C68]	8	![E48]
75	9	10000	![C68]	8	![E48]
76	10	10000	![C68]	8	![E48]
77	!--------	!--------	!--------	!--------	!--------
78					

	F	G	H	I	J
41			'OPTION 1		
42	!--------	!--------	!--------	!--------	!--------
43			^TOTAL	^TOTAL	^DEFLATED
44	!---- CLASS 2 ----		^LABOR	^SYSTEM	^SYSTEM
45	'EMPLOYEES	^WAGE RT	^COSTS	^COSTS	^COSTS
46	!--------	!--------	!--------	!--------	!--------
47	2	+E28	((D47*E47)+(F47*G47))*52*$E$31	+B47+C47+H47	+I47

Exhibit A-2, continued

	F	G	H	I	J
48	2	+$E$28*(1+$E$30)^A47	![H47]	![I47]	+I48/((1+$E$34)^A47)
49	2	![G48]	![H47]	![I47]	![J48]
50	2	![G48]	![H47]	![I47]	![J48]
51	2	![G48]	![H47]	![I47]	![J48]
52	2	![G48]	![H47]	![I47]	![J48]
53	2	![G48]	![H47]	![I47]	![J48]
54	2	![G48]	![H47]	![I47]	![J48]
55	2	![G48]	![H47]	![I47]	![J48]
56	2	![G48]	![H47]	![I47]	![J48]
57	'---------	'---------	'------------	'-------------	'------------
58				@SUM(I47..I56)	![I58]
59					
60					
61			'OPTION 2		
62	'---------	'---------	'------------	'-------------	'------------
63			^TOTAL	^TOTAL	^DEFLATED
64	'---- CLASS 2 ----		^LABOR	^SYSTEM	^SYSTEM
65	'EMPLOYEES	^WAGE RT	^COSTS	^COSTS	^COSTS
66	'---------	'---------	'------------	'-------------	'------------
67	2	+E28	![H47]	![I47]	![J47]
68	2	![G48]	![H47]	![I47]	![J48]
69	2	![G48]	![H47]	![I47]	![J48]
70	2	![G48]	![H47]	![I47]	![J48]
71	2	![G48]	![H47]	![I47]	![J48]
72	2	![G48]	![H47]	![I47]	![J48]
73	2	![G48]	![H47]	![I47]	![J48]
74	2	![G48]	![H47]	![I47]	![J48]
75	2	![G48]	![H47]	![I47]	![J48]
76	2	![G48]	![H47]	![I47]	![J48]
77	'---------	'---------	'------------	'-------------	'------------
78				![I58]	![I58]

	P	Q	R	S	T	U
1	'MACROS		'Instructions		'Description	
2	'---------	'---------	'----------	'----------	'----------	'----------
3						
4	'Alt-G	'\G	'{GRAPH}		'Show graph	
5			'{ESC}		'Wait for Return key	
6						
7	'Alt-N	'\N	'{HOME}		'Initialize	

Exhibit A-2, continued

	P	Q	R	S	T	U
8			'{GOTO}P1~		'Goto Macro area	
9						
10	'Alt-S	'\S	'{HOME}		'Initialize	
11			'{GOTO}A41~		'Goto top of spreadsheet	
12						
13	'Alt-M	'\M	'{HOME}		'Go to menu	
14						
15	'Alt-P	'\P	'{HOME}		'Initialize	
16			'{GOTO}A21~		'Goto parameter and cost	
17					' comparison	
18						
19	'Alt-D	'\D	'{HOME}		'Initialize	
20			'{GOTO}W1~		'Goto Description	
21						
22	'Alt-R	'\R	'{HOME}		'Initialize	
23			'{GOTO}W21~		'Goto Range variable description	
24						

Exhibit A-3
Cell Listing, Smiley County Information System

	A	B	C	D
1				
2		'SMILEY TOWNSHIP INFORMATION SYSTEM		
3				
4				
5		'CAPITAL IMPROVEMENT PROGRAM		
6				
7			'MENU	
8		'--------------------------------		
9				
10		'ALT-I	'Enter project into form	
11				
12		'ALT-M	'Return to menu	
13				
14		'ALT-S	'Shows database	
15				
16		'ALT-P	'Change inflation factor	
17				
18	'Map macros:	'ALT-N	'Macro instructions	
19		'ALT-D	'Description of spreadsheet	
20		'ALT-R	'Description of range names	
21				
22		'INFLATION FACTOR ESTIMATE		
23		'--------------------------------		
24				
25	'What is the expected inflation factor?			
26				
27	'INFLATION FACTOR (R) >>>		0.08	
28	'(ENTER WITH DECIMAL POINT)			
29				
42		'DESCRIPTION		
43		'--------------------------------		
44				

Exhibit A-3, continued

	A	B	C	D
45	' This spreadsheet contains a capital improvement program database			
46	'which is accessed through an input form. A series of macros are			
47	'used to move around the spreadsheet and to perform various tasks.			
48				
62		'DESCRIPTION		
63	'***			
64	'***			
65		'Variable names		
66	'-------------------------------------			
67	'fno	'Project number		
68	'fdept	'Operating department		
69	'fname	'Project name		
70	'f86amt	'1986 expenditures		
71	'f87amt	'1987 expenditures		
72	'f88amt	'1988 expenditures		
73	'f89amt	'1989 expenditures		
74	'f90amt	'1990 expenditures		
75				
76				
77				
78		'Subroutines		
79	'---			
80	'copy	'Copies inpu		

Exhibit A-3, continued

	A	B	C	D
		t form data into database		
81	'erase	'Blanks out the fields in the form		
82	'total	'Calculates totals in the database		
83				
84		'Locators		
85	!---			
86	'formbbegin	'Go to top of form		
87	'form	'The spreadsheet region for the form		
88	'dbbegin	'The top of the database region		
89	'loop	'Takes control back to the data input routine		
90				
195	'CAPITAL IMPROVEMENT PROJECT DATABASE			
196				
197				
198	'Project No.	'Dept.	'Project Name	^1986
199	!-----------	!-----------	!-----------------------------	!----------
200	'G657	'Parks	'Green Foote Hollow	0
201	'R875	'Roads	'Million Dollar Highway	600000
202	'W129	'Water	'Smithville Bags	50000
203	'P341	'Parks	'Happy Turtle Bog	100000
204	'R124	'Roads	'Tory Bend Bridge	30000
205	'P453	'Parks	'Bliss Towers	10000
206	'S786	'Sewers	'Green Smitten	100000
207				

	E	F	G	H	I
198	^1987	^1988	^1989	^1990	"Total
199	!-----------	!-----------	!-----------	!-----------	!----------
200	0	4000000	0	0	@SUM(D200..H200)
201	300000	0	0	0	! [I200]
202	0	0	200000	80	! [I200]

Exhibit A-3, continued

	E	F	G	H	I
203	200000	0	0	0	![I200]
204	230000	0	0	0	![I200]
205	120000	13000	0	0	![I200]
206	20000	40000	30000	50000	![I200]
207					

	J	K	L
1	'CAPITAL IMPROVEMENT PROJECT - DATA ENTRY FORM		
2	'***		
3	'Name of CIP Project >>>		'Green Foote Hollow
4			
5	'Project No.	'G657	'Operating Department >>>>>>
6			
7			
8	'Projected Expenditures by Year		
9		^Dollars	
10	"FY 86 >>	0	
11	"FY 87 >>	0	
12	"FY 88 >>	4000000	
13	"FY 89 >>	0	
14	"FY 90 >>	0	
15	'--		
16	'Note: ENTER will bring up menu of options		
17	' Ctrl-Break will take you out of the macro		
18			
197	"Inflated		
198	"Total		
199	'-----------		
200	@SUM((D200*(1+$C$27))+(E200*(1+$C$27)^2)+(F200*(1+$C$27)^3)+(G200*(1+$C$27)^4)+(H200*(1+$C$27)^5))		

Exhibit A-3, continued

	J	K	L
201	![J200]		
202	![J200]		
203	![J200]		
204	![J200]		
205	![J200]		
206	![J200]		
207			

	M	N	O	P
1			'MACRO NAME	'MACRO INSTRUCTIONS
2			'-----------	'-----------------------
3			'LOOP or	'{GOTO}formbegin~
4			' ALT-I	'/RIform~
5	'Parks			'/XMpanel~
6				
7			'ALT-S	'{HOME}
8				'{GOTO}dbbegin~
9				
10			'COPY	'/Cfno~A200~
11				'/Cfdept~B200~
12				'/Cfname~C200~
13				'/Cf86amt~D200~
14				'/Cf87amt~E200~
15				'/Cf88amt~F200~
16				'/Cf89amt~G200~
17				'/Cf90amt~H200~
18				'/XCtotal~
19				'/XR
20				
21				
22			'ERASE	'/REfno~
23				'/REfdept~
24				'/REfname~
25				'/REf86amt~
26				'/REf87amt~
27				'/REf88amt~
28				'/REf89amt~
29				'/REf90amt~
30				'/XR
31				
32			'ALT-M	'{HOME}
33				
34			'ALT-N	'{HOME}{GOTO}O1~
35				
36			'ALT-O	'{HOME}
37				
38				
39			'TOTAL	'{GOTO}I200~
40				'/RUI200~
41				'@SUM(D200..H200)~

Exhibit A-3, continued

	M	N	O	P
42				'/RF,0~~
43				'{GOTO}J200~
44				'/RUJ200~
45				'@SUM((D200*(1+$C$27))+(E200*(1+$C$27)^2)+(F200*(1+$C$27)^3)+(G200*(1+$C$27)^4)+(H200*(1+$C$27)^5))~
46				'/RF,0~~
47				'/XR
48				
49			'ALT-P	'{HOME}{GOTO}A21~
50				
51			'ALT-D	'{HOME}{GOTO}A41~
52				
53				
54				
55			'ALT-R	'{HOME}{GOTO}A61~
56				
57				
58				
59				
60				
61				
62				
63				
64				
65				

	Q	R	S	T	U
1	'COMMENTS				
2	'-----------------------------				
3	'Goto data input form				
4	'Set up range input				
5	'Goto panel of choices				
6					
7	'Goto database				
8					
9					
10	'Moves fields to database				

Exhibit A-3, continued

	Q	R	S	T	U
11	'beginning at Row 200				
12	'by copying the fields in the				
13	'Data Entry Form to the database				
14	'"flat" file				
15					
16					
17					
18	'Call total subroutine				
19	'Return from subroutine				
20					
21					
22	'Erase fields in form				
23					
24					
25					
26					
27					
28					
29					
30	'Return from subroutine				
31					
32	'Show macro menu				
33					
34	'Show macro descriptions				
35					
36	'Shows macro menu when				
37	'worksheet is loaded				
38					
39	'Calculate totals				
40	' in database				
41					
42	'Format value				
43					
44					

Exhibit A-3, continued

	Q	R	S	T	U
45					
46	'Format value				
47	'Return from subroutine				
48					
49	'Go to inflation factor				
50					
51	'Go to description of spreadsheet				
52	'purpose				
53					
54					
55	'Go to description of range names				
56					

	V	W
1	'Continue	'Put
2	'Continue entering data	'Put record in database
3	'/XGloop~	'{goto}A200~
4		'/WIR~
5		'/XCcopy~
6		'/XGloop~
7		

	X	Y
1	'Erase	'Leave
2	'Clear data entry form	'Leave the data entry section
3	'/XCerase~	'{HOME}
4	'/XGloop~	
5		
6		
7		

	Z
1	'Show
2	'Show the database
3	'/XGprojectdb~
4	
5	
6	
7	

References

Amer, Samy. 1986. "The Use of Expert Systems in Urban Planning: A Transportation Example." Unpublished paper. New Brunswick, New Jersey: Department of Urban Planning and Policy Development, Rutgers University.

Babcock, Charles. 1985. "New Jersey Motorists in Software Jam," *Computerworld* 19:39 (September 30): 1-6.

Batty, Michael. 1976. *Urban Modelling*. Cambridge: Cambridge University Press.

Black, John. 1981. *Urban Transport Planning*. Baltimore: Johns Hopkins University Press.

Bonczek, Robert H., Clyde W. Holsapple, and Andrew B. Whinston. 1984. *Micro Database Management: Practical Techniques for Application Development*. New York: Academic Press.

Bowles, Kenneth L. 1977. *Problem-Solving Using PASCAL*. New York: Springer-Verlag.

Brail, Richard K. 1984. "The Micro in the Classroom," *Journal of Planning Education and Research* 4:1 (August): 55-60.

Brown, H. James. 1969. "Shift and Share Projections of Regional Growth: An Empirical Test," *Journal of Regional Science* 9:1.

Buchanan, Bruce G. and Edward H. Shortliffe, editors. 1984. *Rule-based Expert Systems*. Reading, Massachusetts: Addison-Wesley.

Burchell, Robert W. and David Listokin. 1983. "Fiscal Impact Simulation Model for the ARCORP Planned Residential/Office Development: Technical Appendix." Unpublished report.

Burchell, Robert W. and David Listokin. 1978. *The Fiscal Impact Handbook*. New Brunswick, New Jersey: Center for Urban Policy Research, Rutgers University.

Burchell, Robert W., David Listokin, and William R. Dolphin. 1985. *The New Practitioner's Guide to Fiscal Impact Analysis*. New Brunswick, New Jersey: Center For Urban Policy Research, Rutgers University .

Carter, James R. 1984. *Computer Mapping: Progress in the '80s*. Washington: Association of American Geographers.

Chorafas, Dimitri N. 1983. *DBMS for Distributed Computers and Networks*. New York: Petrocelli Books.

Christian, Kaare. 1986. *A Guide to Modula-2*. New York: Springer-Verlag.

Clocksin, W. F., and C. S. Mellish. 1984. *Programming in Prolog*. Berlin: Springer-Verlag.

Codd, E. F. 1985a. "Is Your DBMS Really Relational?," *Computerworld* 19:41 (October 14): ID1-ID9.
Codd, E. F. 1985b. "Does Your DBMS Run by the Rules?," *Computerworld* 19:42 (October 21): 49-60.
Covington, Michael. 1985. "Programming in Logic, Part 1," *PC Tech Journal* 3:12 (December): 82-93.
Covington, Michael. 1986. "Programming in Logic, Part 2," *PC Tech Journal* 4:1 (January): 145-155.
Covington, Michael and Vellino, Andre. 1986. "Prolog Arrives," *PC Tech Journal* 4:11 (November): 52-67.
Creighton, Roger L. 1970. *Urban Transportation Planning*. Urbana, Illinois: University of Illinois Press.
Date, C.J. 1981. *An Introduction to Database Systems*. Reading, Massachusetts: Addison-Wesley.
Davis, George R. 1982. *The Local Area Network*. New York: McGraw-Hill.
Deken, Joseph. 1981. *The Electronic Cottage*. New York: Bantam.
Dickey, John W., et al. 1975. *Metropolitan Transportation Planning*. Washington: Scripta.
Fishkind, Hank, Neal Sipe and Jerry Milliman. 1983. *The Fiscal Impact Model*. Gainesville, Florida: Bureau of Economic and Business Research, University of Florida.
Foot, David. 1981. *Operational Urban Models: An Introduction*. New York: Methuen.
Frey, Peter W. 1986. "A Bit-Mapped Classifier," *Byte* 11:12 (November): 161-172.
Fridlund, Alan J. 1986. "Statistics Software," *InfoWorld* 8:35 (September 1): 31-40.
Gallant, John. 1986. "Strained Relations: DBMS Debate Turns Bitter," *Computerworld* 20:2 (January 13): 1,8.
Garin, Robert A. 1966. "Research Note: A Matrix Formulation of the Lowry Model for Intrametropolitan Activity Allocation," *Journal of the American Institute of Planners* 32 (November): 361-364.
Gleaves, Richard. 1984. *Modula-2 for Pascal Programmers*. New York: Springer-Verlag.
Godschalk, David R., Scott A. Bollens, John S. Hekman, and Mike E. Miles. 1986. *Land Supply Monitoring*. A Lincoln Institute of Land Use Policy Book. Boston: Oelgeschlager, Gunn, and Hain.
Goldner, William. 1971. "Technical Review: The Lowry Model Heritage," *Journal of the American Institute of Planners* 37 (March): 100-110.

Graham, Neil. 1982. *Programming the IBM Personal Computer: BASIC*. New York: Holt, Rinehart and Winston.

Greenberg, Michael R. 1972. "A Test of Alternative Models for Projecting County Industrial Employment at the 2-, 3-, and 4-digit Standard Industrial Code Level," *Regional and Urban Economics* 1:14.

Hancock, Les and Morris Krieger. 1982. *The C Primer*. New York: McGraw-Hill.

Hansen, Walter G. 1959. "How Accessibility Shapes Land Use," *Journal of the American Institute of Planners* 25 (May): 73-76.

Harris, Britton. 1966. "The Uses of Theory in the Simulation of Urban Phenomena," *Journal of the American Institute of Planners* 32 (September): 258-273.

Hawryszkiewycz, I. T. 1984. *Database Analysis and Design*. Chicago: Science Research Associates, Inc.

Hogan, Thom. 1981. *Osborne CP/M User Guide*. Berkeley: Osborne/McGraw-Hill.

Hogan, Thom. 1983. "From Backyard to Big Time," *Creative Computing* 9:11 (November): 206-209.

Holoien, Martin O. 1977. *Computers and their Societal Impact*. New York: John Wiley & Sons.

Holsapple, C. W. 1984. "A Perspective on Data Models," *PC Tech Journal* 3:7 (July): 113-141.

Holsapple, C. W. and A. B. Whinston. 1981. *Data Base Management: Theory and Applications*. Proceedings of the NATO Advanced Study Institute, Estoril, Portugal, June 1-4. Boston: D. Reidel.

Huston, Arthur. 1985. "Structuring BASIC," *Byte* 10:6 (June): 243-248.

Hysom, John and Stephen Ruth. 1984. "A Nationwide Assessment of Local Government Land Planning Information Systems." Unpublished paper.

Institute of Transportation Engineers. 1983. *Trip Generation*. Third Edition. Washington: Institute of Transportation Engineers.

James, Franklin, and James Hughes. 1973. "A Test of Shift and Share Analysis as a Predictive Device," *Journal of Regional Science* 13:2.

Jensen, Kathleen and Niklaus Wirth. 1974. *PASCAL User Manual and Report*. New York: Springer-Verlag.

Johansson, Jan-Hendrik. 1985. "Simultaneous Equations with Lotus 1-2-3," *Byte* 10:2 (February): 399-405.

Jordan, Larry. 1983. "What Make Modems Run?," *PC World* 1:8 (November): 54-.

Juhl, Ginger M., and Philip Wallick. 1986. "New York: A Map for All Reasons," *Planning* 52:5 (May): 26-27.

Kalish, Candace E., and Malinda F. Mayer. 1981. "DIF: A Format for Data Exchange between Applications Programs," *Byte* (November).

Kendig, Lane. 1984. "Computerized Zoning Ordinances." Presentation at the annual meetings of the American Planning Association, Minneapolis, Minnesota, April.

Kernighan, Brian W. and Dennis M. Ritchie. 1978. *The C Programming Language*. Englewood Cliffs, New Jersey: Prentice-Hall.

Kevany, Michael J. 1980. "Interactive Graphic Systems," in Editorial Staff, with Kenneth L. Kraemer and John L. King, eds. *Computers in Local Government: Urban and Regional Planning*. Pennsauken, New Jersey: Auerbach.

Kindleberger, Charles. 1982. "Reliance on Computers by Large American Planning Departments Past, Present, Future." St. Louis: St. Louis Community Development Agency.

Kinzy, Stephen. 1980. "Urban Geoprocessing: A Staged Development Process," in Editorial Staff, with Kenneth L. Kraemer and John L. King, eds. *Computers in Local Government: Urban and Regional Planning*. Pennsauken, New Jersey: Auerbach.

Klosterman, Richard E. 1986. "An Assessment of Three Microcomputer Software Packages for Planning Analysis," *Journal of the American Planning Association* 52:2 (Spring): 199-202.

Kochan, Stephen. 1983. *Programming in C*. Hasbrouck Heights, New Jersey: Hayden.

Kops, Daniel W., Jr., Lawrence Hall, Jr., Rolf Goetze, and Gerardo Canto. 1986. *Managing Municipal Information Needs Using Microcomputers*. Planning Advisory Service Number 393. Chicago, Illinois: American Planning Association.

Kraemer, Kenneth L., William H. Dutton, and Alana Northrop. 1981. *The Management of Information Systems*. New York: Columbia University Press.

Krueckeberg, Donald A. and Arthur Silvers. 1974. *Urban Planning Analysis: Methods and Models*. New York: John Wiley & Sons.

Krueckeberg, Donald A. and Arthur Silvers. 1986. "Employment Trends and Projections." Unpublished manuscript.

Lamoitier, Jean-Pierre. 1982. *BASIC Exercises for the IBM Personal Computer*. Berkeley, California: Sybex.

Landis, John D. 1985. "Electronic Spreadsheets in Planning: The Case of Shiftshare Analysis," *Journal of the American Planning Association* 51:2 (Spring): 216-225.

Langendorf, Richard. 1985. "Computers and Decision Making," *Journal of the American Planning Association* 51:4 (Autumn): 422-433.

Laudon, Kenneth C. 1974. *Computers and Bureaucratic Reform: The Political Functions of Urban Information Systems*. New York: John Wiley & Sons.

Levine, Ned. 1985. "The Construction of a Population Analysis Program Using a Microcomputer Spreadsheet," *Journal of the American Planning Association* 51:4 (Fall): 496-511.

Levy, Steven. 1984. "Bummed to the Max, Hacked to the Max," *Newsweek/Access* Fall: 101-112.

Lien, David A. 1984. *Learning IBM BASIC for the Personal Computer*. Revised Edition. San Diego: Compusoft.

Lima, Robert J. 1984. *Planning Software Survey*. Planning Advisory Service Number 388. Chicago, Illinois: American Planning Association.

Lima, Robert J. 1985. "Data Structures for Implementation of Thematic Mapping Techniques on a Microcomputer." Unpublished paper.

Luehrmann, Arthur. 1984a. "Structured Programming in Basic — Part 1: Top-Down Basic," *Creative Computing* 10:5 (May): 152-156.

Luehrmann, Arthur. 1984b. "Structured Programming in Basic — Part 2: Control Blocks," *Creative Computing* 10:6 (June): 152-163.

Luehrmann, Arthur. 1984c. "Structured Programming in Basic — Part 3: An Application," *Creative Computing* 10:7 (July): 125-136.

Martin, James. 1976. *Principles of Data-Base Management*. Englewood Cliffs, New Jersey: Prentice-Hall.

Metzgar, Robert. 1980. "Geoprocessing Systems: City of Long Beach Case Study," in Editorial Staff, with Kenneth L. Kraemer and John L. King, eds. *Computers in Local Government: Urban and Regional Planning*. Pennsauken, New Jersey: Auerbach.

Milliman, Jerry, Neil Sipe, and Robert Hopkins. 1983. *Capital Needs Assessment Model*. Gainesville, Florida: Bureau of Economic and Business Research.

Moore, Roland H. and Forrest B. Williams. 1986. "Evaluation of the CD-ROM (Compact Disk-Read Only Memory) as a Means of Distributing Statistical Data." Paper presented at the Business and Economic Statistics Section, Joint Statistical Meetings of the American Statistical Association, Biometric Society-ENAR and WNAR, Institute of Mathematical Statistics, August 18-21.

Olle, T.W. 1978. *The Codasyl Approach to Data Base Management*. New York: John Wiley & Sons.

Oppenheim, Norbert. 1980. *Applied Models in Urban and Regional Analysis.* Englewood Cliffs, New Jersey: Prentice-Hall.

Osborne, Adam and David Bunnell. 1982. *An Introduction to Microcomputers, Volume 0, The Beginner's Book.* Third Edition. Berkeley, California: Osborne/McGraw-Hill.

Ottensmann, John R. 1984. "Analyzing Planning Alternatives Using Electronic Spreadsheets," *Journal of Planning Education and Research* 4:1 (August): 33-42.

Ottensmann, John R. 1985. *Using Personal Computers in Public Agencies.* New York: John Wiley and Sons.

Ottensmann, John R. 1985. *BASIC Microcomputer Programs for Urban Analysis and Planning.* New York: Chapman and Hall.

Page, G. William, and David S. Sawicki. 1984. "Teaching Computer and Policy Analysis Skills in a Case Study Course," *Journal of Planning Education and Research* 4:1 (August): 43-54.

Plum, Thomas. 1983. *Learning to Program in C.* Cardiff, New Jersey: Plum Hall.

Pucher, John and Richard Brail. 1984. *Managing Transit's Fiscal Crisis by Rationalizing Service Policy: A Case Study of New Jersey Transit.* Prepared for the Urban Mass Transportation Administration, U.S. Department of Transportation. New Brunswick, New Jersey: Department of Urban Planning.

Rogers, Everett M. and Judith K. Larsen. 1984. *Silicon Valley Fever.* New York: Basic Books.

Saal, Harry. 1983. "Local Area Networks," *Byte* 8:5 (May): 60-.

Saib, Sabina H. 1984. "An Ada Language Primer, Part 1," *Byte* 9:6 (June): 131-.

Sawicki, David S. 1985. "Microcomputer Applications in Planning," *Journal of the American Planning Association* 51:2 (Spring): 209-215.

Shafer, Dan. 1986. *Turbo Prolog Primer.* Indianapolis, Indiana: Howard W. Sams and Company.

Simpson, Alan. 1985. *Understanding dBASE III.* Berkeley, California: Sybex.

Sosslau, Arthur, Amin B. Hassam, Maurice M. Carter, and George V. Wickstrom. 1978. *Quick-Response Urban Travel Estimation Techniques and Transferable Parameters: User's Guide.* National Cooperative Highway Research Program Report 187. Washington: Transportation Research Board.

Spanovich, Gary. 1984. "Application of the Federal Highway Administration (FHWA) Micro-computer Based Quick Response System

(QRS)." Paper presented at the annual meetings of the American Planning Association, Minneapolis, Minnesota, April.

Standefer, Norman R. and James Rider. 1983. "The Politics of Automating the Planning Office," *Planning* 49:6 (June): 18-21.

Sterling, L. and E. Shapiro. 1986. *The Art of Prolog*. Cambridge, Massachusetts: MIT Press.

Stockman, Robert. 1984. "What's New in Microcomputer Applications," *Planning* 50:8 (August): 21-24.

Stopher, Peter R. and Arnim H. Meyburg. 1975. *Urban Transportation Modeling and Planning*. Lexington, Massachusetts: Lexington Books.

Swaine, Michael. 1986. "Turbo Prolog: The Language," *Dr. Dobb's Journal of Software Tools* 11:9 (September): 36-44.

Toffler, Alvin. 1980. *The Third Wave*. New York: Bantam.

Tsichritizis, Dionysios and Frederick H. Lockovsky. 1977. *Data Base Management Systems*. New York: Academic Press.

U.S. Department of Transportation. 1983. *Microcomputers in Transportation: Selecting a Single User System*. Washington: U.S. Department of Transportation.

U.S. Department of Transportation. 1984. *Microcomputers in Transportation: Quick Response System (QRS) Documentation*. Prepared for the Federal Highway Administration by COMSIS Corporation. Washington: U.S. Department of Transportation.

U.S. Department of Transportation. 1985. *Microcomputers in Transportation Software and Source Book, February 1985*. Prepared by the Methods Division, Urban Mass Transportation Administration. Washington: U.S. Department of Transportation.

Warner, Edward. 1986. "Lotus Unveils RAM-resident Program to Simplify 1-2-3," *Infoworld* (October 13): 9.

Whited, William. 1982. *Using Microcomputers in Urban Planning*. Planning Advisory Service Report Number. 372. Chicago, Illinois: American Planning Association.

Wiggins, Lyna L. 1986. "Three Low-Cost Mapping Packages for Microcomputers," *Journal of the American Planning Association* 52:4 (Autumn): 480-488.

Wirth, Niklaus. 1985. *Programming in Modula-2*. Third, Corrected Edition. New York: Springer-Verlag.

Zaks, Rodney. 1980. *Microprocessors: From Chips to Systems*. Berkeley, California: Sybex.

Glossary

applications software. Computer programs to do particular tasks, such as wordprocesssing, spreadsheets, or database management.

ASCII. American Standard Code for Information Interchange. An alphanumeric 8-bit (or 1 byte) code used with microcomputers.

binary. The number system which contains two possible states, generally referred to as zero and one.

bit. The smallest unit of computer memory. Can take on two states, labeled "on" or "off," or zero or one. The binary number system is used with bits to represent numbers.

byte. A group of bits, usually 8 in number, which can represent a character or machine instruction. There are 256 different ways of representing 8 bits (a byte) in binary notation.

BASIC. Developed by Kemeny and Snell at Dartmouth College, Beginner's All-Purpose Symbolic Instruction Code (BASIC) is a widely used elementary language which is evolving into a highly sophisticated programming environment.

C. A high-level structured programming language widely used in commercial software development. Developed at Bell Laboratories, C is highly portable among different types of computers.

command-driven program. A program in which the user types short instructions to indicate the tasks to be carried out. Often contrasted with a menu-driven program.

compiler. A computer program which translates a program written in a high-level language, such as BASIC or Pascal, completely into a set of machine language instructions prior to being run.

declarative language. A computer language, such as Prolog, in which the user states a goal and the program provides a range of answers in attempting to satisfy the goal.

desktop publishing. The process of designing and producing brochures, manuals, and books on a microcomputer with graphics-based software.

digitizing. The process of creating and storing digital data in X-Y coordinates (two dimensions) or X-Y-Z coordinates (three dimensions) from maps.

disk operating system. DOS. The file and disk management system of a microcomputer.

download. The transfer of information from mainframe computers or minicomputers "down" to a microcomputer using modems or a network.

geographic information system. GIS. A computerized spatially defined database with programs to access this data. Questions of a statistical and logical nature can be asked of the database, and maps and text generated to answer the questions.

icon. A graphic representation of a computer task on the computer screen. The user can point to the icon using a mouse and click a button on the mouse to carry out the task.

interpreter. A computer program which translates a high-level language program on a line-by-line basis into machine language instructions. Interpreters are often used with BASIC.

K. Abbreviation for "kilo," or thousand. For computers, 1K equals 1,024 (the nearest binary value to 1,000). Therefore a 64K byte, or 64KB, microcomputer contains 65,536 bytes.

local area network. LAN. A number of microcomputers or terminals within a confined environment (building or complex of buildings) connected by means of special cabling. These devices will use mainframes, minicomputers, or "file servers" — microcomputers containing high-capacity hard disks — to support file and peripheral sharing, and possibly electronic mail.

macro. A single instruction which carries a set of instructions. Macros are found in programming languages, electronic spreadsheets and wordprocessing packages.

MB. Megabyte. Abbreviation for "mega," or million. For computers, 1MB equals 1,048,576 bytes (the nearest binary value to 1 million).

mainframe. A large central computer connected to many terminals or microcomputers, with the capacity to handle many tasks at once at very high speeds.

menu-driven program. A program in which the operations are controlled by having the user select from a "menu" of choices. Usually contrasted with a command-driven program.

microcomputer. A small desktop computer, usually containing a single central microprocessor chip, which is operated by a single user.

microprocessor. The central chip in the microcomputer which is the "engine" of the machine. Microprocessors are categorized by the width of the internal and external data pathways (8, 16, 32 bit, etc.), and by the speed of the chip.

minicomputer. A small or medium-size computer which usually can perform several tasks at once. The distinction between a minicomputer and the increasingly powerful microcomputer is blurred.

Glossary 319

modem. Short for MOdulator-DEModulator. Permits a microcomputer or terminal to communicate over telephone lines with other computers by converting between the computer's digital signals and the audio tones required for line transmission.

Modula-2. Designed by Wirth as a successor to Pascal. Programs can contain "modules" which are separately compiled and linked through clearly defined relationships.

mother board. The main printed circuit board in a microcomputer. The mother board often contains "slots" into which other circuit boards can be plugged.

mouse. A small input device for a microcomputer which rolls on a flat surface. It directs the movement of a pointer on a computer screen to different tasks represented by text or icons references.

MSDOS. MicroSoft Disk Operating System. A very popular disk and file management system for the Intel microprocesors, the 8088, 8086, and the 80286.

multi-tasking. The computer system, large or small, which can process more than one program at the same time.

Pascal. Developed by Niklaus Wirth, Pascal is a structured, modular programming language which is widely used in teaching. It is verbose and easy to read.

PCDOS. Personal Computer Disk Operating System. The IBM-licensed version of MSDOS (MicroSoft Disk Operating System), the primary operating system of the Intel microprocessors, the 8088, 8086, and the 80286.

peripheral. Refers to input and output devices for computers, including printers, digitizers, modems, etc.

pixel. An acronym for "picture element." The individual elements, or dots, which make up the characters and graphics on the computer screen. Higher resolution screens (e.g., 1,024 by 1,024 pixels) are better for text and graphics processing than low-resolution screens (e.g., 320 by 200 pixels).

procedural language. A programming language in which each instruction is carefully specified in the order to be carried out. BASIC and Pascal are procedural languages.

Prolog. A declarative programming language used to develop expert system applications. The user specifies (declares) a problem and the computer program provides a set of answers.

p-System. The universal operating system developed at the University of California, San Diego (UCSD). The p-System stands for "pseudo-system," a reference to the compiler developed for

UCSD Pascal which generated a universal pseudo-code to be used with a wide variety of microprocessors.

public domain software. Uncopyrighted software which can be freely shared among users.

Quick Response System. QRS. The transportation planning methodology developed to do simplified analysis of regional, corridor and local traffic impacts of development. Originally a manual system, a computer program has been developed by the U.S. Department of Transportation to do QRS analysis.

random access memory. RAM. Information can be both put into RAM and read out of RAM.

read-only memory. ROM. The contents of ROM can only be read, and not altered except by special means.

shareware. A copyrighted computer program which can be shared by users under restrictions. It is assumed that a user who likes the program will send a monetary contribution to the program developers.

software. The programs which are run on the computer system.

spreadsheet. A two-dimensional matrix program, designed originally for microcomputers, which can do calculations, manipulate data, and build models. Permits "what-if" analysis in which alternative assumptions can be tested.

structured programming. The development of computer programs using defined modules, declaration of variables, and legibility of presentation.

Unix. A high-level operating system which permits multi-tasking and contains a variety of program development aids. Originally developed by Bell Laboratories, it runs on a variety of mainframes, minicomputers, and microcomputers.

Trademarks

Amiga®	Registered trademark of Commodore-Amica, Inc.
Apple®	Registered trademark of Apple Computer, Inc.
ATLAS AMP™	Trademark of Strategic Locations Planning.
BetterBASIC	Registered trademark of Summit Software, Inc.
CP/M®	Registered trademark of Digital Research, Inc.
dBASE II®	Registered trademark of Ashton-Tate.
dBASE III®	Registered trademark of Ashton-Tate.
EXSYS™	Trademark of EXSYS, Inc.
IBM,® PC,® PC AT®	Registered trademarks of International Business Machines Corporation.
Lotus™	Trademark of Lotus Development Corporation.
Macintosh™	Trademark licensed to Apple Computer, Inc.
Microsoft®	Registered trademark of Microsoft Corporation.
Modula-2/86™	Trademark of LOGICTECH, Inc.
MSDOS™	Trademark of Microsoft Corporation.
MULTIMAP™	Trademark of Planning Data Systems.
Multiplan™	Trademark of of Microsoft Corporation.
PageMaker™	Trademark of Aldus Corporation
PCDOS™	Trademark of International Business Machines Corporation.
PC-FILE III™	Trademark of Buttonware, Inc.
PCMAP™	Trademark of Criterion Inc.
PC-Write™	Trademark of Quicksoft.
Q&A™	Trademark of Symantec.
Radio Shack®	Registered trademark of Tandy Corporation.
scLASERplus™	Trademark of SOFTWARE CHANNELS, Inc.

Spreadsheet Auditor™	Trademark of Consumers Software Inc.
Symantec™	Trademark of Symantec
Supercalc®	Registered trademark of Sorcim Corporation.
True Basic™	Trademark of True Basic, Inc.
Turbo Pascal®	Registered trademark of Borland International, Inc.
Turbo Prolog™	Trademark of Borland International, Inc.
UCSD p-System™	Trademark of the Regents of the University of California.
Unix™	Trademark of Bell Laboratories.
VisiCalc®	Registered trademark of Visicorp, Inc.
Wordperfect™	Trademark of SSI Software.
Z-80®	Registered trademark of Zilog Corporation, a division of Exxon Corporation.
1-2-3™	Trademark of Lotus Development Corporation.
6502™	Trademark of MOS Technologies.
68000,™ 68020,™	Trademarks of Motorola Corporation.
8088,™ 80286,™ 80386™	Trademarks of Intel Corporation.

Index

Ability software package 217
accessibility equation 85-86
adding a record, in PC-FILE III 220
address space, in microprocessor 18
aggregate models 74
aggregate shift 94-95
Aiken, Howard 13
air quality impacts 40
allocation models 74
Altair computer 4
alternatives analysis 80
ALU (arithmetic-logic unit) 16
Amer, Samy 260
American Planning Association 1984 Conference 37
American Standard Code for Information Interchange 16
Analytical Engine 12
Apple Macintosh computer 5, 19, 20, 21, 32, 41, 46
Apple II computer 5, 15, 49, 50, 51, 208
Applications Generator, in dBASE III PLUS 231
applications program 18
applications software 26, 30-35
arithmetic-logic unit 16
array 154, 209
ASCII (American Standard Code for Information Interchange) 16
Assistant, in dBASE III PLUS 231
Atanasoff, John 13

Atari ST computer 19
ATLAS AMP graphics mapping system 6, 261
atoms, in Prolog 253
attractiveness score 76
attribute 214
automatic recalculation feature, in spreadsheet program 71

Babbage, Charles 12
Babcock, Charles 244
base-export theory 94
base-service multiplier 101
BASIC programming language 29, 38, 39, 139-62
  branching 152
  commands 157-58
  compiler version of 148
  elements of programming 141
  input 144
  interpreter version of 148
  keyboard entry 149
  logical operations in 151-52
  loops 153-54
  mathematical operations in 151-52
  output 144-45
  screen location 145-47
  structured programming 163-208
  text files 148
Batty, Michael 81
Bell Laboratories 27
Berry, Clifford 13
BetterBASIC 211
binary numbering system 13

bit-mapped graphics 21
bit 15
Black, John 86
Bonczek, Robert 248
Borland International 208, 254
boundary files 261
Bowles, Kenneth 167
Boyce-Codd criterion 242
Brail, Richard 38, 141
branching, in BASIC 152, 158
Brown, H. James 94, 99
Buchanan, Bruce 250, 252
Bunnell, David 15, 17
Burchell, Robert 39, 184, 188
Bureau of Labor Statistics 95
bus 17
byte 15

C computer language 46, 163, 212
C++ computer language 212
calculations module 136
Cambridge University 13
Canto, Gerardo 37, 262
Carter, James 20, 37
cathode ray tube 20
CD-ROM (compact disk-read only memory) 263
cell algebra 50, 52, 56
cell listing 54-56
cell referents, in spreadsheets 50
Center for Urban Policy Research 185
central processing unit 16, 17
Chalcedony Software, Inc. 255
chip, microprocessor 16
choropleth mapping 37
Christian, Kaare 211
circuit board 19-20

Clocksin, W. F. 253
clones 27
CODASYL-network 226, 248
Codd, E. F. 226, 243, 244
comma delimited form 205
command language, in dBASE III PLUS 231
command line 50
commands
  BASIC 157-58
  MS-DOS 29
  spreadsheet 58-59
Commodore Amiga computer 19
Community Memory 4
compact read-only disks 263
comparative cost model 125
Compuserve information service 33
computer mapping 7, 37, 40, 249, 261-63
computers in large-scale models 11-13
computing an average 158-61
COMSIS Corporation 6, 36
conceptual flowchart 159
conformant mapping 37
constant share model 99-100
constant shift model 100-101
constant specification in programming 142-44
constrained regional model 70
Control Data Corporation 33
Control Program/Monitor operating system 26
control unit, in microprocessor 16
counting systems 13
Covington, Michael 254
CP/M (Control Program/Monitor) operating system 26

CPM (critical path method) 32
CPU (central processing unit) 16, 17
creating a file, in dBASE III PLUS 232-34
creating a record, in PC FILE III 217
Creighton, Roger 108
critical path method 32
CRT (cathode ray tube) 20
customized template, in dBASE III PLUS 235

daisy wheel printer 23
data element, in file and database management system 214
data input form, use of 225
Data Interchange Format (DIF) 205, 263
data structures
  hierarchical 246
  network 246, 248
database management 31, 213-15
database management system 214-17, 226-38
  definition of 214
  example of 226-38
  functions of 215-17
  See also dBASE III PLUS, dBASE II
Date, C. J. 239, 242
Davis, George 38
dBASE III PLUS database management system 31, 141
  accessing multiple files in 244-46
  Applications Generator 231
  Assistant 231
  command language 231
  creating a file in 232-34
  customized template 235
  displaying records in 236
  entering the data in 234
  generating reports in 237
  linking files in 244-46
  querying a file in 236-37
dBASE II database management system 31
DBMS. *See* database management system
decimal counting system 13
decision support system 250
Deken, Joseph 3
democratization of computing power 1
descriptor module 136
desktop publishing 264
development impact analysis 41
Dickey, John 108
Difference Engine 12
differential shift 94-95
Digital Research, Inc. 26, 32
digitizing 261
disk
  floppy 22
  hard 22
displaying records, in dBASE III PLUS 236
domain expert 250
DOS (disk operating system) 26
dot-matrix printer 23
downloading 35
Dutton, William 7, 8, 9

Edinburgh syntax 255
EDSAC (Electronic Delay Storage Automatic Calculator) 13

326　*Index*

electronic cottage　3
Electronic Delay Storage Automatic Calculator　13
electronic mail　33
Electronic Numerical Integrator and Calculator　13
electronic office　263-67
electronic spreadsheet　31, 35, 49. *See also* spreadsheet, electronic
employment projection model　94-108
　concept　94-95
　location quotient　101-8
　shiftshare analysis　94-101
Enable software package　217
ENIAC (Electronic Numerical Integrator and Calculator)　13
entering the data, in dBASE III PLUS　234
equality and replacement, in Pascal　209
error-checking, in custom programming　42
Excel electronic spreadsheet　31
expert system　250
exponential model　59, 63, 65, 100, 173-79
EXSYS expert system package　260

Felsenstein, Lee　4
field, in file and database management system　214
file conversion　46
file management　213-15
file management system　213-26
　definition of　213
　example of　217-22
　functions of　215-17
file sharing　44
fiscal impact analysis　36, 39
fiscal impact model　184-205
Fishkind, Hank　37, 39
flat file　218-19, 236
floppy disk　22
flowchart
　conceptual　155
　detailed　155
　system　155
FMS. *See* file management system
Foot, David　81
FORTRAN computer language　140
Framework software package　35, 217, 263
Frey, Peter　253
friction factor　86, 87, 123
Fridlund, Alan　34
function keys　20

Gallant, John　244
Gantt chart　31
Garin, Robert　81
GBF/DIME (Geographic Base File Dual Independent Map Encoding) System　262
GEM (Graphics Environment Manager)　32
generating reports, in dBASE III PLUS　237
GIS (geographic information system)　262
Gleaves, Richard　211
Godschalk, David　262
Goetze, Rolf　37, 262

Index 327

Goldner, William 81
Graphics Environment
 Manager 32
graphics generator 32
Greenberg, Michael 94, 99
growth ceiling 66

hacker 4
hacker ethic 5, 6
HAL (Human Language
 Interface) 72
Hall, Lawrence 37, 262
Hancock, Les 212
Hansen, Walter 74, 75
Hansen model 74, 75-80, 179
hard disk 22
Harris, Britton 249
Harvard Total Project Manager
 32
Harvard University 13
Hawryszkiewycz, I. T. 242
Hewlett-Packard printer 23
hexidecimal numbering system
 13, 15
hierarchical data structures
 246
hierarchical file 30
history of computers 11-13
Hollerith, Herman 12
Holoien, Martin 11, 12
Holsapple, Clyde 226, 248
Homebrew Computer Club 4
Hopkins, Robert 37
Hughes, James 94
Human Language Interface
 72
Hysom, John 37

IBM AT (Advanced Technology)
 computer 5, 19, 262
IBM Corporation 12, 27

IBM PC (Personal Computer)
 5, 17, 18, 26, 31, 132, 208
icon 32
IDEAL relational language
 244
indexing computer files 245
industrial shift 95
inference engine 250, 251
inflation factor 193
information-processing tasks 7
input, in BASIC 144
instantiation 254
Institute of Transportation
 Engineers 109, 113, 121
integers 143
integrated software package
 31, 34-35
Intel 19, 20, 27
Iowa State University 13
IPT (information-processing
 tasks) 7
ITE (Institute of
 Transportation Engineers)
 109, 113, 121

Jacquard, Joseph Marie 12
James, Franklin 94
Jazz electronic spreadsheet
 31, 49
Johansson, Jan-Hendrik 138
Jordan, Larry 39
*Journal of the American
 Planning Association* 44
Juhl, Ginger 262

Kalish, Candace 205
Kaypro computer 17
Kemeny, John 211
Kendig, Lane 37
Kernighan, Brian 212
Kevany, Michael 262

keyboard entry, in BASIC 149
keyboard 20
Kindall, Gary 26
Kindleberger, Charles 6-7
Kinzy, Stephen 262
knowledge base, in an expert system 250, 251, 252
knowledge engineer 250, 251
Kochan, Stephen 212
Kops, Daniel 37, 262
Kraemer, Kenneth 7, 8, 9
Krieger, Morris 212
Krueckeberg, Donald 32, 59, 73, 74, 75, 94, 99
Kurtz, Thomas 211

labels, spreadsheet 50
Lamoitier, Jean-Pierre 155, 167
LAN (local area network) 33, 38, 264
Land Use Information System 37, 262
Landis, John 94, 99
Langendorf, Richard 249, 250
largest number program 164, 165
laser printer 23
Laudon, Kenneth 8
Levy, Steven 4, 5
Lima, Robert 261
linear model 54, 56-58, 169
linear model program 169-173
linear thinking 143
linking files
 in dBASE III PLUS 244-246
 in relational models 238-242
LISP 252, 253, 254
listing a file, in PC-FILE III 221

Listokin, David 39, 184, 188
local area network 33, 38, 264
location quotient 101-8
logical operations, in BASIC 151-52
Logitech 212
loops, in BASIC 153-54
Lotus 138
Lotus 1-2-3 electronic spreadsheet program 18, 25, 31, 38
 concept and command structure 49-72
 and data transfer 205, 221
 ease of use 35
 file management capacity of 217, 222, 225, 227
 and model development 73-138
Lovelace, Ada Augusta 12
Lowry model 75, 80-93, 123
Luehrmann, Arthur 166
LUIS (Land Use Information System) 37, 262

Macintosh computer 5, 19, 20, 21, 32, 41, 46
macro module 136
macros 132, 134
main unit, of microcomputer system 19
mapping
 choropleth 37
 conformant 37
Mark I computer 13
mathematical operations, in BASIC 151-52
matrix manipulation 93
Mayer, Malinda 205
MCI Mail 33
Mellish, C. S. 253

menu module 136
Meyburg, Arnim 86, 108
microprocessing chips
  Motorola
    6502 17, 26, 50
    68000 19, 20, 27
    68020 19
  Intel
    80286 19, 27
    80386 19, 27, 262
    8080 26, 27
    8088 20, 24, 26, 27
microprocessor 3, 16
microprocessor structure
  16-19
Microrim 265
Microsoft 27, 140, 164, 253, 263
microtechnology
  current applications in planning 35-38
  effects on society 1, 3
  evolution of 45-46
  future uses in planning and management 249-67
  past utilization in local government 6-10
MicroTrips software package 36
Milliman, Jerry 37, 39
MINUTP planning package 6
MITS 4
modal split 110
model
  aggregate 74
  allocation 74
  comparative cost 125, 130-36
  constant shift 100
  constrained regional 70-71
  employment projection 94, 107

  exponential 59, 63, 65, 100, 173-79
  Hansen 74, 75-80, 179
  linear 54, 56-58, 169
  Lowry 75, 80-93, 123
  modified exponential 59, 66-67, 69, 174
  multiplier 59, 67, 70
  population allocation 75-80
  Super Ingrow 99, 100
  transportation planning 108-125
model of a metropolis 80
modem 23, 33
modified exponential model 59, 66-67, 69, 174
Modula-2 programming language 42, 163, 212
module
  calculations 136
  descriptor 136
  macro 136
  menu 136
Moore, Roland 263-64
mother board 20
Motorola 19, 20, 27, 262
mouse 23
MS-DOS operating system 27-30
MULTIMAP computer mapping package 261
Multiplan electronic spreadsheet 31
multiplier model 59, 67, 70
multiplier, base-service 101
multiplier effect 93

network data structures 246, 248
networking of microcomputers 33, 264-65

Index

Neumann, John von 13
New Haven 37
New York City 262
normal forms, in the relational model 239-42
normalization criterion 242
Northrop, Alana 7, 8, 9
numeric data, in spreadsheets 50
numeric formats 147

OBERS employment projection series 100, 107
operating systems 18, 26-30
Oppenheim, Norbert 73
optical storage devices 22
Osborne, Adam 15, 16
Osborne 1 computer 4
Ottensmann, John 138
output, in BASIC 144
output unit 145

p-System 28, 208
Page, William 138
Pascal, Blaise 12
Pascal computer language 163, 208-11
  equality and replacement 209
  procedures 209
PC-CALC computer program 45
PC-DOS 26, 27
PC-FILE computer program 45
PC-FILE III file management program 214, 217-22
  adding a record in 220
  creating a record in 219
  listing a file in 221
PCMAP computer mapping package 261

PC-WRITE computer program 45
People's Computer Company 4
per capita method, in fiscal impact model 187
PERT (project evaluation review technique) chart 31, 32
pixel 20
plotter 23
Plum, Thomas 212
pointer 151
Popular Electronics 4
population allocation model 75-80
population allocation model program 179-84
population projection model 51-72
postrelational database model 226
Postscript page description language 264
PRC Voorhees 36
pre-declaration 166, 168
predicates, in Prolog 253
primary field 243
printer
  daisy wheel 23
  dot-matrix 23
program
  computing an average 158-61
  fiscal impact model 184-205
  identifying the largest number in a set 164-65
  linear model 169-73
  population allocation model 179-84
  three model projection 173-79

program legibility 166, 168
project scheduler 31
Prolog language 253-59
   atoms 253
   predicates 253
   with Prolog V-Plus 255
   rules 253
   traffic impact program 255-59
   variables 254
proportional shift 95
proposed development, and fiscal impact model 185
pseudo-code 28, 208
Pucher, John 38, 141
punch card 12

Q&A database management system 231-32
QRS (Quick Response System) 36, 40
querying a file, in dBASE III PLUS 236-37
Quick Response System 36, 40
QuickBASIC 211

R:BASE System V database package 265
R:base relational system 244
Radio Shack computer 17
RAM (random access memory) 3, 18
random access memory 3, 18
random accessed text file 148-49
raster scan 20
read only memory 18
real numbers 143
record, in file and database management system 214
regional population projection model 53-72

regional shift 95
register, in microprocessor 17
relational database model 226
   linking files in 238-42
   normal forms in 239-42
Remington-Rand 13
replacement concept 144
replicate function, in spreadsheet 58
Ritchie, Dennis 212
Roger Creighton Associates 36
ROM (read only memory) 18
Rutgers University 185
Ruth, Stephen 37

Saal, Harry 38
SAS statistical package 34
Sawicki, David 138
screen location, BASIC 145-47
segment, in file and database management system 214
sequentially stored text file 148-49
shallow-network database model 226
shareware 217
shift
   aggregate 94-95
   differential 94-95
   industrial 95
   proportional 95
   regional 95
shift-share analysis 94-95
Shortliffe, Edward 250, 252
SIC (Standard Industrial Classification) codes 95
Silvers, Arthur 32, 59, 73, 74, 75, 94, 99
Sipe, Neal 37, 39
Smiley County Information System 222-26

software
  applications   26, 30-35
  availability of   41
  commercially packaged   41, 42-43
  custom   42
  future development of   45
  operating systems   26-30
Software Arts   208
Sosslau, Arthur   109, 110
Source information service   33
spaghetti code   163
Spanovich, Gary   36
spreadsheet, comparative cost model   125, 130-31
spreadsheet, electronic
  appearance and reality   54
  Auditor   87
  automatic recalculation feature in   71
  cell referents   50
  command line   50
  commands   58-59
  conceptual base of   50
  as file manager   222, 225-26
  labels   50
  map   132, 136
  numeric data   50
  recommendations for improving   136-37
  replicate function in   58
  structured design   73, 134
SPSS (Statistical Package for the Social Sciences)   34, 39
Standard Industrial Classification codes   95
statistical package   34
Statistical Package for the Social Sciences   34, 39
steady state variables, in fiscal impact model   187, 189

Stockman, Robert   37
Stonehenge   11
Stopher, Peter   86, 108
storage devices   22
string constants   143
string variables   143
structured BASIC   163-208
structured programming   163-212
structured spreadsheet design   73, 134
sub-directories of files   30
Summit Software   211
Super Ingrow model   99, 100
Supercalc   31
Superproject   32
Symanytec   231
Symphony software package   34, 35, 263
system flowchart   155

Tabulating Machine Company   12
telecommunications   3-4, 31, 33
telex messages, and electronic mail   33
text files, in BASIC   148
three model projection program   173-79
TIP (Transportation Improvement Program)   40, 227-31
Toffler, Alvin   3
top-down programming   166
Topview   32
traffic assignment   108, 110, 112, 125, 126-29
traffic impact program, in Prolog   255-59
transit studies, use of the microcomputer in   38-39

Transportation Improvement
  Program 40, 227-31
transportation planning model
  108-25
  concept 108-12
  travel times 124
  trip attractions 121, 122
  trip distribution 108,
    109-10, 114-20, 123-24
  trip generation 108, 109,
    114-20
  trip productions 121, 122
TrueBASIC 211
tuples 214, 239
Turbo Pascal 208
Turbo Prolog 255

U. S. Department of Commerce
  107
U. S. Department of
  Transportation 36, 40, 208
UCSD (University of
  California, San Diego)
  p-System 28
Univac I computer 13
University of Pennsylvania 13
Unix 27
urban transportation planning
  model. *See* transportation
  planning model
Urban Transportation Planning
  System (UTPS) 36

variable specification in
  programming 142-44
variables, in Prolog 254
Vellino, Andre 254
video display 20-21
VisiCalc electronic spreadsheet
  program 25, 38, 49, 50, 51
VisiFile file management
  program 38

Wallick, Philip 262
what-if analysis 71
Whinston, Andrew 248
Wiggins, Lyna 37, 44, 261
Williams, Forrest 263-64
Windows operating system 32,
  263
Wirth, Niklaus 163, 208, 211
word processor 31, 34
Wozniak, Steve 4, 5

Z80 microprocessor 17, 26, 50
Zaks, Rodney 16, 18